The Mad Mosaic

Other books by the same author

The Devil and the Fool
Nobody's Nothing
Last Seen Near Trafalgar
It's Locked in with You

The Mad Mosaic

A Life Story

Gael Elton Mayo

Q

Quartet Books
London Melbourne New York

First published by Quartet Books Limited 1983
A member of the Namara Group
27/29 Goodge Street, London W1P 1FD

British Library Cataloguing in Publication Data

Mayo, Gael Elton
   The mad mosaic
   1. Mayo, Gael Elton
   I. Title
   973.927'092'4   E878

   ISBN 0-7043-2360-5

Typeset by MC Typeset, Rochester, Kent
Printed and bound in Great Britain by
Mackays of Chatham, Kent

This book is dedicated to
GEORGIA
and written at her request

Contents

Illustrations

Preface

Strange though it may sound, I wrote this story partly by mistake. It all started when my daughter, Georgia, was fourteen and we used to have dinner together in Sussex (dinner was always a great event) and discuss almost every subject imaginable. Sometimes it was about Australia – stories of 'Granny's' adventures with snakes or untamed stallions – and Georgia asked me to write them down. I started with Joey the kangaroo, but although there was enough to fill a few chapters, it was not a book. Then I thought of short biographies – perhaps sketches – of various people, and an article about White Russians, a subject I was close to, and about which I encountered nearly always complete ignorance. Again, since I am not Isaiah Berlin, this was not a book. Finally, I followed the advice of a publisher and wrote what we call 'my story'.

Unlike the preface to novels, where it is stated that 'any reference to real people is coincidental', this, on the contrary, is a true story. The reason for writing it however, and the reason that makes it worth the telling, is not that it is 'my' story, but that the events described in it form a strange pattern.

Since it is these events that are the point, I have written only about the people directly concerned. I would like to have written also of others, of whom I am fond, but since they did not form part of this picture, I have not done so. On the other hand there are two people here I would rather not have mentioned – but they played a large part indeed in the shaping of things, and so they are here; sketched in as briefly, and I hope as kindly as possible.

So here is a true story, and all the people in it are real.

G.E.M.

Part One

On 4 June 1940, while evacuation from Dunkirk was taking place in the north, my son was born at Cauderan near Bordeaux; we were part of the exodus which was surging down the roads to the south throughout June, at times under bombs from Italian planes. The hospitals in Paris were closing and there was a general, undirected and frightened emptying of the capital, like water running out of a lake; at the Gare d'Austerlitz Maurice Chevalier was on the platform, jostled, but still one of the remaining faces appearing to belong to a separate individual, rather than the amoebic swill. There were no other familiar faces. Our idea was to try and reach Biarritz; but we never did get there.

The crowd in the train seemed to reach the ceiling. Stuffed all together, it was impossible to penetrate the thick, solid mass in the passage to get to the lavatory, so this function was performed by sticking one's buttocks out of the window, held up by other people against the train's jostlings. In my case it was frequent and mortifying, as my baby was due.

I had married a White Russian when I was seventeen, because of strange and rather fatuous circumstances mainly outside my control. It was a loveless marriage and a waste, but companionship was formed by the war. I promised to help him leave France where he was not allowed to work; we were waiting for his never-delivered exit visa.

We got off the train in anxiety at Bordeaux. My French doctor had told me I had far too much *albumine* which could apparently 'cause convulsions at childbirth'. It sounded terrifying. I was eighteen and would have been frightened even without these forewarnings. Bordeaux was a port, but we were not allowed on any boat, though I would dearly have loved to sail for America where my parents were living at the time.

There was nowhere to stay. The Bordelaise mother of a friend, with a large empty house, refused to take us in. We spent the first night on benches in the Place des Quiquonces, the second in a brothel. Nine thousand other refugees arrived in hordes from the north, some on foot, others with mattresses strapped on to their roofs. They also looked for rooms. Eventually we found a hospital outside the town; on the third night my son was born: Vladimir Stephen Elton Gebrovsky von Schneeuhr, later known as Steve Gebb. When Bordeaux was bombed, the director of the clinic got into his car and drove away, the staff gradually disappeared, and I lay with mounting fever in an abandoned hospital.

Part One of this book is reconstituted from a diary I kept during the war, some of it direct from pages lost and refound. When we escaped across the German lines, we imagined we were free, but a day later we found it had been an illusion; the free zone was another sort of imprisonment. Freedom was the Grail; England winning the war felt certain, but to get a White Russian out of France was a perpetual broken promise, an illogical and iron–clad refusal, always out of reach.

Maybe the last war was indeed the 'last war' that was fought with complete faith in the idea of freedom. In the middle ages wars were for loot or adventure, the later wars for terrain or power. Last time the ideal was purely for man – to prevent him from being tyrannized. The war was won and then followed by various brainwashing doctrines designed to deceive. Poor man.

But to explain how Vsevolod, the White Russian, and I came to be on the train to Bordeaux when there was no reason for us even to be together: my sister and I were brought up in America until I was eight and she was fourteen, at which time we were sent away from home permanently, never to return. Our parents had met in Australia at my grandfather's house, Cressbrook, named after the one in Derbyshire left behind by his father, David Cannon McConnel as a younger brother. This Scot introduced Herefords into Australia, imported Reugny (a winner of the Grand National) for breeding, and built the first stone house in Brisbane, called Bulimba, which is today under conservation order. As children we heard much talk of Cressbrook – in fact we dreamed of it, and though I have never been to Australia apart from being born there and leaving aged one, I had seen photographs in a 1911 album of this long, low building – perhaps the only one in what could have been described as native style, not imitating English architecture. It was very glamorous, very romantic – *Gone with the Wind* Australian version and, though unattainable, entirely real to us. (There were no aeroplanes in those days and it was the other side of the world.) Tales of it seemed like the garden of Eden, with the pomegranate and quince orchard and the tall bunya tree. Lagoon, creek and river skirted it with water on three sides. Racehorses and polo ponies galloped in the paddocks. But as my mother said, the land outside was so silent, so empty, so lacking in European civilization. . . She went to Italy, to Russia before the Revolution, then spent three years in Paris reading history of art and writing a thesis on landscape gardening. When she returned, she met my father, who came to Cressbrook as a visitor, a young man who had read medicine in Edinburgh but decided not to finish. He had travelled to Africa in search of his own ideas, and was now working with shell-shocked soldiers returning from the First World War. He was the future Elton Mayo of the revolutionary Hawthorne Experiment of the Western Electric (*The Human Problems of an Industrial Civilization,* 1933) with a Rockefeller Foundation Life Research Chair at Harvard, but this was not known then. At that time he was a freckled Australian with very blue eyes, who waltzed, swam and played tennis excellently, and had astonishing new ideas. After three weeks they were married; she was thirty-five, he was thirty-two; she saw to it that he left Australia as his ideas were not understood there at that time. His name was George, but she did not like it, and called him always by part of his surname: Elton.

We had a happy home in America in Cambridge Massachusetts. We lived in a house with a veranda and a huge wistaria vine that reached my father's bedroom, where he left pear cores for a squirrel who came in off the vine regularly. My mother made us wreaths on our birthdays, plaiting flowers into little crowns. Once my father bought the entire bunch of balloons from a street seller and rang our doorbell pretending to be a stranger. We were loved and cherished and yet we were sent away. This is the first enigma. Our parents had an intense intellectual life of their own. My mother was over fifty when we went away, so perhaps they were too old to cope. But they meant the best for us: to give us what they missed and wanted us to have: Europe, and a European education. For this they made great effort and even sacrifice. Consciously and intellectually it was rational, but they did not realize, when applying the theory, that the only thing children really want and also need is a home, any home, anywhere. We never had one again. Family life after that was two months' summer holiday in a hotel when they came to Europe. During the year we did not see our parents, but stayed for some of our holidays with a great aunt in Norfolk, or if that was not convenient, with someone found in the agony column, an arrangement which sometimes meant separation from my sister. On one of these visits, while staying with strangers on Porlock Hill, I collected stray dogs and caught ringworm, and in order to be accepted back at boarding school I was given deep X-ray treatment which caused my hair to fall out by the roots. It could easily have been cured at home, but we did not have a home. First my head was shaved and marked with blue crosses; the hair lay golden on the floor. I returned to school wearing a mob cap and was jeered at, like a Hindu untouchable.

The alternate visits with our great aunt were happy, too wildly so, and unsettling. For two or three weeks at Christmas or Easter, we lived in a beautiful house where the silver shone and breakfasts were enormous; there was a picking garden for violets and white raspberries and our uncle had a private broad with a cut leading through to the river. My sister used to row us through the rushes in an old boat, and we would stare down at pike. This was our own family, the house of our grandmother's sister, yet not for us except in snatches – so instead of belonging we felt lost, and hated more than ever the return to the institutional life of boarding school, uncertain where the next holiday might be.

To the Australian aborigine the past and the future are the same;

he calls both the Dreaming. If a member of this oldest race is asked when he was born, he will not give a date, but will say, 'in the Dreaming, at time of flood', or 'at time of bushfire'. Reality is the visible present. Our reality was 'at the time of home' – or even the knowledge of Cressbrook, swimming somewhere in space, with mimosa in the garden and cedar panels in the rooms. Happiness was intense and brief during our summer holidays in a hotel, but leaves turning yellow meant the end of summer and no more parents, and caused despair. From the age of eight, there had never been a home. The autumn, bringing the new school year, stretched ahead filled with longing.

However, the last summer before the war was spent not in a hotel but in a house lent to us by a friend in Asolo, Italy. It was where Robert Browning had stayed and was named La Mura, having been built into the old town wall; it had a long, mysterious garden. By now I was sixteen. This was the summer of Mussolini and pollenta bread, Fascist slogans written on walls: 'Geneva, the city of lies'. The streets in Asolo were white and dusty, with donkey carts. There was one long black car belonging to Fabriz, the taxi-driver, and only one other, a Topolino, driven fast by a young man who had a method of stopping in front of the cafe in a wild, abrupt swerve. People sat about in this one cafe in the piazza; my father used to chat in Latin with a lawyer there. This was our first vision of the south: Via Roberto Browning with arcaded streets, the white light of southern heat and dark cool stone interiors. Behind the town rose the green foothills of the Dolomites as in Giorgione paintings – there were rushing streams, so the gardens bloomed with roses and jasmine in spite of the heat. The cook in our house, called La Nina, produced chicken with fried melon flowers and the markets were piled with peaches and figs. My father laughed and chuckled at the amount of peaches we ate. Below the town the plain of the Veneto stretched into a blue haze that looked like a Grecian sea.

An English friend brought a group of young Italians to meet us. One of them was Paolo, who had grey eyes and blond hair, and was the owner of the fast Topolino. He was twenty-two and he spoke with a soft, northern Italian voice, which was quiet and deep, making everything he said sound like music. I understood little at first but we spoke broken French and I gradually learned some Italian. We drove over the small white country roads in his little car, and we danced on wooden platforms in village piazzas. Small orchestras played American jazz set to Italian words and sung in velvet voices. Brown children from the mountains threw bunches of tiny wild cyclamen into the car shouting 'Ciclamini!' like an exclaimed greeting. The idea of ever leaving him was impossible. The anger of my parents was therefore terrifying, and they became like strangers. My father was an immensely kind man, almost never cross, but when he did lose his temper he turned white and caused gooseflesh. In his rage he threw a chair out of the upstairs window on to Paolo's car when I was brought home; he shouted down that if I saw him again he would return to America at once. But we wanted to marry.

They said that sixteen was too young, which was true, yet now over forty years later I can see his face clearly as if it were only yesterday; he is unchanged and completely real, not belonging to the past but part of my person. It probably would have worked, and at least so much better than the subsequent disasters. The first love, when each tree, each thing viewed together is a discovery seen in new light, is understandably dangerous from a parent's point of view. Mayo came from old puritanical stock, and his daughters were not to be fooled with; any Latin father would have felt the same. But the curious thing was their change of attitude less than a year later.

Paolo came to say goodbye wearing a black shirt. Although he disliked Fascism and Mussolini, (and had read me Eugenio Montale's poetry, which was outside the pattern and later censored), he did not know how to avoid his duty when first called up. He wrote me letters saying the sun had gone out of his life. For many months I cried in a world that looked grey and torn from its roots.

The next spring while I was living with a French family in Paris and taking a diploma at the Sorbonne, I went to an American club with another girl, and met members who were mainly Turks and Armenians. There I met the White Russian Vsevolod and went often to his house in Auteuil where his very small mother lived; she told me she had the smallest feet in Russia and that she had known Chekhov. There were many Russians there drinking eternal tea from a samovar. There were also French writers, like Jean Cocteau and Romain Rolland who encouraged Vsevolod's poetry, laughed at his jokes and were drawn by his warmth. Vsevolod suggested that I type for him and translate his writings, which was a form of marriage proposal. In June my parents had rented a house in London, and I told them, rather vaguely and uncertainly of this offer, not expecting to be taken up on it since I had only recently been too young. I think I half liked the idea of a home, rather than not knowing where to go next, since there was apparently no plan for me to return to America with them, and school was now finished. But when the idea was accepted I was shaken and lost. I had not meant it, or had I? It was a joke – yet what was the alternative? Though I did not really want it, I could not say what I did want. At this point, guidance would have been useful, and not only for me, for logic seemed lost to us all. From my parents' point of view, love for Paolo might rightly have been regarded with suspicion, but at least security should have mattered. Paolo had passed his law degree, owned a Palladian villa in the country near Asolo and a small palace in Venice. He would have been a good worldly match. Vsevolod was a stateless Russian with a Nansen passport. He had had one of his poems accepted by the *New Statesman* but he had no means of support. My father looked grey and sad in the registry office, my mother flushed and feverish. ('What else can we do with her?' she said.) The whole thing was fearful and mad, yet I was only half conscious of what was happening and dared not upset plans – I felt I was being pushed into it by some insanity larger than my person. Any alternative road seemed to be fog; I followed through in a state of downcast hypnosis and cried on the wedding night.

What had in fact happened? Perhaps my parents were traversing some problem of their own as they approached old age, or perhaps they just could not cope with young girls. My sister was twenty-two and at university, not at a loose end. Why, she asked later, couldn't I have been married off to someone suitable, or sent to university as she had been? She was older when we left America, so it was luckier for her, though still difficult. There was a strange lack of organization of my future.

I have never been able to explain these events, which led to my finding myself on the train to Bordeaux, I can only recount what happened. In later life I have found something shaming and embarrassing about being accused of choosing 'ropey fellows' – but I didn't choose them; I chose someone else. He, Vsevolod chose: he happened; it all happened and nobody stopped it. Mayo had been a psychiatrist, yet as is often the case, this fact did not apply in his own family. My parents were exceptional people who made one vast blunder, but were in every other domain outstanding. It was forty years before I managed to link this event to another which took place in Australia long before, in my mother's own childhood. I was married to Vsevolod without either love or worldly gain, and remained wistful for Paolo and a white gown.

2

We had a home of sorts at first, and an unreal, nearly white marriage. On our honeymoon in St Tropez we quarrelled most of the time, to the amusement of other people (*une lune de miel originale*) including a Dutchman, Gussy Miesegaes, who owned a yacht, and lent me his Rolls-Royce which I drove about in, penniless. But the war that started almost immediately after our marriage made us 'brothers of the road', companions of hard times, and there grew a bond between us. I thought of Vsevolod as 'this chap', and without ever feeling really connected to him, I was sorry for him and once I became aware of the immense difficulties facing White Russians in France, I developed a sense of mission to get him out of Europe. Our meeting was a fluke of useful fate for him; I was the instrument that changed his life. My father paid his debts and also for our honeymoon. He had nothing, and seemingly, after meeting him, nor had I.

At that time St Tropez was still a small port and the countryside around the outside was wild – old women dressed in black tended goats in the fields, and dusty white tracks, bordered with oleanders, led to the sea. The beach at La Moutte was strewn with tiny pink shells and no people. In the port there strolled a mixture of millionaires and poor painters, complete contrasts. There were not yet the masses of middle kingdom people who came later, looking all more or less the same. There were no modern flats or car queues – just one luxury hotel and many lodgings in rooms above cafes.

It was the last superb summer of old Europe as it was then, light on the green leaves and sunburned skins with the tango Violetta playing *Chez l'Amiral*. My feeling of sadness, that I had lost something precious, was as nothing compared to the greater waste that was soon to start. Suddenly the music stops – as if everyone is listening to hear what is coming. It was not just the war, which had started with a whimper – it was the divide of Europe, the death rattle of the end of a whole period. Everybody drove away, flew to Paris, or England, and only the cicadas remained. The old south was never the same again. Elton Mayo was right when he took my sister on the grand tour in 1937, saying Europe would soon be finished, even if it would take a long time dying. The civilization that had produced such a degree of aesthetics, traditions, rooted habits and cultures became a levelling-out into sameness of buildings and pretentious, yet ratty people. Change had to come, but it brought discontent instead of happiness. The war came before my turn for the grand tour with my father.

In Paris the house in Auteuil was surrounded by overgrown trees, so close that they dwarfed it and made it dark. Many other people lived or camped there, the youngest being thirty years old. They were kind to me and amused, but treated me like a doll, and dolls are not expected to think, just to be quiet, which was easy as I was shy. However there was an Alsatian dog called Mars whom I loved with passion. I had a small income which partly kept this community going until it was cut on the arrival of the Germans. Vsevolod was a nucleus for all sorts of people, and had a kind of magnetism which drew them. In peacetime there had been much laughing and drinking and discussions – but underneath now there was anguish.

The White Russians, *apatrides,* were not allowed work permits, and this prevented them from applying for normal jobs. They were allowed to freelance in the arts if they had talent, but talent is not universal. Some of them, like Eugene Rubin (*Vogue*), and Harry Meerson, worked in a fashion photographer's studio which adjoined the house, but most failed to find a means of existence since salaried jobs were denied them. Vsevolod's writings were not published. Kyril Volkoff was so poor, he dressed in clothes from the morgue given to him by a friend who worked there. Sometimes when they did not fit, or the shoes hurt, he would say: 'The corpse was too small this time.' He had one shirt of his own which he washed in our house and then sat about waiting for it to dry, playing cards and drinking tea from the samovar with the others. Even those with homes or at least places to sleep, gravitated to our house to spend most of their time in it. There was a great amount of bridge-playing, which I found a colossal bore; I could not understand how it could last so long, sometimes all the day and until the early hours of the next one, like a substitute for life.

At the beginning of the war these Russians were told they were going to do 'prestations', as opposed to military service which only French nationals could do. There was a slight slur on not being French, as if not worthy to be in the army. But what were prestations? Nobody knew.

At the first air-raid siren we went to a cellar, rather futilely, and sat there with Yousoupoff and his dignified wife, the Grand Duchess Irina. I stared fascinated at the large red hands of this man who had murdered Rasputin, and was mesmerized by the brilliant blue of his eyes. This was the only time we went to a cellar; it was the phoney war, but the siren was a presage. Most of the Russians spoke bad French – if they spoke it at all – and that even after twenty years. They printed their own newspaper, *Poslednye Novosti,* drank endless tea and vodka and grew nervous about what would happen to them. The photographic studio closed. There was no money except for my allowance, which was not enough. The studio had been working on debts and the war ended its prospects. The Russians signed their prestation papers and waited, stamping about and swearing. Vsevolod frequently shouted a word that sounded phonetically like Hibidashumai, it apparently meant grandmother's corpse. His grandmother's corpse played a large part in his anger; the *apatrides* did not have the rent reduction allowed to the French. The Russians felt they were *sales étrangers,* and the trees outside seemed to play grandmother's steps and creep nearer the house, casting gloom. A Pole called Boris discovered that prestations would be a form of hard labour. He had volunteered for the army and been refused. This made him feel insulted.

Gradually I belonged with these Slavs, this colony of people who had lost their country; we were equally lost, the only difference being that I had a passport. Occasionally there were wild evenings in a Russian nightclub, where minor-key Russian music was played – a music whose rhythm gradually accelerated until one could feel the Cossacks galloping with raised swords; it was exhilarating – the glasses were thrown and smashed against the wall. In *Shéhérazade* there were twenty violins of gut-tearing intensity.

We applied for an immigration visa to America for Vsevolod. America was a reality where he would surely be naturalized and able to work. My father supplied the affidavit required for immigration; we obtained the American visa. But more than that was needed: an exit visa from France. Incredibly this was refused. The law said that a stateless person obtaining entry to another country on a permanent basis would be allowed (obviously) to leave; but this law was quite simply not applied. They did not let him go. The *Chef de Section* in the Prefecture said, 'I cannot grant the exit visa. The law has not been *put into practice.*'

What Lewis Carroll nonsense was this? We stared at the man's face and pondered the meaningless phrase he had uttered, feeling dense. Vsevolod had brown eyes which at moments like this slanted downwards, making a sad Slav expression. I could see his fear showing, and growing from then on; he felt trapped.

'If these people are so undesirable, why not let them go?' I asked angrily.

'I cannot grant the visa,' he repeated.

'I would never come back; you would be rid of an *apatride*,' said Vsevolod.

'I usually have a letter as well as this stamped paper,' said the *Chef de Section* mysteriously, without explaining further. A letter from whom? Was it a bribe, an 'arrangement'? Was the law in practice only under certain conditions? He sat solid behind his desk, as if red tape were wrapped all round him, like a mad Magritte.

We trailed away feeling frustrated and impotent. It was necessary to know someone, but whom? To offer money direct could make matters worse. For if that was not what was expected, it could cause a scandal, maybe an arrest.

We drove back and forth to various ministries where we had

introductions. We dreamed of a stamp on a passport as if it were a ticket to salvation. We met a man called Tarazov who knew another man who might arrange it. He failed. It was a Kafkaesque impasse, blind. What had Vsevolod done to be made to feel like a despicable pariah? What was he guilty of? There was no explanation. We grew afraid even to ask for one, in case the anger of the petty official would make the situation worse. It was a question of balance . . . I learned how it felt to be stateless, to have no consul for protection; a person becomes frightened to stand up and ask for his rights. An *apatride* cannot have natural reactions. Anger is a luxury. A man must belong somewhere before he can get cross, in public at any rate. But if these people were not allowed to work, what were they supposed to do?

We waited in crowds that smelled of fear and sweat. Fear has a smell. We tried continually new 'tips', each time hoping, and then losing hope and growing superstitious. There were many others whose papers were not in order. The Prefecture in those days was a place of endless waiting, occasional hope, but at that time the *apatrides* were at the mercy of any small, sadistic clerk imposing his mean power. Vsevolod's flair for organizing and attracting people, for launching ideas, had got him by (albeit in second gear) in peacetime. He had once opened a nightclub, Le Boar, in the *15e arrondissement*, he had started the fashion studio, but no more. The luxury of the thirties had gone.

Things grew monotonous, fear became familiar. The undercurrent of sickness had highs and lows, but there were times when it was just a way of life. Mars had long elegant beige paws with long toenails which I painted red. We drove about in the Renault Nervasport with him in the open back seat, sometimes hopelessly, sometimes high on belief with a new tip. Polish were hanged in Varsovie. The Maginot Line was spoken of with pride. In the spring I was sick. I was pregnant, unlikely though that was. The chestnut trees bloomed in their thousands all over Paris, and in May guns were heard. Shrapnel fell in the street and cut Boris on the forehead. The suspense grew.

Hospitals closed. We did not want to leave, but there was the baby, though this seemed unreal. We were told that the French army was invincible, Weygand being in charge. Pétain, hero of the Great War, was on hand. But people were leaving Paris like a stream of rats. The rich had gone first – now *hoi polloi* were on the move. A new rumour contradicted invincibility and said the troops were retreating. Anti-aircraft guns were heard in the distance, the German offensive was launched, and reconnaissance planes circled the sky.

Newspaper headlines still said, *'Nous vaincrons parce que nous sommes les plus forts,'* but the French had ceased to believe. They had nothing to hold on to. The Maginot Line was now said to be worthless, that money had been spent on it for nothing. Each statement contradicted the last, like the needle of a compass whirring in circles, having lost its north.

We left in the last train out of Paris from the Gare d'Austerlitz. Crowds oozed along the platforms, their faces showing anger and egotism. They fought each other and kicked and scratched to get into the carriages. Once inside, they were on each other's laps, piled into human walls. Everyone was going away. But where was away? This journey lasted one day and all the night; we were twelve hours late on the schedule for Bordeaux. Biarritz was unreachable.

3

Bordeaux was hot, with a sickening muggy smell that hung over it. It was a port, but the sea was invisible – a disappointing city. I dreamed of Cambridge Massachusetts and my parents. There were the clanking noisy trams, the awful smell, and nowhere to stay. We slept once in a brothel but only one night was allowed. We sat on a bench in front of a twelve-bedroomed mansion where Madame de Sillac, the mother of a friend lived, hoping that if we stared at the door long enough it would open and she would change her mind about taking us in. Other refugees like us thronged the streets looking dazed. Even the army apparently had no plan. Everyone was fleeing to nowhere. News came that the Germans were near Beauvais and would soon enter Paris. More people appeared in carts, in vans, on horses, or in Belgian cars with branches on their roofs.

The last doctor I had seen had put me on to a diet of milk and fruit, with no salt; I had very swollen ankles, and I dragged myself along in the high tide of beings that jammed every cafe, park, or space. At times I lay on the ground of the main square. Once some soldiers were carried on stretchers from a Red Cross train. One soldier was vomiting. A man jeered and said, 'I didn't think we *had* an army.' I cried for the sick one, feeling abject and sick too – then the jeerer looked at me and said, 'It's a pity she's got such fat legs.'

That night we found a room in a hotel. Outside trams whined in their gritty rails, and the noise of the tramping and breathing of thousands of people came in at the window. For this one night we planned to relish the luxury of privacy and sheets, but so much for plans: after two hours I had my dreaded primeval pain, and I was very frightened. I was taken to the only hospital not to be requisitioned.

The sky above the hospital was red and swollen with noise. When the bombs fell the director got into his car and drove off. I had a private room but the hospital was left with almost no one in charge. An old man came and peered at me through bi-focals. He turned out to be the father of the usual gynaecologist who was in the army. I held his hand in terror, hoping he would stay with me. The pain was lonely and prehistoric, not human – but the old man had gone. I had to run, or be split in two. I ran out of my room looking for a nurse. The passage was hollow like a tunnel; there was nobody there. I waited on all fours for someone to come.

In the long night a woman came in with a bundle and said, 'Your son.' The bundle looked very small. I held him and gingerly kissed his cheek; it was so soft it was almost a shock. He was so entirely clean and new, so tiny and private and apart, that I was filled with immense love for him and clutched him tight. Suddenly he was real. He was the smallest person in France. He was mine, the only thing to belong to me, my family. We were together. I was very hot; I clung to my bundle and outside bombs exploded.

Reynaud said, 'We will defend Paris street by street,' and Pétain made his extraordinary announcement which stunned the nation. My fever rose. Someone said they had bombed Bordeaux because the government was there, but not on the night I thought; my high temperature gave me its premonition. There was a magnolia tree outside, crickets chirping, and tanks in the road. Italy had declared war. We were at war with Paolo, with Asolo and the red roses and La Nina and her fried melon flowers. The Italians bombed the old and poor people escaping along the roads of France on foot, people pushing prams filled with their clothes, bird cages, and various belongings. My baby slept in a basket and I was delirious. Vsevolod appeared with a Greek friend he had found in the street. All of France was on the move; people ran into each other everywhere. The Greek was on his way to Spain and said black rain was falling on Paris. The army had been ordered to run. He told us to hurry up and leave as the frontier would soon be closed.

There was another woman in the hospital who had had a baby, but she was cool and well. She invited us to go to her home since no one would look after us in this hospital.

When we waited for the ambulance at the front door, people stared at me and said, 'That is room twenty-two,' as if something were wrong, something they did not tell. The ambulance arrived at the same time as planes and more noise; the driver said to hurry as he was not really allowed to be mobile; we bumped off down side roads through explosions and flying clods; the baby lay in his basket and stared at the roof. French troops were guarding the bridge we crossed. A head at the window asked for our papers. Then there was an enormous bang. 'They got the powder factory,' said the driver.

Later there were hedgerows with flowers like stars, moonlight brilliantly white on miles of vineyards, a smell of honeysuckle and complete quiet. We reached a farmhouse near Fronsac. The woman who had befriended us was called Madame Dormeau. She owned many hectares of vines but worked them alone with an old aunt and partially paralysed father. Her husband was a prisoner of war in Germany. A dog called Ignace howled.

They took me to the attic, to a bed with a feather mattress. They said I must be kept separate. Next day the local doctor came and said I had puerperal fever. The maiden aunt said I should be sent away, but Mme Dormeau let me stay, though she would not come near me, fearing that my 'childbed fever' would be contagious to 'recent mothers'. I was burning hot. The doctor suggested ice on my stomach, but they had none. 'Never mind,' he said then, 'it is probably too late.' Did he mean I would die?

The old aunt, called Madame Laure, gave me water during the night. It had a sour taste, but I could not drink enough. The next morning there was a discussion with Vsevolod. The French bank in Libourne had blocked the money we had sent for by cable, even though the Germans had not yet arrived there. The doctor said I should have a curette, but without money it was impossible. Vsevolod was incredulous and frantic.

Mme Dormeau said then, 'Take her to the hospital, I will pay. They can pay me back after the war.' The doctor drove me away to Libourne in his car; he did not take Vsevolod since it was too far to return at night.

'Don't worry,' Vsevolod said as we left, holding my hot hand for a moment, 'he has promised to operate at once. I will come tomorrow.'

But I lay in the operating theatre hearing merely talk: the doctor argued with the matron, who said he was not allowed there because he was not attached to the hospital. So where was the hospital doctor then? He was away, but would probably be back in the morning. Misery overcame me violently; they had said it was urgent, that there was no time to lose.

'*Please* don't let me die.'

'How long have you had the fever?'

'I don't remember. Maybe seven days.'

Incredible. The wildest nightmare: childbed fever, blood poisoning, what did it matter who operated? It could not be true, if each hour, each extra night counted. They could not really behave this way . . . yet they did. I lay there helpless in their hands.

The matron pressed a hand on to my belly.

The doctor told the matron that an old man had delivered the baby.

'Maybe he could not see and left some pieces inside,' he suggested. But they took me away to a bedroom. The proper doctor was not there and as far as the matron was concerned, that was the end of the matter.

The next morning I was not dead; they wheeled me back into the theatre, and again they stood over my stretcher and argued; they evidently had decided the operation should be done, but now it was a question of who would get the money.

'This is my case, I brought her here.'

'But it's against the rules. You *can't* operate.'

My life was running like sand in an hour-glass. A good stranger had lent us the money, now these bad strangers would not even get it if I died first.

I tried to say: you are ridiculous, I shall knock your heads together, but was too weak and too hot, and fear overcame my anger. A nun came into the room billowing like a black sailing ship; I grabbed her hand and held it in both of mine, imploring, 'Please make them hurry.'

'I can't supply you with patients for nothing,' the man's voice said.

Another day passed. I heard Vsevolod's voice in the passage shouting, 'All the decent doctors are at the front! You are rats! Not even human rats! I come to see her and nothing has been done! Hibidashumai, shall I kick you, shall I take the knife and operate on *you*?'

A new doctor was produced; he was deaf, so he did not hear Vsevolod's abuse, but he was apparently the retired doctor and so had the legal right to use the theatre. The rules were now in order. So finally after a nine-day fever, this simple yet vital act was done. Heads were nodding, too late, too late. In time for the funeral perhaps.

The next day was peaceful and often blurred, as if sometimes I was levitating above the bed. Into this haze came a clear picture: yet another doctor was there, a new one! This one was young. He was the official hospital doctor who had been away. He never would have allowed such behaviour, he was telling me. He said, 'The war is over and I have come back. I was with the army.'

He looked like Ronald Colman wearing a misty halo and I loved him. Then he was surrounded; two other doctors appeared, the deaf one and the first one from Fronsac. The deaf one said goodbye; what were they all doing? It was mad. Was he going to retire, or was I still going to die? With Ronald Colman on call, surely it would be safe.

When I was alone there was absolute silence; I could not remember where I was. Then sound returned like a rushing river. Two nuns came and looked at me. One said, 'She is foreign.'

'The fever has risen,' said the other.

Vsevolod's voice drifted through from somewhere invisible, swearing once more on his grandmother's corpse: 'Puerperal fever comes from dirt. I'm sure it doesn't exist in America! Can't

21

you wash? I spit on your grandmothers.'

'She didn't catch it *here*.'

'You are all despicable.'

I had the impression it was essential to get out and away from this place – I got up and imagined myself in a railway station with a man saying they would give me a job. Then the nuns found me in the passage in my nightdress and took me back to bed. They tried to take my passport away but I snatched it back and put it under the pillow; it was precious, it would be the only means of escape.

'They go temporarily mad,' the nun said. 'It can happen.'

After this they performed a medieval act. It was called an *abcès de fixation*. An injection was given in the thigh to make a festering boil, which would apparently concentrate the poison of the blood in one place, so that it could then be squeezed and pumped out of the body.

I lay in furnace heat with multi-coloured dreams until two days later they pressed this thing they had made and announced proudly that nearly a litre of pus had come out of it. An achievement indeed, but it made no difference to my temperature, which was 105°F.

The Mother Superior brought me the priest. He said, 'God calls his children to him. Would you want to make a confession?' So I was condemned.

Suddenly I became lucid, awake, and very, very angry. I knew I had a baby, a life to live, parents in America and a sister in England, and that the war we were fighting was about being free. Freedom from tyranny of any sort. And we would win. The priest leaning forward in his cassock filled me with a strong, sure fight. I said, 'Go away. Your God is sombre and sinister, but I am counting on mine and he does not want me to die. My God gives life. And light and stars. I *plan* to live. Go away.' My anger gave me strength.

After that I slept for a long time.

In the street in Libourne, Vsevolod happened to run into Eugene Rubin, who was staying with a friend nearby. Eugene told him of a new drug called Sulphanilamide. It was still new and barely heard of, but Vsevolod procured some and it was given to me.

During the long sleep I had beautiful dreams: I saw the white gate at the bottom of the garden at Cressbrook, separating the pastures where the thoroughbred horses galloped in splendour. As a young girl my mother swung on this gate upside down, her hair trailing. The Cressbrook girls were famous for their beautiful hair, full of light. My mother picked muscat grapes from her bedroom window. She could hear snakes catching frogs in the gutter pipe. There was still an echo of ghostly music that was played when she opened the dancing at the ball with the head stockman. A pet kangaroo called Joey, six foot tall, would steal the bread from the dinner table. Then I saw my parents waiting at Harvard, sitting on a veranda, and I knew it was all right, that we would get there.

When I woke, they gave me a delicious lemon drink; I felt cool and rested.

The Mother Superior brought me a white rose and put it beside my bed. She said white was pure. Then she brought visitors to see me and said, 'This girl has lived because of her faith.' They looked at me as at a miracle. I slept and woke and sometimes saw them. Their faces were soft and sweet.

Vsevolod said it was also a miracle that he had met Eugene quite by chance, and found the new sulphur drug, but it might not have been enough alone. Vsevolod believed in strength of will. Something remarkable had happened, against all odds.

Mail was sent by Vsevolod's mother from Paris. During a storm with thunder crashing outside, Vsevolod arrived in a dripping raincoat and held out a telegram from my sister which read: 'Married Walter yesterday.' It was as if I had new vision to see Vsevolod clearly, to place everything once again and realize where I was. We were in Libourne, France . . . the war. I had returned to earth from somewhere else. He removed the paper indicating my nationality from the head of my bed. He also took my passport away, and though I felt unsafe without it, I understood that it meant that the Germans had arrived. He washed my face with warm water and gave me my hairbrush, then held up a looking-glass. It was a shock. Who was that? A small white face with eyes too big and a mane of hair. He shook his head and smiled, saying, 'Phew, it was a close shave.' Dear Vsevolod, dear old friend, what a rum road we had travelled.

'In my dreams I could hear music,' I told Vsevolod, 'isn't that odd?'

In all this time I could not remember having eaten, and I was very hungry. They had not washed me or turned me over in my bed, so we now discovered I had a fearful bedsore; acid was poured on to it which burned. There was talk of gangrene. What was gangrene? Something soldiers get. So I was a soldier at least.

'What has happened to France while I was away?' I asked.

'It has fallen.'

Two German officers entered the room and stared at me.

'Aryan,' they said.

'Is the war over then?' I asked Vsevolod when they left.

'We are occupied,' he said. 'But England fights on.'

'*We* fight on you mean.'

'Not many in France, I think. . .'

We prepared for my departure. They weighed me; my weight was thirty kilos.

4

Vsevolod fetched me from the hospital in the Dormeaus' car; it was like leaving prison. Since I had been inside, the conquerors had come. They were striding the streets in impeccable uniforms or driving around in their tanks. Outside Libourne I looked at the countryside with hunger and thirst; it seemed to slide and lap by as we drove along the winding roads over the hills. There were blue chicory flowers, nasturtiums in masses against farmhouse walls; I was filled with joy at discovering the world again, at not having died. Being alive seemed to course through my body like rushing blood. But the Germans in the villages looked grim. The red sky I remembered over Bordeaux seemed to have been in another life, yet it had led to this: Vsevolod said it had been four weeks. He had also learned in the mail from Paris that my two first cousins had been killed, one shot down in the Mediterranean, the other in the navy.

When we arrived at Fronsac, there was Stephen, one month old, lying in a basket beside the other dark baby, born to Mme Dormeau. They were on a table under the trees. I was given a big bed in a room on the ground floor where I could see and hear what happened through the window.

'We can hide here for a while and hope they won't discover us,' Vsevolod said. 'You are not registered yet as an enemy subject.' The old man of the house passed outside the window. He wore a hat with a feather and propelled himself in a wheelchair because his legs were paralysed. Chickens strutted and crowed. The master had been reported missing in Germany, but his place at table was laid every night, because now that France had fallen he might come.

Apart from the wine which flowed, the meals were frugal. There was usually clear soup made of stock and vegetables, with chunks of bread floating in it, followed by salad and cheese. Meat was eaten only occasionally. Once when there were sardines, Mme Laure took only one, but looked longingly at the box. The dog called Ignace was not fed. They occasionally threw him scraps, or flung the remains of something into the yard. He was a mongrel with golden eyes and he pulled the old man's chair when his arms grew tired and he was unable to propel himself further. Ignace had a shaggy coat and strong shoulders; I felt sure he was always hungry.

There was a new iron, but in order to conserve electricity it was not used. Instead they used the old one that Mme Laure heated on the wood stove. Yet one day the father buried gold dollars in the vegetable garden. How paradoxical and strange I thought, watching him dig his treasure-hole and surveying the beans and lettuces and the miles of vineyards, which seemed to signify riches and security; how could they fear to become poor?

Mme Laure wore her apron back to front, but turned it round when there was a visitor. She disapproved of Vsevolod sitting in the deck chair.

'What is the chair for then?' he asked.

'For company,' she said.

'Well I'm company,' he answered, rather cheekily, I thought, because after all they had taken us in and we should keep our place. So after that, as I suggested, he helped dig out weeds in the vegetable garden, which they did not realize was an amazing gesture from him, being physically very lazy. Mme Laure was shocked when she saw him with a bare chest.

One evening, after Ignace had pulled the old man all the way to the village and back, (his strong shoulder-blades pushing up and down like pistons, his tongue hanging out) and he had drunk gallons of water on his return, I gave him some of my food at dinner. Mme Dormeau and the old man were furious.

'How can you be mean to him and generous to us?' I asked,

embarrassed at my own outspokenness, but carried away by anger.

'That is different,' Mme Dormeau said, 'you will repay us. It is written down.'

'But he pays you. He pulls the chair and guards the house. It is foolish to let him grow weak.'

They glared then at Mme Laure who had cashed in on this distraction to replenish her plate furtively.

When Ignace escaped at night to hunt, they beat him and then chained him. I could not understand their mixture of cruelty to him, kindness to us, lavish wine, gold dollars and miserly economy.

The Germans were expected to set things on fire and rape; there had already been a few cases, but mostly the girls were willing. One day a mild-looking blond boy came to borrow a ladder. He was timid, as if ashamed to be the enemy. Mme Laure spat with splendid venom, though this particular boy hardly even seemed German, until he looked at the babies and then as usual said, 'Aryan,' about mine.

This family life we were leading among the roses and leafy sunlight was complete happiness, in spite of the Germans prowling outside and beyond. There were days of picking greengages in the hot afternoon with the bees drumming in the flowers; or sitting in the kitchen peeling vegetables. They told me I looked like a skeleton and gave me extra bowls of soup; my hair was falling out, and there was a plague of red fleas that made us all itch, yet I was convalescing and happy. They sprayed their vines, the bandages were removed from my back, and one day I rode a bicycle, flying down the hill with the air rushing past, feeling giddy and singing out loud.

In Fronsac there was a cafe in a courtyard full of flowers where we sometimes had a glass of wine under the gaze of a German sentinel, until the mayor told us to refrain as it was unwise. The mayor of Fronsac lied for me; when asked if there were foreigners in his village he did not give me away. But I knew then that our serenity would be short-lived, that once I was well we would have to leave and that we would lose this strange wartime peace, when misers were generous, foreigners friends, and the farm seemed to be our home.

Already in Libourne an undercurrent of panic was growing: pastry was rationed and allowed only two days a week, and the trains departed for Germany every night packed with food, so that soon there would be nothing left. Gradually – but surely – the shop windows looked bleaker and grew empty. Food simply disappeared. The Germans were called the *doryphores* because they took everything. They filled the streets with the ringing of their boots, trudging about and looking disdainful. There were exceptions, however; I saw two young German soldiers one day seeming to be embarrassed. They were in a shop, not managing to make themselves understood, so I translated for them; it was like a game, with their not knowing I was the enemy. Was this handbag real leather, one wanted to know. I answered with my rudimentary German that there was nothing *ersatz* here. Perhaps I seemed slightly indignant at their insulting question about the quality, because they became suspicious and asked my nationality. I quickly lied: American. They at once leapt with fervour into a discussion about America, fortunately not thinking to ask for my identity papers (not that it was the duty of soldiers, but it did happen). They said they were longing to go to America. As I left, one of them whispered to me as if it were a secret, 'We are not happy in France.'

At home that evening we listened to the radio. This was a rare event because the old man was afraid of being caught and would not allow it if he was there. But on this occasion there was no one in the room. Outside Mme Laure was calling, '*Viens pouli pouli pouli*,' as she scattered grain and bread from her apron to the chickens. Alas, the profile of the old man appeared in the doorway before we could get the BBC but we heard on the French news that Vichy had broken off relations with England.

Vsevolod unexpectedly got a job in the railway station, translating between the Germans and the French. Workers' cards were not necessary for this sort of job, which was likely to encourage other White Russians to work for the Germans. Vsevolod was paid and earned some money. This produced an incredible feeling, but it did not last long.

He went to the station each day and came home with things to tell. The Germans were saying they would be in England in three weeks. They did not like the women's make-up, but since they were conquerors, they would make rules about it later when they had time. One day the German stationmaster said to Vsevolod, 'Consider the lavatories. What filth.'

This was true, but Vsevolod answered, 'Consider Pasteur, Balzac and Voltaire. Consider the wine.' The Germans hated the French with a sort of frenzied jealousy.

There was complete incomprehension between the French stationmaster and the German stationmaster: the French had no respect for laws, which in their view were made to be broken. The Germans on the other hand obeyed and respected laws with the result that every day the German stationmaster, lean and fanatical, would ask, 'Where is the train? It is late. Why is it not on time?'

French trains had always been on time but the war made things different, Vsevolod told him.

'But we have signed the peace! There is no war.'

'Call it disorder,' Vsevolod said, and then he was asked to translate the question, upon which the French stationmaster shrugged and walked off. 'Is that all? The train is late? Why bother to translate that? I thought he had something real to say.' Yet the Frenchman was puzzled, according to Vsevolod, because he had seen him staring with sneaking admiration at the German soldiers who arrived looking handsome, immaculate, groomed and rather impressive.

One day two Arabs arrived. They had been demobilized but were still in uniform. They had been despatched to Marseilles, but were completely lost, scruffy and dishevelled. The German was asked for a permit to send them through, and at this he flew into a rage and said, 'It is not civilized the way the French use colonial troops. Look at these specimens.'

'As if war could be civilized,' said Vsevolod.

Sometimes I went to the station. Once we met a Bavarian soldier who accompanied us part of the way home. When we reached a crossroads, he leaned on his motorcycle handlebars and said, 'You don't know my name and you will never see me again, so I will tell you this: I hope England wins! I hope the invasion fails! Germany is mad, and unless England wins we are lost!' and then he roared off fast and we stood there gaping and watching the dust subside. There were blackberries in the hedge which reminded me of the blackberry and plum cakes we had eaten one summer when I was twelve and we had spent our holidays with our parents in Kyllburg in Germany. The people in those bright little homes had been kind and smiling. *Pflaumenkuchen* with cream. Were those people now the ones who were baking Jews instead of cakes? The Bavarian soldier wanted England to win. . .

The Gestapo sent for Vsevolod; the *Kommandant* wished to see him; he was accused of spreading British propaganda, and of having an English wife who had not been declared. Why was she not registered? We were told I must register as an enemy subject and not leave Fronsac until the end of the war. English women were not allowed to move from their residence. We therefore decided to attempt to get on to the train for Paris the next day, pretending to the stationmaster that our journey was official so that he would not ask for travelling papers. This could only succeed if done immediately, before anyone had time to notice, or follow up my registration. We could not stay in someone else's house forever, even if it had become home. . .

So suddenly, with hardly time to think, we said goodbye. The Dormeaus stood at the gate and watched us go. They had been trusting; considering how suspicious and miserly they were, it was all the more generous. How could they be sure we would repay them? Anything could happen. The departure was sad. A man from the vineyards took us to the station in the cart. We sat high up on the suitcases, watching the broad rump of the white horse swinging from side to side along the lanes of honeysuckle where we had spent six weeks and where I would rather have stayed on.

When we reached the station, the German stationmaster said, 'Ah so you are leaving. I thought the English were not allowed to circulate.'

'Yes, I arranged it yesterday at the *Kommandatur*,' lied Vsevolod.

'Oh, is that why you were there,' said the German, 'I thought *they* called *you*.'

'They did,' I said quickly, 'and we came to this arrangement.'

How long would the train take to come now, considering it was always late? How late would it be today? If the German police paid their daily visit first, we would be caught. Even this stationmaster might telephone the Gestapo to check . . . he was looking at us wonderingly.

Vsevolod tried to interrupt his thoughts by saying, 'Look at our son, you have not seen him yet,' and the German looked, and immediately said, '*Wunderbar*, he is a blond!' and we were saved by the Aryan obsession. The train came at this moment; we climbed in, and as it slid further down the platform past the French stationmaster, he winked at us and I blew him a kiss. Then Fronsac and Libourne became the past.

We swayed and rattled along, lurching slowly with heads looking out of the window as we crossed a repaired bridge. In the passage a man brushed past, saying to me in English, 'It's too damned hot,' and was gone. There was a feeling of unseen allies. Some people in France might be eating and sleeping with the Germans, but there were others, not conquered, holding on. The man who had spoken to me probably jumped the train while it was going slow and had now gone back underground. He would not have risked his joke otherwise. As it was, he had vanished as suddenly as he had appeared . . . An Englishman at large: the invisible resistance . . .

5

In Paris the English women, the students and the Jews had to sign the police register every day. Once when I forgot, the police came to see me, so evidently a thorough check was kept on us. There were ration tickets but very little food; the tickets hardly applied and were fairly useless. The black market had started, but this required money, or fraternizing with Germans. Arrests became frequent. Segovia's son, who was simply out walking without identity papers in the Champs-Elysées, was put into a van and deported to Germany. It was the French police who did the rounding up. At night there was curfew. There was a grim feeling that many French had gone over to the 'other side'. They made merry and we heard of parties with caviar. When questioned, they were not in fact pro-Nazi, but just sure Germany would win; they wanted to be on the safe side and also to eat. I thought this worse than being a Fascist which, however base, was at least a belief to hold. Vsevolod said the Germans probably despised these people and that after the war they would have a surprise. We never had one moment of doubt about the outcome, we never lost faith, though there were many French who did not believe in England and who seemed to care about nothing other than their personal comfort.

To all of us in our house a Thing had descended, a feeling of disgust, but also anxiety. What were the Germans going to do?

Kyril Volkoff moved in to stay with us, as did two Turks, one of whom was Prince Fevzi, an enormous bear with a loud laugh. He was kind, generous and spoke little French, but his allowance from the Egyptian Consul helped us all survive. The other Turk, Rafet, used to sit up half the night, wrapped in a Caucasian dressing-gown, copying into his notebook the thoughts and sayings of various writers.

Vsevolod's mother appeared and disappeared in the background, usually wearing a white cotton coat over her clothes like a doctor; Vsevolod said she was a scientist. I was impressed and also somewhat awed by this idea; was she making discoveries or inventions in that room behind the kitchen? Although she was small (she measured about four foot six) and seldom in evidence, she nevertheless seemed to dominate Vsevolod and the house in an obscure way. She spent a great deal of time in her study upstairs or in general behind the scenes – and then suddenly she would be with us, listening and commenting. She had escaped from Russia with her older son who lived in England. She was an ardent admirer of England and its 'spiritual strength'. Vsevolod's father had been in the Imperial Guards. In her study there was a newspaper clipping of him wearing a fur hat and charging on horseback. He had been brave and dashing – but one day had left their house in Russia never to return. No one knew where he was. Eugenie von Schneeuhr, as she was called, seemed to me to be very old. While we had been away she had stayed in Paris with Mars. She had not worried, believing that 'God would provide'. In a strange way he did, for she always seemed to have something to eat, however meagre, and to survive on it as if it were a feast. She wore shoddy clothes, and rouged her cheeks. She received odd-looking visitors, old ladies in ragged coats, trying to retain their appearance with a fur tippet and hat. They were greeted in floods of Russian at the front door and then somehow inhaled up the stairs to the region of the study.

One day it came out by chance in the conversation that by 'scientist', Vsevolod had meant Christian Scientist. He laughed and said, 'People bring her their problems and she emits rays like a healer.' It was mystifying, since there were many icons in her study and the Russian Orthodox priest was also a frequent visitor. And why the white coat? She did hardly anything in the kitchen, as cooking bored her – so it couldn't have been an overall. In spite of his tease, Vsevolod was very fond of his mother and admired her. She exuded strength and self-sufficiency, whereas he himself was perhaps somewhat weak. She rather spoilt Vsevolod, over-praising his slightest poem. There was never a useful criticism; always his poems were the greatest.

Fevzi used to get lost in Paris, then telephone and ask us where he was. 'Where do I live?' he would roar, and we would have to tell the taxi-driver who could not understand Fevzi's accent. He entered a tailor's shop one day shouting, 'Falanelle!' to their alarm – they rushed out looking anxiously into the street – until we explained he wanted a flannel suit. Everything about him was large: his person, his voice, his heart.

But during all this time we were hungry. We had no money. I did not regain strength. Many of the houses round us were empty, their owners not having returned after the exodus, so the rats came from their houses to ours, adding to those we had already. Rats ran up the curtains and the walls. It was very cold, since we had little coal, and the house was damp. Drops ran down the wall and mould formed on the coats that were left in the hall. Outside our house people did not trust each other. A Frenchman who lived opposite denounced us for being spies; he said that so many odd-looking foreigners together must be up to something. This was foolish, because obviously spies take trouble to look ordinary and innocuous; they would not roar like Fevzi or wear skull-caps and brilliant dressing-gowns like Rafet.

Fevzi gave us tickets for the Opera. We arrived at the same time as Goering, who sat in a long car between two officers. The crowd stared. Two people cheered, but one spat and was hustled away. Postcards were being sold with pictures of the Eiffel Tower or the Arch of Triumph, with the inscription: 'Greetings from Paris, Germany'. These were sent home by Germans to their families. The Opera outing was disturbing, and we felt depressed and unsafe until we returned home. But when I talked of safety to Rafet, he said, 'You may be sure they are watching this house. Say "dirty German" once and they will rush through the window and drag you off.'

'You've just said it,' I said, and we laughed, but it was not funny.

'Do you think they know we listen to the English radio, when we can?'

'Probably. They will use it against us in time.'

'How calm you are, Rafet.'

'No, just sad.'

That night the English dropped bombs; we ran out to watch, feeling elated. They fell on to a factory by the Seine.

I had to go to a doctor. He talked to me a long time because I was English; he told me that listening to the English broadcast was his life-saviour. He said that the Germans had shipped nearly all the food away except for their own needs, that not enough was being produced, that growing children were not forming their bones properly, and that the hunger would become desperate. He said he would give me and my son vitamin injections as long as he could obtain them. He told me he no longer saw many of his friends, who were collaborators and dined with the Germans every night; they were opportunists who cared for nothing, believed in nothing – and *dis*believed in England. He said it was tragic that there was no ideal left in France, and seemed exceedingly upset. I had not thought that coming to see a doctor would cause such a watershed.

'My heart is broken by what has happened to France,' he said. 'They have deflated.'

'But the resistance?'

'Oh yes, the resistance. But in such small pockets. Look at Cocteau, Leautaud and so on. None of them care. Leautaud at least was always anti-Jewish, anti-English – he hasn't changed. I hate him but can accept. But look at the others; they are just flabby.'

We had not seen Cocteau lately; he used to be a friend of Vsevolod's and I felt appalled.

'My father was killed at Verdun,' said the doctor. 'That was a different war.'

His name was Maurice. In one meeting we were friends. One hour with him was more than any vitamin injection.

Persecution of the Jews started around that time. Posters were put up with caricatures of the most typical Jewish features. Harry Meerson came to stay with us. He had the exceedingly Semitic face the Germans stereotyped, to such an extent that he was stared at in the street and wanted to hide. He was superb, the type they called ugly.

But it was the French who stamped J for Jew on his passport. The French police summoned him to the Commissariat and turned him over on arrival to two German officers for questioning. His excellent German impressed them, and he was able to bluff his way out of the immediate snare by saying he worked in America, pretending it was the place where he still really lived. The French police did not understand the conversation and he was released. But since he had a Nansen passport like Vsevolod, the French would not let him leave France. He was born in Warsaw, so the *agent de police* called him a Polish ally of the English. 'Your days are numbered,' he said.

'What a fool I was ever to have left America and come back here,' Meerson said, striding up and down, up and down in our small drawing-room on his long legs. 'Those yellow *Vichyssois* . . .'

'Well, get your warm coat ready,' said Rafet, and I prepared another bed upstairs. The third bedroom had become a sort of dormitory. Only Rafet remained downstairs all night because he liked to be alone, he liked the silence of the small hours, he wrote quietly and painstakingly and then slept in an armchair.

The feeling of evil grew. When would the whole of France be occupied? When would they deport all the Jews, arrest the English women? Meerson was planning his escape methodically, but he felt time was closing in. Pétain was allowing young men to be deported to Germany. In our house we despised Pétain for hiding in his old man's clothing. He was admired by many as the hero of the Great War, but he was now the great betrayer. Vichy was vomit to us. We fought with some of our old friends for this cause. There was much hate, and no team spirit except in small groups. But when we heard Churchill's voice coming through on the radio it was like hearing Christ. He gave us certainty, a passionate shining torch and we were uplifted – while outside the boots echoed like the Devil's pulse beating in the streets.

We were so hungry, so increasingly hungry, we thought and talked about food almost all the time. We described meals remembered to each other, or invented meals dreamed of. In the meantime anything available was gobbled but there was never enough to prevent the pangs which made our stomachs gurgle.

We made one black market attempt: someone gave us an address for meat. I bicycled many miles across Paris to fetch it. It was very expensive and wrapped secretively in newspapers; I was told in a whisper that it was pork. I bicycled back, already dilating my nostrils at the imagined smell of roasting meat. There were no potatoes, but we could cook it with apples and onions. I sometimes fried apples in salt, as a vegetable. When I got home Fevzi, Rafet and Vsevolod crowded eagerly round me and we unwrapped the joint together. It was crawling with little white maggots.

The rat plague grew worse. Heat was available now only once a week, and on this day we all had baths. After three o'clock cafes were not allowed to serve coffee. The coffee was in any case foul; *Café National* tasted of road sweepings and chips of wood. I worried about Stephen's diet.

At this point an English woman called Joan du Guerny appeared in our lives. Her husband was a French prisoner of war and she had been sent to us by a friend. She was in her eighth month of pregnancy and wanted to escape before the general arrest. She said she was on the track of a *passeur*, who got people through to the free zone . . . This was legal only for the French, and even then only to those with a valid reason to cross the line. She took me to visit a hospital where there were English prisoners of war: two officers and a soldier with a septic wound after a leg amputation. On this day he also had stomach pains and I remembered Libourne. When we returned a week later he was dead and the officers had been removed to a prison camp. But one of them had given Joan du Guerny an address. She told me to keep it safely, to use it for ourselves as soon as we were able; it was a secret, but she allowed us to give it to Meerson.

A few days later, like a bluebird plummeting out of the sky, a letter came from Lloyds Bank saying they had received money for me. There had to be some mistake in view of the fact that the

Germans controlled the bank, but there was just a chance that they had overlooked my nationality because of my Russian name. We decided to risk going to collect the money – a vastly alarming enterprise.

Vsevolod went into the bank with me and said in German that I was his wife, but showed his own papers. They then asked for mine, and I showed a French identity card. We waited. . . They said, 'Counter Number Eight'. We crossed the bare polished floor with resounding steps feeling we were attracting the maximum attention, desperately hoping they would not check my card again. Since their French was poor, they seemed not to have read it thoroughly. But it was I who had to sign for the money because my father had specified, when I married, that Vsevolod could not sign for me.

We stood transfixed while the man behind the wire bars counted out the money and handed it to us. We tried to walk, not run into the street – but once outside we rushed.

Now we had money we could also escape to the free zone!

When we got home, Meerson had gone. Rafet said he had told him farewell. A man called on us then with a message from my parents: they had sent the money on a gamble, through the Foreign Office. They had no news and were devoured by anxiety. What should he tell them?

'That we got the money, thank God and thank them. We are well.'

He looked at me, rather surprised.

'Don't say I am thin, just say we are all right.'

Now it was essential to get away fast.

The next morning was 19 December. At six o'clock there was loud banging on the front door. Outside the window was a sinister black Citroen. Vsevolod went down, telling me to stay in bed and look ill.

It was the *garde mobile*, come to fetch me. All English women were being taken to Besançon, to a camp in the military fortress up in the mountain above the town. We had been expecting it, yet when it happened, I was sweating and frozen. What would Stephen eat? He would die of cold in the mountains.

'She has fifteen minutes to get ready,' said the voice downstairs, as I listened from the doorway on the landing.

'She is sick,' said Vsevolod, 'she can't get up today. Wait, I will give you a medical paper.'

He came upstairs and we rummaged frantically in the drawer for the registration card from Libourne; luckily we found it.

I got back into bed and lay there trembling. But the man left and Vsevolod came back.

'He has orders to bring everyone,' Vsevolod said, 'whether or not they are sick, or ninety-five, or pregnant. All the women are to go. He has only gone away to order an ambulance, so what shall we do?'

'Telephone Maurice, for a start.'

I put on a dressing-gown and paced restlessly around. Meerson had gone, Joan du Guerny had gone; we too had to get on to the *passeur*. Each time the bell rang I dashed back to bed.

Maurice came. He was wearing a big coat with a fur collar. Outside it was snowing, the light stark and white and the window panes like ice. Maurice was furious. 'There's been an armistice,' he said, 'they can't take the women.'

'There's no armistice with England,' said Vsevolod.

Maurice wrote a new medical certificate with the December date. He held it out uselessly, not believing in its efficacy. He said, 'Your only hope really is that they may not get the ambulance organized immediately. Try to leave at once.'

Then he looked at me rather sadly and said, 'Will you promise to come back to France and see me when this is all over? If you don't die of cold in Besançon, if you succeed in escaping across the lines, it means you will go far away. Do you promise?'

Outside the snow started to fall more heavily and the hushed silence was total. Looking into his kind face, in the silence of my frozen room, I realized that he loved me. It was an honour; he was a beautiful, manly, sad idealist.

'After it is over,' he said again, and stared out at the perpetual snow falling on to our close trees like cages round us. I did not move as I listened to the engine of his car as he drove away. It was the end of my first friend since I had grown up. I never saw him again. I went back after the war but he had died.

The bell rang that afternoon. It was another doctor sent by the Germans. He looked at Maurice's paper with his mouth in a thin line.

'You must realize you are under arrest,' he said then. 'We are coming to fetch you, maybe today, maybe in a few days. There are some other people like you to be picked up and we organize the ambulances per district.'

He again examined the certificate and said, 'It says sickness after childbirth. In your file at the Prefecture there is no mention of a baby.' I was amazed. Were the English women so important? Had they time to check each one? I did not know I even had a file.

'I lived here as a student,' I said. 'My marriage was in England so I suppose it was not registered. The child was not born in Paris, but you may see him.'

They were certainly very thorough, taking time for each person; nothing was left unchecked.

He said no more, but when he saw the child I saw his eyes lighten softly, fatuously, because Stephen was a blond and very perfect baby with small regular features.

He said to Vsevolod in the hall, 'She is under arrest and must not leave the house.'

We now had a possible dividend of more time, but it might only be hours. We had to find the *passeur*. Joan de Guerny had crossed the line alone with her brave large belly; we had received a postcard with merely '*Souvenir de Nice*', as a sign that she had succeeded. The *passeur* was a greengrocer, but we grew desperate because there was no answer to his telephone. The afternoon passed and no ambulance came – a faint hope grew in us. We waited until dark, then went out in the Metro to his address. He was there; the telephone was out of order. He was a grey-haired man with large features who pretended to drive round the countryside fetching vegetables, though in fact he was also getting people across the lines.

'My car is broken,' he said. 'We will go by train. It will take me three days to arrange.'

'Oh God,' I said, shattered, 'they are coming to fetch me any minute.'

'They may not. They always talk that way to make sure people don't try to get away.'

'Please make it soon.'

'I can't do it before. Don't think about it. Or hide somewhere. But prepare to meet me at the Gare de Lyon, in the restaurant at seven p.m. three days from now. You will hear no more from me. Don't try to telephone. Just be there.'

We went home. I could not 'hide somewhere', as he had suggested – not with a baby. Whoever took us in would be arrested. There was nothing to do but hope he was right when he said they often did not return at once . . .

The next morning there was a man in civilian clothes, walking about outside the house. We were being watched. Optimistically, I thought this might be a sign that they would not come at once. It was two days before Christmas. We could not sit down, we could not read. Our nerves were raw. What could we do to pass three days? We bought a Christmas tree and also miraculously found a turkey and we feverishly set about organizing a Christmas dinner. Mars stole the turkey which we retrieved, mangled. Whenever the doorbell rang blood rushed through my ears. I listened, trying not to breathe, to hear who each visitor was.

On Christmas Eve the visitor was an old Russian man, wearing a black fur cap. He had heard Vsevolod's name in the Russian church in the morning, where his mother had gone to take parcels of clothes; this old man had realized Vsevolod was the nephew of an officer under his command of the fortress of Sebastopol. Another war, another time . . . What was even more astonishing, he had known Vsevolod's father, the father who was a legend and whom Vsevolod had never known himself (his mother never mentioned him) . . . So this stranger came to dinner, bringing a feeling of fate and balance and hope. There had been so many wars – ours was just one more, its proportions diminished. We learned that Vsevolod's father had flown in the very first aeroplane. This father whom nobody knew became real, a daredevil, a hothead, a man of action. Looking at the baby, the old Russian said he was pleased that Nikolai had a grandson. I clutched the tiny grandson and prayed: Nikolai Gebrovsky and Elton Mayo, two grandfathers, please make magic with God so we get away.

Fevzi said I should leave Stephen behind so he would be safe, but I told him never.

I made a sack out of blankets sewn together and put Stephen into this with almost his entire wardrobe. This was convenient for travelling and had the added advantage that he could not possibly be cold. We observed the Russian custom of sitting down for a moment for good luck before leaving the house. Then as we stood in the doorway to say goodbye to Vsevolod's mother, who appeared that evening to be especially small, her dark button eyes piercing, she said, 'Keep this in mind: spirit doesn't travel, you are already there.'

We walked out through the snow and away, carrying Stephen and one suitcase. Her words must be one of what Vsevolod called her Z–z–z– messages, I thought, and tried to hold firmly to the thought: we are already there. I tried repeating it when fears came to me, and was grateful for the snow which seemed to hide us. We took the Metro, where the Germans stared at us. This made my hackles rise since I knew we did not look local – and they knew the English had been rounded up. I stared back at them saying inside: they can't really see us. We're invisible. We're going to make it. It was very difficult to hold these thoughts since other fears crept into my mind constantly, especially the one about Stephen, who was already undernourished and might easily die of cold in Bensançon.

In the Gare de Lyon our morale was strengthened because the *passeur* was there and he took charge. He seemed quite different in his big coat and large-brimmed felt hat; he looked like an old actor. Two other men were with him and were to travel with us. No one was introduced by name. We ate sandwiches that tasted of nothing and were hard to swallow. Then we got into the train.

Once inside the carriage I felt excited; this was our escape train and we were hidden. But the thought was foolish and premature because inspectors come through trains – and how could such a large group not be noticed? Our fellow passengers were probably Gaullists. However, we had to trust the *passeur*. It was after all his organization; the best but most difficult thing was not to think at all.

There was one stranger in our carriage. When the train moved and the platform started to slide by, I sighed. At this the stranger looked up sharply, and the others frowned at me. Control yourself. I folded my arms, holding my body tight, my nails digging through my sleeves: it is now. Now this thing is really happening. Goodbye Paris; there must not be one slip.

6

The stranger in the carriage starts to chat as the train jogs along. How far are we going? He has an *Ausweis* through to the free zone. Are we going through too? Our men grow restless and maybe impatient with this, and go out to stand in the passage. Now I am alone with the stranger, apart from Stephen lying in his large bundle on the seat; the train is cold with black window panes.

The stranger looks at me curiously and asks again where we are going. I tell him we are going to stay with friends.

'In a few hours we will be at the frontier,' he repeats. 'Are you crossing?'

'No.' I am not prepared for this and wish the *passeur* would come back. Is it a questionnaire or is he just chatty? And I think: Yes, we are crossing too, but not your way.

The train stops after a few hours and we change to a smaller one. We sit in the station. There are no lights and it is even colder than in the last train; we grow numb. Stephen, however, is red-faced; his complete wardrobe of clothes seems to be serving him well. The night seems very long but the train finally moves and gradually the diluted light of a new, wet, cold morning appears.

We get out at Montceau-les-Mines. Without speaking, we follow the *passeur* and go into a cafe. He tells us then that the plan is to wait here all day and cross the line at night. He sends me to the kitchen so that I do not stand out and look displaced, all day in a cafe with a baby. The night will be spent in an inn known as Nenesse; it is called Chez Erneste and is five kilometres away. We will walk there casually along the road, once it is evening. We will have dinner there and retire to bed. At two in the morning he will waken us to make the crossing. It seems that it will be a long day first . . .

Outside the window there is a poster on the wall depicting an English Tommy laughing, standing astride miserable starving people and children who are lying at his feet. Not only have the Germans taken the food, they also paste lies on the walls.

I sit in the kitchen looking at this poster, and we wait. All day Stephen and I wait. The men are luckier, since they can walk about without attracting attention. Our two travellers are wearing workmen's blue overalls. Our *passeur* strolls off with them and Vsevolod, just a group of unnoticeable men. I sit in the kitchen where the *patron* gives us some soup. This is the great action we have been expecting, but for the moment it is static, though all my nerves are alive. The *patron* comes in and out frequently and talks to me. He tells me people are often questioned here because it is so near the frontier of the free zone. He says if anyone should ask what I am doing, I should reply that I have come to look for potatoes or coal. He does not know or ask my nationality; large numbers of French also pass without permits. In spite of their blue overalls, the two men who are with us do not look like workmen to me; there is something about them . . .

Now Vsevolod comes back looking pale. The two men and the *passeur* come with him into the kitchen. The *passeur* tells us the game is up: last night at Chez Nenesse the people were caught and are now in prison. The *auberge* is surrounded by German guards. The *passeur* says that this was his only plan; he has no other and does not know what to do. He sits down with his head in his hands. We look at each other; it is quite unreal. Here we are in a kitchen. The *patron* won't want us here forever. We have left Paris . . . we have nowhere to go . . . it is ten o'clock and broad daylight – the *passeur* continues to sit with his head in his hands.

I suggest going to the hotel across the street, taking rooms and lying low all day until we think of something – no one would see us there. But the *passeur* starts violently and says that hotel is the Gestapo headquarters.

'All the more reason,' I hear myself say – 'they would not expect people to hide in such a place.' And I am thinking that by now they must have been to fetch me in Paris and know I have gone. *We have to disappear . . .*

'A disaster,' the *passeur* says. 'The fifteen people who were caught last night were Jews who had come from Germany and brought their valuable possessions with them. They will probably be shot.'

'We will go to the hotel,' I repeat. 'We've got to get out of here. If people have been caught they will start going through the cafes. You can't leave us now. Please think of something – and when you do, come and tell us. Just ask for the Russian name.'

We are in a hotel room with the door locked. The lobby was full of Germans when we went through. Vsevolod chattered away in French and they did not take much notice of us. We told the blue overall men to come and tell us as soon as there is a new idea. But Vsevolod is now becoming frantic, though we are here alone. With me, it alternates; I am strangely calm, but know it won't last. He says they will imprison me. Of course, but what else was Besançon? Maybe I will be shot, he says. He says he is losing his nerve, it was all right as long as we followed a plan, but this oasis, waiting in a nest of Germans, with the plan suddenly stopped short . . . I tell him they will certainly not shoot me, since I am only a prisoner of war. He says they may have orders to shoot because I was told not to go away and they may think I am a spy . . .

'Stop talking,' I say then, as we start to snap at each other. 'You talk too much. You talk all the time.'

'We can't stay here. It was mad to come here.'

'We aren't going to stay here. Let's eat something,' I say then. 'It looks like a place where there must be food.'

'Eat?' he shouts. 'Are you crazy? All you can think of is that we should eat?'

'Yes, I am growing. I am hungry, hollow and famished. Never can I get enough.'

'Even when we may be about to be shot?'

There is hammering on the door; at this I also panic. But it is only a maid who gives us forms to fill in. Name, nationality. Last address. Destination. Reason for travelling.

Could she not overlook it, Vsevolod asks, we are only resting here for an hour and will not stay. But the maid says no, every new arrival must fill in their passport numbers.

'All right,' my voice says. 'Leave them here, we will fill them in and bring them down when we leave. Now please bring breakfast.'

She goes away. I dream of toast; crisp outside and soft inside, with melted butter. Why is toast so delicious? The symbol of home when one is at school . . .

We have greenish tea and greyish bread with no butter, and jam made of fermented grape sugar that hurts the teeth. Pangs like small sharp arrows rise into the jawbone. Stephen has concentrated milk I have brought with us. It is the point when the action stops and we have time to think of what might happen, that it is the most difficult to control oneself.

Luckily, as this meal finishes, one of the blue overall men comes to fetch us. He says, 'Come back quick, we have discussed it and decided to cross in daylight. After the arrests of last night, and because up until now people have always crossed by night – they will not be expecting it. It is anyway our only chance.'

So we fill in the forms; I write English and I hope we leave the hotel before they have time to read it. The maid comes for the tray, and we point with largesse to the forms and rush away. I imagine I see her gaping – but she is French – why should she betray us? She might even put them at the bottom of the pile . . . and now we are out in the street and away.

Once again in the kitchen of the cafe opposite, the *passeur* introduces us to two gamekeepers who are to be our guides. One of them is tall, with a bony mountaineer's face; the other has a wall-eye. They both have sticks.

'Do not talk unless essential,' they tell us. 'Follow us, but not in a group – straggle along the road.'

The wall-eyed one points to the other, 'My friend will go in front and communicate with me in his fashion. It is a fifteen kilometre walk from here to reach the safe zone of the other side. We leave now.'

I give him my passport, which he puts in his pocket. We say goodbye to our *passeur* and give him some money; we are elated once more because action has returned. It is a feeling like bursting. The *passeur* says he will wait here until the guides return, to hear whether we get across.

'That will be a great help,' says Vsevolod sarcastically.

'*Ça va, ça va,*' says the old man, and smiles for the first time. He keeps our suitcase and says he will check it through to Marseilles.

We set off along the road, the men straggling ahead separately, Vsevolod and I together with the baby, trying to look relaxed and detached. One guide is quite far in front of the other – they both glance back occasionally but not at the same time, and never directly at us – they appear to re-read a signpost or look at a hedge. Stephen is already very heavy so we take it in turns to carry him. On the edge of a forest we see an inn with Chez Erneste written above the door; here is the scene of our failed rendezvous. There are no guards; did the gamekeepers know their change of patrol time, or is the watch only at night, since no one has yet passed this particular path by day? We leave it behind and head into the woods; here there is no longer a road; we follow the men who make their own track, and they do not seem to mind now that we walk in a group. But as the curve of road disappears from sight, a car appears on it; one gamekeeper points towards it with his stick and beckons us to hurry. We reach the slope and get over it out of sight. It feels safer in the trees. The guide speaks now: 'That was a German car. They probably saw us but it may not matter. But they may think it over and try to cut us off – so we must go faster.'

We quicken our steps and follow up a hill into thicker woods. The baby grows heavier and my spine cannot hold straight. We are hot but the air feels like knives of ice. Sticks snap under our feet and snow thuds down off branches. Everywhere there are animal footprints. There is the noise of people panting; we must not make a noise but cannot help it. The guide in front occasionally whistles like a bird to his colleague, only two or three notes, very soft. Then as we turn right and go downhill again Stephen slips right into his bag and disappears. I wonder if he will suffocate, but we cannot stop. We keep going – I try to pull him up and adjust – and on we go at the same pace, no matter what, diarrhoea or puking – the speed remains even. For God's sake let the baby not cry. One guide is waving his stick and we are out in the open again. The other guide whistles his bird call and points – it seems we are changing course. It feels vulnerable out of the protection of the trees.

Now we pass a lone farm. Dogs bark; perhaps they will give us away. Who would have thought of dogs? For miles it is now known there are strangers. As we pass the gate there is an old woman leaning on it; she nods and says: '*Bonne chance*. The patrol passed this morning; they change time each day but must be due back, so hurry.' She gives momentarily the feeling of an ally, but also extra anxiety. As we walk on, taking less care as we hurry, as the distance mounts and we feel we must be near the end – the rhythm of feet can be distinctly heard. The taller of the blue overall men is coughing – the noise barks out like a fox. He looks purple and murmurs that he can't help it. Vsevolod says Hibidashumai under his breath. There is a feeling of things disintegrating. We were told not to speak.

Now the guides stop. There is a wooden board on a tree with the words: *Ligne de Demarcation*. Can this be true? One guide says softly, 'I will take the short cut which runs along the line itself, and I will join you later. You must all follow my friend now. You must not take a chance. If I meet them I will try to detain and delay them – they know me and as a gamekeeper I am allowed to circulate.'

As he finishes, and we set off behind his friend, five German helmets appear round the corner of the hill, five bayonets, five fixed faces. For one second we stare. Then the guide shouts, 'Run!' – and the tall one runs ahead up the hill and we follow. Now we either get there or we will be shot, for this *is* the line – and how far beyond it does their authority go? There is shouting behind us: Halt! There are two shots, a soft whistling noise, but we are running, running and running up the hill with our throats and bodies bursting, torn apart with the maximum over-effort beyond our physical powers. There is a line crossing our path and continuing across country. We stumble and jump over this ditch, and in spite of the speed and the rush, there is time to think: is that all it is? A little ditch? And now we are a mass of animals, gone berserk, with no direction . . . We career up the hill, following the guide, hanging on to each other, amok. Another shot whirrs past, then we reach the top of the hill and we are rolling and running with loose collapsing legs over and down the other side, screaming and laughing and crying. Over the hill and beyond: we are there. The Germans won't come any further, this is FREE FRANCE – they may shoot as far as they can aim but not through a hill! We are there – across the border and away; we have made it.

The guides both grin now, the tall blue overall man is lying in the snow panting, saying, 'Of all times to have a liver attack . . . But we are free!' We laugh and laugh as if we are all mad. This is the free zone. We hug and kiss each other and dance, though we are so weak our legs cave in. We are rag dolls and we are drunk. Now we can make a noise, it is all right to talk, and we all chatter. The second blue overall tells us that they are indeed Gaullists, as we had thought. One asks to carry the baby; he has one himself that he has never seen. Talk, chatter, prattle, verbal diarrhoea. The men tell us they are carrying documents to England; if they had been caught they might have been tortured for information.

We reach a cluster of houses where the French flag is flying on a tall pole. The sight of it smites us with patriotism and faith in winning the war. There is a bus waiting; the guide says it always waits in the middle of the countryside in case there are escapees. He gives me back my passport. We say goodbye. I think: for the rest of my life I must see with a special lucidity each person, each leaf, each thing; nothing will be the same again, nothing taken for granted.

The bus starts its engine. The baby gets his usual attention from old women on board, country people going from the inn to Cluny. We wave at the gamekeepers and they now grow smaller and smaller. I wish we could know more about these men of the forest, but they are gone forever, waving their sticks and watching us go with their mountaineers' eyes.

At Cluny the bus stops. We change to another. In Macon we have baths, dinner, a vast amount of wine; we are giddy, we are soaring because we are free.

7

The next day our feeling of freedom rapidly vanished. Vsevolod could not travel without a special permit because he was of military age, as well as an *apatride*. We all boarded the train for Marseilles, where an inspector tried to detain us but we managed to push him off the train as it started to move, the questioning having taken place by the door at the end of the coach in front of the lavatory (a fortunate detail) – and with us murmuring lies about having *lost* Vsevolod's permit. This was how we discovered he needed one.

When we reached Marseilles it began again: there was a guard outside the station. One of the Gaullists had lent Vsevolod an extra set of military papers which got us through the exit. We were *there*, in Marseilles – but now what?

The streets were crowded with people milling back and forth; they wore a hunted look and did not appear to be going anywhere. There was talk of boats to Tunis. Faces looked strained. This was our longed-for freedom. Identity papers were asked for frequently, we discovered, and any homeless person was arrested; these were the rules of Free France. It was therefore necessary to establish a residence. A person had the right to exist as long as he stayed in one place but any form of travel required documents. Our Gaullist friends were leaving for England the next day since arrangements had been made for them. We decided to go to Cannes, as it would be better to be 'stuck' somewhere smaller. But this first night, as hotels were all full, we applied the usual solution and went with our Gaullists to a brothel where Stephen, their youngest customer, had fresh milk. There were fewer police checks here than in hotels so we hoped to get safely to Cannes the next day before being questioned. At night the feet of trudging herds of people resounded up and down the Canebière. Nobody seemed to know or care who they were, whether they were left over from the exodus or just lost people.

Cannes was a complete contrast – balmy air, quiet sunlight, and a small surf on the shore of the tideless sea. In the bar of the Carlton Hotel there was a Welshman in a baggy suit. He was real, and at liberty . . . it seemed to be paradise.

We learned 'the system'. Money could be paid to a man in New York, his correspondent would then produce the equivalent at this end. A cable was worded in terms of fur skins: a fox meant a hundred dollars. We were in touch with my parents. The police allowed us to stay, provided we never moved at any time without notifying them, so we decided to register, even if this amounted to swearing to remain. We felt free and the view looked like a free place, though the people we met told us they were trapped, as we ourselves would discover later. For now, it seemed very beautiful: the old port, the Grand Hotel with its huge palm trees where my sister had stayed with my father on part of their grand tour. It was warm – no more rats or cold like in Paris.

Without notifying the authorities, we went to Nice for the day to see what the chance of an exit visa from a different Prefecture might be. There was no chance. No exit visa was allowed for a stateless foreigner, even with an immigration visa for America; the world of papers and stamps had returned.

Cannes was small like a village and strangers came to know each other soon. Pedro was a political refugee who could not return to Spain; he took his bicycle to his bedroom every night so it would not be stolen. There were few cars and bicycles were worth gold. There was an Englishman called Jimmy who was taken prisoner at Dunkirk and managed to get away. He said he was trying to find a way back to England, but did not seem to be trying very hard. He sat in the sun, not complaining, and the consul gave him a survival allowance. He said Marseilles was the place for intrigues; you could go anywhere from there but it required 'arranging'.

Vsevolod met people he played cards with and I went for walks with Jimmy and Pedro, pushing Stephen along the Croisette in a pram lent by our rooming house. The owner of this *pension* also had a grandmother who liked taking Stephen to walk under the pines, where she said the air was good. We settled into a non-life, marking time.

Posters said: 'Those who follow de Gaulle betray their country. Long live Pétain. Frenchmen: remember Mers El Kebir.'

All the books in the bookshops were Free French literature: *The Life of the Marshal, The Friends of the Marshal, The Pure French Blood*. Soon there would be books about Aryans.

Pedro knew a Yugoslav whom he thought we might bribe for Vsevolod's exit visa. We returned to Nice to meet him, but to no avail. He said to come back in a month. Indeed, it did seem that everyone was waiting for visas, or some sort of fraudulent ticket for a boat out of Marseilles – and there was much talk of total occupation. It was certain to come, but when? At this I felt alarm; there was a file on me, they would find me and what then? When I heard feet marching in the early morning I looked uneasily out of the window; it was the French Youth parading, bedraggled and out of step.

We met a man called Barry the Beachcomber who had been a film actor but seemed to be drinking himself to death. He had also got into the Foreign Legion by faking his papers and pretending to be Dutch. He told me contradictory stories about Marseilles, saying that all the ports were blocked and it was too late to try to go anywhere. He was always very well dressed and explained he put his trousers under the mattress each night. 'Always look after your wardrobe, kid,' he said. I wondered why he had wanted to be in the Legion, which was supposed to be for fierce drop-outs or people with a record. What could have happened to this outwardly cheerful Canadian?

Vichy passed strict laws; there was midnight curfew, anyone found in the streets after hours would be arrested. I dreamed of chocolate and bananas. We were always hungry; there was even less food here than there had been in Paris. Food was mainly *rutabaga* and *topinembongs* (types of Jerusalem artichoke and swede) without salt, because there was no salt either. One day when I was walking in cold rain with Barry, an overwhelming smell of herbs and garlic came wafting out of a side street. He did not look surprised, as he knew the black market restaurant. He reached for his wallet, counted his money, then took me to lunch where we ate snails. I was famished, but still English and had never eaten them before. Added to this, I could not remember eating anything that could be called food for many months. I will never forget the degree of satisfaction a greedy lunch gives to a famished stomach. But neither of us was used to rich food, or eating so much, and after the sensuous licking of oil was over and we were back on the cold Croisette, we both had cramps and were sick.

Jimmy had one suit, Pedro usually wore a black sweater and red scarf, Barry had a surprising Hollywood wardrobe and a white linen suit ready for the summer. He repeatedly gave the same advice without waiting to be asked; it was his sort of lifeline: 'The more you are broke, the more you must look after your clothes. Always be clean and immaculate and don't let them guess. Broke is not poor. But if you let yourself go, then you grow poor. The good luck event will not come, the change will not happen . . .'

A man on the Croisette took a photograph of me. He was André Ostier, a *Vogue* photographer from Paris. He hired me as a model and I made some money. My picture came out on the cover of *Marie-Claire* and Jimmy saw it up in the mountains where he said (mysteriously) he had been to investigate an escape route.

I was growing impatient about Vsevolod's visa, afraid the Germans would arrive before we got out – and irritated with his card-playing. I was tired of being sorry for him, tired of being 'nice'. It was normal to have tried to help him, up to a point; anyone would have done so. But now all he did was gamble. What of Stephen, stagnating here in this first year of his life? He was not eating properly, and I was sick too of the grape sugar that made the jawbone ache and stained the teeth black. Stephen should have a better chance. We still followed up each tip, each new name of an official who might help. It was right – and yet . . . *Apatride*, Nansen; who was Nansen anyway? When I asked

Vsevolod he did not know himself beyond the fact that he was a Norwegian who had tried to help displaced people. No one seemed to care. What was a Nansen passport to an average man? Another word for stateless. N for no one, a non-person, never. It was like a street name, which most people associated only with the street, not wondering about its origin. I wanted to leave all this and take Stephen to America where he would be safe. My parents had been staying in Wiscasset Maine, which was the latest telegraphic address. What a name . . . Were people at least really free in America, the home of our childhood?

At this time I met and made friends with Micheline Presle, who was about my age and just starting on her acting career. It was exciting to talk of her future, and made me also want to do something 'real' – apart from nursing Vsevolod. I told Micheline I wanted to be a dancer, and then realized it was true. At school my music had been good and my teacher said I should never give it up. We talked of Micheline's plans, and I sensed her dedication and knew she would succeed.★

Pedro took me for a drive into the hills in a cart he had hired, with a horse who was so weak he could hardly reach the top. He apparently only had beetroot to eat. Mimosa was in flower, a smell of arbutus and the maquis; spring was coming. We had crossed the line in January; now it was nearly April – how much longer would it be . . .? There were villas with blank faces, shutters closed, their owners absent somewhere safe.

'Who are you Pedro? Why did you have to leave Spain?'

He tried to tell me about the complications of Spain, the 'apart-place', and the war that had been fought when I was at school.

'Why do you stay here?'

'My family are all dead. Here I am not yet in prison. Where else could I go? America? That is *your* dream. I'll never get there.' (Would we?)

It was the last time I saw him. After that he disappeared. What would happen to a Republican from Spain? Three days later, Barry was no longer around. Anyone 'not there' was presumed arrested. Our friends diminished in eerie fashion. We started to

★This was six years before her greatest film: *Le Diable Au Corps*, with Gerard Philippe.

feel that the 'something dreadful' we expected would happen before we had time to get out. The newspaper that morning said: 'Why not arrest all foreigners and have done with the trouble they are?' We were hated simply for being foreign, we felt illegal, that we had no right to exist. But what harm had we done? I began to feel as much a pariah as an *apatride*; the English were enemies and hated more by Vichy than the *apatrides* who were only despised. In some ways Vichy was worse than the Germans. Yet foreigners had 'made' the Côte d'Azur, Jimmy had told me. In 1835 Lord Brougham had made the first garden in this climate of natural beauty, considered until then too hot to live in. There were sixty-three sorts of flowers in his garden. After that came Sir Herbert Taylor, followed by Woolfield and Leader, who also made famous gardens . . . then came those of the White Russians who were rich – a minority, but large enough to bring prosperity and glamour to this coast where the land and its people had been poor. Now all was resentment and hate. They loathed us.

During the daytime, those of us who were left formed a group in which I felt relatively brave; but at night as I lay in bed I was frightened of everything I could think of; each noise must be the Germans arriving. Total occupation was surely coming any day now, any week . . . Stephen was not building his bones with only flour and dried milk mixtures to eat . . .

The grocer had been insulting one afternoon, saying that the English blockade was the reason he had nothing for sale. Did he believe the lies? A notice which was nailed on to the tree outside his shop said: 'England is a plutocracy led by the Jews.' Poor deluded grocer. Or was he a lousy Fascist grocer? He did not *have* to believe, did he? But this was the New Order, Free France; most local people just swallowed it down and digested sour bile; it was perhaps agreeable to have a scapegoat to hate. The express train rattled through like the ghost train each night, taking provisions and whatever was left to Germany or Italy.

Jimmy was out after the midnight curfew. The police beat him with a leather whip and he was put in prison in Grasse where there were rats in his cell; this was how Vichy treated a minor offence. They seemed zealous far beyond acceptance of defeat; it was their faith. They were not the conquered; this made them aggressively active in their own cause.

Some people disappeared, but others appeared. Maurice Chevalier, last seen at the Gare d'Austerlitz, was seen bicycling along the Croisette one day, saying his teeth would fall out because of the food. He got little sympathy because he could afford black market and was notoriously mean. There was much bitterness and envy about food. Ration tickets were meaningless and produced nothing; fairness was non-existent. Pierre Brasseur was angrily drunk in a bar one afternoon. Poiret, who was once a famous couturier but now an old man, was reduced to reciting La Fontaine's Fables in a nightclub in order to survive. He chose *Le Chêne et le Roseau*, with obvious allusion to the reeds that bent in the wind, winning out over the strong oak. This dispelled the rumours that he had collaborated in Paris. His message was: wait, and be supple.

On the Croisette I met a girl I had known at school. She had been let out of the concentration camp at Besançon after three months because she was Australian. They might possibly have let me out too, since I had been born in Sydney, but during those three months Stephen would probably have died of cold, as had two old ladies she told me about.

'Anyway,' she said, 'with an English passport you would have stayed inside. They keep track of each person and they obviously have a cross by your name, since you got away. What on earth are you doing, hanging around here? You must be mad. Get out while you can and let the Russian follow.'

'He would not manage – it's a promise I made – but we'll see.' After that I was confused.

Then we discovered the casino. I was under age but allowed in because of being married. There were people who went there every morning after breakfast, like going to an office, and stayed all day until it closed. Amnesia and fascination enveloped them. They gambled their escapes, their visas, their bribe-money; when they lost, they lost their chances, but at least during the time they spent enclosed in these walls, they forgot. It was warm, there was a bar, people walked about when not gambling and met each other. A Greek lost large sums frequently, but no one was sorry for him because he was known to eat lobster on the black market and could therefore afford to lose. I liked him. Why should he not eat lobster? Anyone would, given the chance.

I learned the game *trente et quarante* which I played in a mild sort of way, excited when I won. But not having enough money really to gamble I did not risk much and soon got bored. Besides I felt guilty because even the small amount we had for our escape and our life came from my parents, and to a lesser degree from my earnings as a model. Also, I became bored with the place itself which was airless and enclosed and its players obsessed. Outside one afternoon when I heard the palm trees crackling in a wild mistral, I decided to give it all up and leave. I would look for Stephen on the Croisette where our old Provençal granny-lady would be pushing his pram.

When I went to tell Vsevolod I was leaving, I found him white-faced. He said he had lost all our money. And then I was angry; I scorned and despised him.

'Why are you at the baccarat table,' I said, 'which is for millionaires? Why can't you at least play roulette which is small-time, like we are?'

And I turned and walked away trying to control conflicting emotions: tragedy, disgust, pain, hurt, despair. Damn the Nansen passport – then shame at myself. Who really was Nansen and why could I not be great and altruistic like him? But this was Stephen's escape-money too, Stephen's chance; that was why.

The door was held open for me by an Italian whose familiar face I had seen a few times in this village life of the casino where people knew each other by sight. Outside we stepped into the huge racing wind with a smell of green spring growth.

'Come and have a drink somewhere,' he said, and I jumped at it gratefully, not even wondering who he might be. I got into his car, so upset by Vsevolod's losing all our money that I did not register or remember immediately that it was unusual for anyone to own a car. We drove off quite normally, looking out at the wild swishing palms. Still preoccupied, I asked, 'Who was Nansen?'

He told me. Fridtjof Nansen, a Norwegian explorer who experimented with icebergs, was the High Commissioner for Refugees at the League of Nations in 1920; he championed their cause and created their passport, for which he won the Nobel Peace Prize in 1923.

I gasped. How well-informed this man was to reel it off like an encyclopaedia, and as we drove happily along the coast in his car I was furious with Vsevolod for not knowing more about his own saviour. Perhaps, though, he was not saved. It was up to me to wait here for him. I would not let him down now. He was my mission. The temptation to leave passed, my pity returned, but the excessive boredom with his weakness remained. His mother had always over-bolstered him: he was an Adonis, a poet. Romain Rolland's letter praising his poetry was regularly produced. He was handsome and a success with the ladies. But what was a poet in the twentieth century? It was not enough to be just a poet and nothing else.

We seemed to be driving for miles. So this man had petrol, I observed at last, forgetting Vsevolod. He told me he had read law and studied political economy. Like Paolo. How beautiful Italian names sounded when he pronounced them. Could he have known Paolo? I asked him. He knew Asolo! He talked then of Elenora Duse's house there . . . and back came my lost summer, where the world had spread itself out at our feet, promising and sure, and the future had seemed like the view of the endless Veneto plain seen from the piazza, blue like heaven.

I remembered the special sound of last year's northern Italian voices, and these gentle people, so different from the southerners. Above all I remembered Paolo's voice saying: '*Ti voglio bene,*' and I said to this strange man, 'Do continue to tell me all this in Italian, not French, for I love the language.' Suddenly the car stopped and I was grasped in an enormous hug, a mouth was pressed against mine with a hot tongue tasting of all the things we were deprived of: Béarnaise, chocolate, cigars. I was stupefied. Oh God, of course: the car and enough petrol . . . he must be in the Armistice Commission. What a dumb blonde I was!

'*Sono abruttita,*' I said. After all it was my fault; no one could blame him. What a pity. He was a rather attractive man, with a face like a Roman coin – in spite of his belched-up luxury. I had enjoyed his company.

'Can you please take me back?'

'What does it matter who is the enemy?' he said.

'It does. My sister is bombed in London. My two first cousins are killed. We fight for belief in this war, not territory. It is special.'

'Your lover Paolo is a Fascist like me.'

'No. He thought Mussolini was a pompous balloon. I don't

know what he is doing now, but he is not like you.'

He drove me back, polite and respectful. I was eyed by the Greek when I got out of the Italian car.

In our room I found Vsevolod fallen apart like a heap of rags, and crying. He needed consoling. He needed a mother, perhaps not his own, but another mother. He was thirty-two. I could just have been his daughter, but I tried to be maternal. It was difficult, the more so since I was remembering Paolo and would have preferred a virile man who would have looked after us and coped.

'Dear old Vsevolod, never mind,' I said. 'Just keep out of the casino. It is now out of bounds. O.K. We agree?'

He smiled his charming slightly sad smile, and we were brothers of the road again.

'What will we do?' he asked.

'I'll sell something. My gold bracelet.'

When he had his sad-Slav expression, and his eyes slanted downwards, it changed the set of his features and made him, in my eyes, look nicer than his usual perfectly proportioned face, famous in Paris, admired by Cocteau. But now he was not proud but humble and contrite; the whole lost continent of Czarist Russia was showing through his brown eyes. Poor old wretched fellow. Obviously it was tempting to try and double our money. It was a Russian tradition anyway. He had never had a chance.

We stood together and looked out of the window at the clouds of the evening sky. The pawnshop and the jeweller would both be shut now, so there was no money for dinner that night. I thought of the Armistice Commissioner tucking in somewhere.

I told him then about the Italian incident and we both laughed. I told him also of Paolo and found that he knew the name of his family, who had been famous for their honour throughout history and had fought for the various kings. What *was* happening to Paolo now, an anti-Fascist in Italy?

It was spring and there was a smell of jasmine. Were there still sixty-three sorts of flowers in Lord Brougham's garden – was it still there even?

We had been in this cul-de-sac five months.

8

On 25 May at last, unbelievably and quite suddenly, the exit visa was granted. It was on our seventh trip to Nice. The Yugoslav had discovered who to pay. He handed us the passport, having obtained its small, trivial-looking stamp.

He grinned. 'Now hurry away,' he said.

But in order to leave France we also needed a Spanish visa, and to obtain this we needed boat tickets, to prove we would not stay, because people were only allowed into Spain on transit. So we began the new job of obtaining berths on a boat, the only possibility of space being on ships going from Bilbao to South America. Now that we were so nearly there the terror of time running out was acute; each night I dreamed I heard the noise of boots marching, like in Paris and Libourne . . . We must race to the frontier first. There was an agreement between Spain and Germany that men of military age would not be allowed through; was Vsevolod considered of military age? We contacted an American doctor friend of my father's then in Marseilles with the Quaker Friends. We waited for him to confirm our tickets in an eerily empty Cannes; when his telegram arrived we went to Marseilles to meet him and spent our last night in France.

'You have passage to Buenos Aires,' he said, 'it was all I could get. The conditions are dreadful. Do you mind?'

I laughed.

'Do not talk politics to anyone on the train or say where you are going. You can be denounced for anything at all, or rather for nothing at all. Even if you have the right to travel, a form of hysteria has set in.'

At five the next morning the noise of endless lorries leaving the port was shattering. Could German tanks have arrived? A form of hysteria now set in at our hotel room. We were frantic to board our train which would not leave till the afternoon. The streets were still seething with faces, as on our last visit, but they seemed different, as if they had lost hope; feet tramped evenly like automatons.

On the train our anxiety was heightened even more, and the nearer we grew to the goal, the more important it was to reach it. But the train was so slow, taking so long to reach Toulouse where we had to change. A much delayed postcard from Kyril Volkoff said the Germans had been angry not to find me when they came to the house. I thought of this now and felt pursued. There was still this day and a whole night to pass in trains. We stopped again at Sette, the port for 'German fish'. The next train went even more slowly.

And then, as time passed, something strange happened: numbness gradually overcame me as if I was ceasing to care. I looked at Vsevolod whose face was like those in the crowds in Marseilles, fatalistic and resigned, so the feeling was evidently mutual. This was our eternity. We had always been on a train, unwashed and dirty. We would never really arrive anywhere. The long anti-climax after the long suspense had turned into a permanent state. We were travellers in a never-ending search for a destination in which we only half believed. Perhaps arrival, like freedom, was just an idea, and when we reached it, it would turn out to be an illusion. We had no power of decision, just the power to go on. And on. Sit in a train, hungry, smelly, and go on. I tried feebly to fight off this gloom. In the hospital in Libourne I had had faith which I tried to summon up now and to keep on summoning it, and hold to it but I was tired. Completely tired.

I thought of Jimmy with his sculpted but growing-flabby face, Pedro with eyes like a bull and a gold tooth, Barry with dark red hair like an Irish setter, smiling and putting a face on misfortune. So where had they gone, our friends? Into limbo. We would never see them again, we could never know how to find them. I wondered if the Gaullists had reached England safely, and thought of the sadness of Maurice. Now it was dark, the train jolted up and down, and Stephen swung in his hammock slung between the luggage racks. I fell asleep.

In the morning Vsevolod bought coffee from a trolley in a station. A severe-looking woman got into our carriage with her daughter. They chattered and jabbered, apparently unafraid of being denounced. The woman did not like the Germans, nor did she like the English whom she considered low and false. 'Are you English?' she asked me.

'No, Australian,' I said, 'but I am also low and false,' and I suddenly giggled and knew it would be all right. It had to be. Yesterday was *over*. This was a new day, the last day here! The country was growing steep and wild and France was beginning to disappear. We went through a tunnel; it was the Pyrenees. I began to believe again.

And so – at last – we reached the frontier. A French soldier looked long and carefully at Vsevolod's passport with its exit visa, while Vsevolod watched with the green 'unprotected-*apatride*' look on his face. Did military age truly cease at thirty? The soldier handed back the passport and got off the train. We entered another tunnel and suddenly it was Campfranc and we were in Spain. We changed trains. Dark men like Pedro were running all over the platform. I gazed at them, hypnotized. One old lady came through with us from France. Our passports were checked and stamped again, and as we boarded the new train it filled with people.

As we crossed Aragon it became fiercely hot. The land was ochre and red, the sky white with brilliantly luminous clouds. The beauty of it was grandiose and I was struck by the astonishing power of the heat, by the fact that we were really away. We had gone. I believed it.

The view was forever-land; the lines of mountains did not enclose, but folded into each other range upon range like the sea. The horizon did not end; it was a long swell of brown, red and violet – there was no green. A farm stood out in sharp light, white on dry brown earth. Our escape and the realization of it was growing, which made me want to shout. Zaragosa smelled of oil; donkeys with loaded saddle bags walked beside their dark-skinned owners. 'What is the filth they use to cook with here?' asked Vsevolod.

There was indeed a dreadful smell, yet I was overwhelmed with pleasure, since my high faith had returned, it went up and down like a fever chart.

We spent the night in Zaragosa and ate an oily dinner of nevertheless real food: meat, vegetables, cheese and rasping wine.

Bilbao was humid, the heat hanging like a muffling curtain, completely different from the dry heat of Aragon. It was a disappointing town, as Bordeaux had been, in that it was built far from its port with no waterfront. This was a different, dirty, industrial Spain, with heavy nineteenth-century buildings. Once again, we could find no room; it was crowded, and it seemed as if everyone was leaving Europe from this grimy springboard. We went to the shipping office of Ybarra and Co where we had been told to pick up our tickets. But we were told that no confirmation of our reservation had been received from their head office in Buenos Aires. I waved our telegram at the manager, showing him our confirmation from Marseilles; but it did not tell which ship, which day. He just said to call again.

We managed to find a room in a hotel, and we waited. Nothing could be done until the confirmation arrived at the Ybarra office. We ate cakes called *mantecados*, made with oil and sugar. America again seemed like World's End.

We went to a bullfight. We sat in the arena enveloped in very heavy, cloying heat, and I felt sick into the pit of my stomach, where it felt as if a lift was going up and down. I got up to leave, and a man sitting beside us said, 'Are you afraid?'

'No,' I said, 'I am curious, I have never been to a bullfight. It must be the rich food, I feel poisoned,' and I fainted.

The fight had not yet started. They carried me into the room where the bullfighters were taken when wounded. Surrounded by cool stone walls, I lay on the operating table and felt better. The *torero* arrived, looked down at me with dark eyes seemingly filled with the heat of the desert and all the strength of Spain. He was fierce, detached and dignified; he allowed us to leave in his car. A crowd collected at the exit: who was the *señorita* in his car?

We returned to the hotel and the smell of the sweet oily cakes came in through the window from next door, where a machine like a small steam engine made *churros*. We put Stephen on the floor, as it was cooler to lie on stone. And so we never saw the fight.

The next day was July. Still no confirmation from the Ybarra office. Other people waiting in the crowded office shouted noisily for their tickets, and some panicked. The next ship to leave was rumoured to be the last, and it was also rumoured to have engine trouble. There was no space on the Clipper for three months.

Our visas, which had been granted for two weeks only, were soon due to expire. After that they apparently would not be prolonged. We would simply be arrested and experience Spanish prison. Freedom evaporated once again; we were corraled, with nowhere to go if the tickets did not arrive in time. A cable from my parents said: 'Hooray at last *bon voyage.*'

A new rumour said that belligerents would not be accepted on board. There was a Polish couple in the hotel with us who were now in despair; they were elderly: to reach America was their last dream. They spent each day in the Ybarra office just sitting there and refusing to move. Feelings were stronger since Germany had invaded Russia. But the next day a counter-order cancelled the rumour: Poles would be accepted, and the boat was mended and due to sail. Now I was the one who panicked.

With a sudden intuitive hunch, I went into the director's office and started to search through the pile of telegrams and ticker-tape messages on his desk. He was angry and protested, but so utterly harassed and overwhelmed by the crowds and noise that I was able to continue. I found our telegram. Confirmation from Buenos Aires that the tickets had been paid and that our reservation was in order. This had been sent to Marseilles, forwarded from there to Bilbao and then filed under the wrong alphabetical letter.

If there had not been engine trouble, the ship would probably have left before this incident. Life was a fluke. We clambered into the crowded train to the port and saw the sea at last.

9

We stood waiting, standing in the sun all day before word came that we could board the ship, whereupon we were herded and stuffed and pushed up the gangplank: German refugees, Poles and Spanish immigrants going to Argentina. The longed-for ocean looked grey and dismal. Outwardly the ship was white and beautiful, but when we were aboard it appeared we were to sleep in the *entrapuentes*. We descended a ladder of sticky wet paint to reach quarters in the hold where there were bunks for men. Another ladder led to a second hold below, with tarred walls and straw mattresses in double bunks: the women's quarters. It was perpetually dark with only small night-lights, and there were rats. Halfway up the ladders between the two holds there was a room with a slimy floor streaked in wet dirt, like mud, containing six basins and lavatories. This was called the Bathroom. It was indeed what the American doctor had meant by dreadful conditions, but we were on our way.

A bell clanged for dinner and we clambered back up the ladders to a room with long wooden benches and trestle tables, where we ate oily food. We were more like prisoners than fare-paying passengers. The tickets had been oversold; there were two thousand people on a ship with space for only eight hundred.

At dinner we met a Belgian film producer and a Belgian boy who was going to Canada, by way of South America, and eventually to England to join the army. There was also a Swiss; since the Swiss had no need to escape, it seemed an odd pastime.

We decided to bring our mattresses up on to the deck, where there would be air and no rats. Many followed this example, so eventually there was a mass of mattresses with people sitting about playing cards, or crouching on lifeboats or the machinery for unloading. We made a separate camp using our luggage as barricades. We were stared at all day by thousands of eyes, the Spanish immigrants staring with the curiosity of animals. Sometimes, however, there was an interval when they went to the far end of the deck where one of them would play a concertina and then, like strutting cranes, they would do a strange, angular dance. We did not wash since the squalor of the basins in the mud-room was worse than our own smell. The men grew beards and we were tramps, but we were in the open, and if torpedoed would not be caught in the hold.

The first stop was Vigo, and at the second stop, Lisbon, we were allowed ashore.

Lisbon was astonishing: a clean white town with shops full of cakes, not oil-cakes but fluffy sponges, cream buns and old childhood memory-cakes of forgotten existence. Stephen had never seen a banana. His little face looked puzzled as he bit into it with his two teeth. We ate too much and were sick.

There was a whole day in Lisbon. In order to cash money we drove by taxi to the jetty where the Clipper landed. As we arrived, there it was, flying in out of the sky, swimming through the horizon of red clouds of sunset, landing on the water like a huge powerful bird in a swishing spray. Then it floated, with the American flag painted on its side, a symbol of our longing. The next day it would glide away again and take only one day to reach the other side of the Atlantic, a voyage that would take us five weeks: three to Argentina and two more after that northwards to New York.

We returned to the boat. More immigrants came on board, this time Portuguese bound for Brazil. They settled down, wearing pyjamas and heavy walking shoes.

The next day we did not leave but remained in port, no longer allowed to go ashore. A machine drilled with ear-splitting noise and the new immigrants hung together in clusters. The purser came to call on us behind our barricade. He gave us a newspaper that told of a Turkish ship sunk as a result of mistaken identity, but he said we were more likely to hit a mine than be torpedoed. The Spanish flag on the side of the ship was illuminated so that the Germans would know it was neutral. We were blocked all day in port. No one knew why, but since every person's visa had expired there could be no return; we waited, floating, a world apart.

I crossed into first class on a reconnaissance tour. It was cool and carpeted, with elegant officers in white uniforms. We had paid first-class fares but there had been no room left. I asked the purser if I could see the captain. The difference between first- and second-class comfort angered me, and I felt we had been swindled and that it was disgraceful to treat the second-class people as animals.

'Immigrants don't care how they travel,' he said.

'How do you know?'

'They live that way, it is like their homes.'

'It isn't like mine,' I said, scarlet with rage at his condescension.

He became friendly and said he would arrange for me to see the captain, who spoke English. 'You are the only English person on this ship,' he said.

I returned to the region of rancid sweat, to our mattress-fort, where Eli, the Belgian boy, was playing a guitar. The purser brought people to the bridge above our quarters and they stared down at us as at the zoo.

At midnight the engines rumbled; we lay in the glare of lights and felt the ship move. At night part of the herd went below, which created more room and made it possible to stroll. But now we were made angry by the first-class passengers who stood in groups on the bridge and stared down at us as if it were their main occupation. We were never unwatched and their constant stare was worse than that of our own animal herd.

We stopped again at Cadiz, which looked Moorish and gaunt; Europe had gone. I went into first class and had a bath; the experience of being clean was almost spiritual.

All day men unloaded cargo; in the evening they remained on board and watched us eat, standing round our tables like wolves, though our food seemed foul to us. When the meal was over they collected all the bits of gristle and bread that were left on the plates and stuffed these chewed remains into their pockets. Then they went off, gaunt haunchy men returning to their gaunt, beautiful city, while we steamed away again out to sea.

At night when the heat of the day cooled, the metal of the loading machines contracted and made gunshot sounds. Though the heat was intense and grew like a furnace as we approached the Equator, the immigrant women continued to wear their thick black stockings.

Two days later we were stopped in mid-ocean. A dinghy came alongside with four British sailors. I dashed headlong into first class to the deck that was just above the dinghy, and waved to them with passion. They waved back. An officer climbed on board wearing shorts with a dirk in his belt. A German would have clicked his heels pompously, trying to impose. But the power of this phlegmatic Englishman gave the feeling he had controlled the seas for a very long time.

A few hundred yards away a small steamship with a black flag waited. The officer checked our ship's papers. When the dinghy rowed him away, the sailors said something and the officer looked up and waved to me. I shouted, 'Good luck, bless you, bless you, bless you,' crying and laughing with pride and patriotic excitement. My voice was carried away and lost, but I waved and waved until they were nothing but a dot on the water, then turned and found the purser standing behind me looking on.

'Well – you see who owns the ocean?' I said, with nostalgia for my own people, both happy and sad.

'My name is Rafael,' he answered, his hair gleaming blue in the sun, his uniform immaculately white.

Then he took me to see the captain.

The cabin was cool with cross breezes blowing through it. Now that I was there, I was not sure how to start. I tried to describe our conditions.

'The ship is full,' he said, 'I cannot help it.'

'But do you know what the *entrapuentes* are like? You could perhaps report it, at least. The ship is dangerously overloaded. Why can people only wash in first class? I have a baby, please find me somewhere else to sleep with him.' As I talked I was spurring myself into ever greater anger.

'You are a little lady to be so violent,' he said.

'I hate injustice. Come down and see us and maybe you will be violent too.'

I returned to our quarters, feeling futile and fatuous.

But later in the day, the captain came. His visit caused a stir among the pyjama crowds. When he saw my baby on the dirty mattress he saluted.

After that, Stephen and I were allowed to sleep in the ship's hospital which was a cabin in first class with six bunks. There were four sick people in the cabin, but at least we had our own bunk with sheets. Stephen had started a fever. I discovered his flour mixture was not cooked, but merely warmed raw, so from then on I went to the kitchen myself and took care of his food. The cook gave me fruit juice for him, but his fever did not go down. The heat continued to grow, and the male nurse told me a baby had died on the last trip. This nurse used the sterilized surgical scissors to cut the soles of his shoes. At night the four sick people coughed and spat into bowls.

I went out on to the deck and prayed. Rafael found me, took me to his cabin and gave me a glass of Fundador, Spanish brandy; he was soothing and kind and told me babies ran higher temperatures than adults. Here, surprisingly, was a friend. The next day Stephen's fever started to subside.

Rafael introduced me to a Belgian film actress called Annie Vernay. She was nineteen and occupied a luxury cabin with her American fiancé who was president of Tokalon. Like Stephen, she was unwell with a fever, so she did not leave her cabin. We sat there and talked and became friends. There are people one meets who at the first joke cease to be strangers; here was an affinity as if we had always known each other. She was tall, with long yellow hair, no make-up, and a sweet gentle expression. But she was not well.

A French reporter with a monocle and a penchant for gossip, told me their cabin cost three thousand dollars and that she had a certain notoriety for having had an affair with the Belgian king.

On the other side of the ship, the immigrants threw a little dog into the sea. The owner was a woman, weeping tragically. They were savages and I ceased to be sorry for them. Now I stood on the bridge and looked down, doing in effect what I myself had so resented. It was incredible to see them perched like monkeys all over the loading machines in their eternal unfresh pyjamas. We had made the last stop on the eastern side of the ocean, and Europe finally receded altogether.

When we crossed the Equator there was a fancy-dress ball. I dressed like a little girl, which was singularly unimaginative, but simple and requiring no effort to find clothes. I simply wore pigtails and a short skirt. They gave me first prize, an earthy perfume called Jungla. I danced with the captain, the doctor, and Rafael who held me in a vice-strong grip.

Vsevolod danced all evening with a pretty Spanish woman. Their tango was superb. I admired the way he placed his feet, the smooth movement of his body and thought what a beautiful dancer he was. How odd that we had danced together only once, in St Tropez; we had never led the life of an ordinary couple, dining out, prams in the hall. Now as the war was left behind and our troubles were diminishing, this man, my husband, was becoming a stranger.

As we crossed the Equator, the ship blew its whistle, the orchestra played paso dobles, and I went to sit with Annie who lay in bed with a rising temperature.

10

We reached Rio de Janeiro on 21 July. Here was another continent, the other side of the ocean. The saved people went ashore and as we looked at the quay it seemed that hundreds of Portuguese were meeting their uncles and brothers and hugging each other. Jagged mountains surrounded the bay, with a façade of skyscrapers in front. Our ship then went on to Santos, where men with long brown limbs unloaded crates; it was green and steamy here and it rained. The old straw mattresses were sodden, but no matter, most of the monkey people had gone.

At Montevideo Annie grew worse. I went ashore with her fiancé to do some shopping. It was growing still cooler. 'When we reach Buenos Aires it will be winter,' he said, sounding somehow sombre. This man, who was called Ben, had a strong rather fleshy face and smoked a pipe. I asked him why people threw dogs into the sea, but he just said, 'Someone will hurt you one day.' He was odd; he spoke in parables.

On 26 July we finally arrived: Buenos Aires, our destination for the first round. But the consul in Marseilles had given us the wrong visa so we were not allowed to land. We should have had tourist visas, but had been given transit. This meant embarkation on to another ship, but not going ashore. Everyone left the boat except for one Jewish family, also in transit, but they were to embark on another ship the next day and did not mind.

It was cold, after crossing the Equator. It was also confusing and the disappointment of being virtually interned on this ship was deep. Vsevolod reverted to his grandmother's corpse, which we had been doing without for a long time. 'Hibidashumai,' he swore, 'and what do we do when this ship *leaves* again?'

We telephoned the embassy, and asked them to send us a saviour to bale us out. Ben returned to the boat, bringing us chocolates; also stockings and Guerlain perfume for me, a kind gesture from a seemingly tough man. When I thanked him he said, 'I am just a materialist. Who knows? You might be my next girl.' He added that Annie's fever was worse, which made his joking the more peculiar.

In the evening the Jewish family prayed, wearing little black skull-caps and standing up. One of them told me Israel meant wrestling with God. He pointed out that in our religion we knelt prostrate in church and took our hats off. They stood, he said, looking God in the eye, and asked, 'What about it God?' And they put their hats on to see him face to face. This family helped us through the evening; the empty abandoned ship would otherwise have been a nightmare.

Our saviour came from the embassy in the form of a tall Scot like a Viking. He whisked us way in his car . . . and all was transformed into a miracle again: here was a new capital, Buenos Aires, even with Harrods and Argentine men wearing an English type of greenish 'pork pie' hat.

Our saviour was called Hadow but known as Shadow. There were flowers in our room in his house, his cook made a succulent dinner, he played the piano, our clothes were washed and ironed, and the blankets on the bed were soft to the skin. I rolled in the bedclothes laughing with happiness. The whole thing was a kaleidoscope of mad changing colours; one minute despair and being interned in a port, the next, freedom and flying along the road in the car of this lovely Shadow and discovering the world. The streets of Buenos Aires were full of people who did not realize how lucky they were to have food and peace. Cars ran on petrol, not gazogene.

I took flowers to the Plaza for Annie. She was lying in bed very hot, her hair in a great mass around her like mine had been in Libourne. The sight of her hair and her delirium filled me with dread. Mine had grown the same sudden way – and I had nearly died. Ben told me she had typhoid and paratyphoid at the same time. For weeks before, she had been on a slimming diet and so had little resistance.

Then he said, 'Let's go out to dinner. There are tango places here.'

I looked at him in amazement. 'But she is ill . . .'

'What can we do?' he said. 'She sleeps mostly. We have to eat somewhere. We have to live. I arranged for a nurse to be on call.'

Annie looked beautiful, lying with her eyes closed. I was very afraid. She did not know where she was, or that we were there. I held her hot hand very tight: I love you Annie. Please fight. Please know we are with you.

'You could be a winner,' Ben said. 'You have all the requirements, but you may turn out a loser.'

What did he mean? I was terrified by the thought that Annie was dying.

'You could be a winner if you lose your pity.'

I did not want to dine with him; I went away.

We booked on an American ship, the Moore McCormack Line, for New York. On the day we left Annie was still in her coma. In our cabin I found a basket of roses and carnations, sent by Ben. For some reason this made Shadow angry and he took them away. There were more goodbyes, the continual departures of life; Shadow gave me a photograph of himself.

And so we went back up the same coast once again, but this time on a very different boat, full of returning American holidaymakers who did not believe there really was a war, and certainly did not want to know about it. They thought concentration camps were propaganda and any mention of Europe produced expressions of either incredulity or boredom.

We passed the wreck of the *Graf Spee* outside Montevideo. We reached Rio de Janeiro again and moored opposite another ship, the *Cabo de Buena Esperanza*. It was our Spanish ship – that stinking, sweaty, puking ship now clean and going back to Europe empty. We went ashore for the day to climb the Sugarloaf mountain with a kind white-haired American man and his grandson, adventurous in their gym shoes. When we returned there stood Rafael on the quay, changed into a dark blue uniform. We showed the Americans our Spanish ship, white and ghostly, with only two passengers on board.

Returning to our cabin I found a note from Rafael that said: *Siempre iras en mi pensamientos*. On the American ship there were floor shows and no worries. People dressed for dinner and went to 'get-together parties'. It seemed unreal. But why shouldn't they? On the first night out of Rio the alarm bell rang; a steward had committed suicide by jumping overboard, but the search for him lasted less than half an hour because the waters were full of sharks. Dancing resumed.

In Trinidad where we stopped on 11 August there was a telegram saying Annie had died. Ben had looked after her in the only way he knew how, covering her with jewellery and furs and luxury cabins, but perhaps not tenderness. And now she had gone before her life had started. We ploughed on through the grey waves and the frequent flying fish. I mourned Annie. I thought of Rafael returning forlorn across the ocean.

I puzzled about the Americans on board and the frivolous way they were not even slightly interested (except for the old man and his grandson) in a war that might later be theirs. After all, the Great War had been theirs too at the end.

In spite of the excitement of finally reaching America, I found to my surprise that I also missed Europe – a paradox, since all we had wanted was to leave it. But what had happened to Meerson, to Vsevolod's mother (God will provide) to shaggy unhugged Mars? And Maurice, the sort of Frenchman who made France the centre balance-point of Europe? . . . I was confused.

Drinking iced water from lily cups was like already being in America, the home of our childhood. We were going to see my parents and we were saved. Yet somehow Maurice and Meerson were betrayed by these good-time Charlies on board who did not know freedom was something that had to be fought for. They did not even realize they were lucky . . . They did not feel like my people (yet we were going *home* to them – the idea of seeing my parents was overwhelming). The thinking and quick under-standing of Europeans seemed more familiar . . . At eighteen I seemed to have absorbed a nostalgia that was never to leave me, like Russian minor-key music that would always haunt. Whatever a person had, something was often missing or lost. Happiness existed, but was contained in small shining moments, transitory, precious, not with permanence. Yet America was looked upon as a star of salvation, the end of the crusade. The old Poles with the dream in their eyes were bringing this dream to the promised land.

So – what did it matter then? Americans were kind and generous, and if they did not want to hear that we slept with rats or were shot at by the Germans, or that Meerson had J for Jew stamped on his passport – maybe after all they were right. Better not to know. In the meantime, Stephen was eating puree of peas with bacon and drinking fresh orange juice. We had been cold and famished – so now we were eating as if we had never eaten before, as if we could not remember ever having eaten properly. We were safe, stable and saved.

On 14 August we steamed up the Hudson, and we saw, far away at first but growing larger, the statue of liberty, representing the sunrise which boatloads of refugees had been watching for. This time, perhaps, we really would be free.

Vsevolod was standing on the deck, shading his eyes to see the statue clearly, trembling with excitement. I prayed for him not to be disappointed ever again, for him to have a job, a country, a nationality . . . In America everyone was foreign so the label 'foreigner' would fall flat. And how foolish, since at last we had truly arrived, we had reached the end of the road, mission accomplished and achieved – how foolish then, that I should be crying, wishing him luck, holding his hand, saying, dear old Vsevolod, dear old America, here is one grown man and one little new one, don't let them down. In the long winter when we had heard Churchill's voice on the radio saying, 'Frenchmen, I am with you –' we were all fighting in our various fashions to hold on. This was what all that holding on and not giving up had been for – for this moment, this special day of arrival.

As we approached the dock we could begin to see details in the waiting crowd. There was a white straw hat that must be my mother's. My father would not be here, but in Cambridge Mass., with his long cigarette holder and the far-distant look in his eyes. The impossible was true. Perhaps it was not the finish; perhaps it was only now beginning.

Part Two

11

After leaving Australia, and in spite of his eventual success (once
the first lean years in America were overcome) Elton Mayo never
acquired a home of his own. He had a Rockefeller Foundation
Life Research Chair at Harvard; his books were translated into
Japanese and Spanish; *Fortune Magazine* was due to call him
'Philosopher of the Picket Line', saying: 'If there were a Nobel
Prize for Labour Relations Elton Mayo should have it' – yet he
lived with my mother in a rented flat. Perhaps it was partly
because neither of my parents wanted to finish their lives in
America. My mother dreamed of a garden; the plan was
probably a house in the English countryside. Her garden was
frequently referred to but never finally achieved. Marriage was
the great adventure, my father used to say, and part of theirs was
to be homeless, though they collected some beautiful furniture,
many Shirvan and Anatolian rugs and a superb library: their
rented flats had their own climate.

In the summer of 1941 a colleague of my father's, Professor
Henderson (called 'Pinky', because of his red beard and strong
views) lent my parents his house. It was here that we arrived: thin
and hyper-excited refugees with the feeling of coming home to
America. It was *someone*'s home at least and it was also in
Cambridge Massachusetts where I had lived as a child and had
memories of going to school on the handlebars of my sister's

bicycle (forbidden and sensational); and at last, and incredibly, it was the present abode of my parents.

America rediscovered: there was a wide wooden veranda with rocking chairs, red cardinals flitting in the trees, chipmunks watching us with bright eyes, sitting in their tiny striped jackets in the fork of a branch. Everything seemed large and generous: the streets were wide and lined with tall elm trees; the gardens all opened on to each other with no barriers between neighbours. Men who passed wore straw boater hats with coloured foulard ribbons and said, 'Hi.' (Had it a Red Indian origin? Vsevolod wondered.) The heat was balmy and humid, but the house was cool inside and had screen doors to keep out the fearful American insects.

We reached this peace on the crest of the wave – flying high, believing the escape had been ordained and that we had special work to do. But first there was the summer . . . Each morning we stretched in bed, realizing the luxury of having arrived – relishing the unbelievable: American breakfast with bacon and cereal, seeing a large American robin (really a thrush with a red breast) hop across the lawn just ahead of Stephen who dragged one leg when he crawled, but was now safe. He was treated for undernourishment by Dr Ganz, the Boston paediatrician. My mother had grown up with four younger brothers and had always wanted sons. Here now was their sudden grandson, the tiny boy Elton Mayo invented games for and stalked the wood-chuck with. The safety, the garden, the calling of whippoorwills at night, the peace – all seemed unreal and yet it had somehow been attained.

It was like surfing: the wave we arrived on was a long roller – but eventually it had to break. Money was the first reason. Any wealth that I might have had as a dowry or for a university education had been spent on the escape and Vsevolod's debts. Now his American future must begin to be the present.

In September we went to New York with various addresses and much hope. Stephen stayed with his grandparents. We rented a room in a brownstone house in 63rd Street between Madison and Park Avenues, and in order to distract from the dingy plush furnishings, I painted some large water-colours, covering the walls with imagined subjects: two Negroes looking over a hedge, surprised at their first sight of snow; a crowd leaving a penthouse roof after a party. My parents waited for good news but it was slow in coming. There were times when hope turned to anxiety, imperceptibly at first, and quickly dispelled by the lavish American promise.

By degrees, Vsevolod and I snapped at each other, no longer held together by a state of emergency. New York was electric with a feeling that anything might happen. There were no negative refusals as in Europe, and yet in spite of the huge potential, the promises did not crystallize. We were sent on to another name and address, always with smiles. They called this 'passing the buck' which amounted to a sort of cowardice in not admitting outright that there was no job. 'Nice to meet you. You've got what it takes. Very interesting. You should go and see John G. Come to my house for drinks tomorrow.' (Now get lost, I'm busy and can't quite face the responsibility, let John G. have a go.)

But drinks and open houses there were in plenty. Hospitality was vast, so was friendship in the end, though at first it was superficial.

We were out of work. We had not yet been *in* work, so there was no name for us. But Madison Avenue was a place where all the world seemed to meet and Vsevolod often ran into friends. French was often heard on the buses. I met a girl I had been at school with in Switzerland who had married Maughan Gould; he looked rather like Fred Astaire only taller. He had been brought up until he was seventeen in France and so spoke French with no accent. '*Alors, ça va?*' he asked, with a wide grin, (the *boulevardier*), pouring out double martinis. American martinis are neat gin with a dash of bitters, shaken with ice for a few minutes only. Then a twist of lemon, or an olive, or a small onion was added, accordingly. After a few of these all was very well.

The owner of El Morocco, John Perona, presided over a round table which was the territory of mainly South Americans; they had olive skins and small, elegant, degenerate feet like lemurs, shod in well-polished custom-made shoes. The languages spoken at this table were Argentine-Spanish, Italian, Brazilian-Portuguese, and infrequent English. Perona was Italian; white truffles were sent to him from Italy; a mysterious, silent power seemed to surround him. He sat at the head of his table (though it was round, he quietly and subtly dominated) amid the circle of dark-skinned playboys with sometimes a European or American too. This area was usually men-only but occasionally a girl would be asked to sit there; it was an honour of sorts, and though a dubious one, it made the other girls in the room vaguely jealous. Perhaps the very young felt that something emanating from this corner controlled part of the world. They walked between the tables, in their tight dresses exposing their breasts, hoping to be seen.

There was a smaller room in El Morocco, dark and rather strange, called the Champagne Room. There was no orchestra here, and it seemed to be used for private dinners or talks . . . or something else perhaps? We wondered. Intrigues, propositions? Or just old millionaires who were tired. We found its purpose unclear and fascinating. It was known to be still more expensive than the main nightclub – yet after glancing in through the door when it was open, it seemed a bit dull and too quiet. We preferred to be in with the music, the movement, the zebra stripes and palm trees.

Howard Hughes, silent and remote, would arrive sometimes (before he decided to disappear), threading his way to a reserved table for two with some pretty girl of that evening's choice. He never sat at the 'round table'. Other legendary characters came and went, and for this reason I preferred El Morocco to that other high spot of those times, the Stork Club, which had a sameness about it. With its Ivy League and ex-débutantes, it was all-American and lacked variety.

After the gloom of Europe this life glittered. And there was food. Just food. Everyone ate – that was normal. But we were not yet used to the normality of being able to. Not to be hungry was a conscious state. We would often return home late at night after too many martinis and a sketchy dinner (Americans invariably drank more than they ate) and feel the hollow cramps of our old war. But we simply telephoned for food, and even at three in the morning a black boy, whistling happily, would deliver an order, as if it were a normal time for him to work and for us to eat. Not only was there plenty, but it was also available at any time. New York City never slept. The rest of America called it a place apart, 'not really America at all'. It was unique and extraordinary. The Puerto Rican quarter (street fights), the German quarter (swastikas hanging out on flags, America not yet in the war), the Italian quarter with the only decent coffee, (American coffee being foul), Chinatown with paper dragons, the Bowery, where a large eye painted on a barber's shop meant black eyes could be made up and repaired. And then there was the central part of town – Madison, Park, Lexington – where people had only Christian names and were, with few exceptions, immediately friendly.

Devil's food cake, chocolate layer (remember *rutabaga* and no salt?) 'Two rare cheeseburgers on cracked wheat with relish please,' . . . Delicatessens with liver sausage and smoked turkey, sturgeon – European, yet un-European – drug stores with fudge sundaes. The delectable restaurant the Colony, where we were invited sometimes on first meeting by open-handed, warm-hearted acquaintances. Broccoli Hollandaise (an Italian-New York cuisine) first started in America, and Vichyssoise (a French-New York cuisine) we had never eaten in France even before the war shortage. I wondered if the ex-patriates had invented it when they reached America . . .

At the St Regis hotel a drawer of ice was pulled out over the dance floor for the show, and then skating took place. This ice-show in a warm room made Vsevolod roar with laughter. 'Anything can happen here, what a country!' he said, and saw someone he knew who was apparently involved in running the hotel, Serge Obolensky. They chatted together and I heard names like Dolgourouky that my mother had also mentioned as someone she had either known or stayed with in Russia, Troubetskoy, Shcherbatov. I saw that old photograph of my mother in front of the Kremlin in the snow as I listened to accounts of their various escapades and watched the skaters. Obolensky was successful, rich, grander than Vsevolod and exceedingly handsome, but they both spoke the language of the Imperial world and their talk seemed to hold some faded glitter of ghostly Old Russia.

And there was jazz, and being able to dance. But what were we actually doing together? And was this *all*?

City of contrasts, New York was also squalidly dirty. One night a file of cockroaches too wide to step across, came out of the gutter hole like an army manoeuvre and crossed the pavement. People waited for this thick black band to finish, or else crossed the street. Papers floated about held up by air currents, a page of newspaper seen from an office on the fortieth floor appeared to dance, to swoop as if to settle and fall and then leap up again; winged garbage waltzing in the sky.

One day, suddenly, Vsevolod got a job. The Office of War Information hired him to broadcast on the short wave frequency to Europe. A little later I also got my first job, as a Conover model. His work was interesting, mine was dreadful. Out-of-town buyers came to a big Broadway hotel; the models walked along a floodlit horseshoe raised above the dining-room tables and showed off clothes (I thought them hideous). The horseshoe sparkled with sequins and we were instructed to smile. I found it silly to smile to order, a fixed grin like an American president – (what was so funny about these lousy clothes anyway? No one in their right mind would buy them.) I hated the whole arrangement, and what was worse, found it embarrassing. I felt cross and sulky and probably looked it. Luckily this was not repeated. Afterwards I worked with photographers; this I had been used to in France and could cope with, I even liked the chatter and jokes and the way each one was so different. 'Say, what a name, Gael Mayo, how long did it take Harry Conover to think that one up?'

'Ha, ha, it happens to be my real name,' and at once it became easy.

There was great jealousy in the modelling business. Sometimes a specific girl would be requested by a photographer who wanted her particular face or long *Vogue* body – but there were also general calls. When not working, the girls would sit around waiting for these calls, lacquering their nails and eyeing each other.

'Blonde, medium height, good legs,' the loudspeaker would announce, and a group would rush, each girl pushing to get there first.

I made some money and appreciated the positive feeling it gave, but hated the work. One day I was sent to Peter Arno. He drew caricatures of the old, the fat and the ridiculous mainly for the *New Yorker* magazine. His drawings were cruel, sometimes funny, usually bitter. He did not need model girls but liked their company and grew bored working alone. So I just sat there feeling slightly nutty while he drew something else. It was odd to look at a girl, then down at his pad, where with vitriolic strokes of his clever pen he would draw some poor old hag.

He did not write his own gags. One morning I suggested a joke. We laughed together and he was pleased, his pleasure encouraging and sparking off more jokes. We giggled and shrieked with laughter about nothing special, just anything . . . a feeling of well-being. He made some coffee double strength to please my foreign taste and we ate Danish pastries.

'Say,' he said, 'you could be my gag writer.'

'Who is usually?'

'Various.'

'I like that. When they ask my name, I would say "Various", and they'll say, "How long did it take Harry Conover to think that one up"?'

'I'll ask for you again baby.'

But I was not there when his call came through, and several times, the girls who should have made appointments for me deliberately said I was unavailable, in order to take the job themselves. They lied to the answer-girl secretary. Their inter-bitchiness was entire. Peter Arno was dark, handsome and desirable and they were all on the make. Their life-aim consisted in securing future husbands or rich men who would keep them. I never discovered whether friendship existed between any of them because I never really got to know even one – but the atmosphere seemed phoney and false. I had learned the necessity of money but not respect for it. Nor could I understand their haste in wanting to be put into a mould when the world was still a colossal arena. So one day – on impulse – I quit.

Vsevolod said I was a fool; I answered it was impossible to work at something I loathed.

'The American dream is based on security and you have never been safe,' he said.

He was right, but there had to be another way. It was delightful to wake up the following morning to the thought of not seeing the beautiful girls with green barracuda insides hidden behind their glossy magazine exteriors. Some of them must be nice, I supposed, so good luck to them; I would never know now. It would of course have been possible to work for Conover by relying on the telephone and not going to the office, but then half the work would have been lost.

I sat in our brownstone and wrote a short story which was very corny – not intentionally corny – but clichés come out by mistake. I quoted Shelley, 'The lamp is shattered' referring to a love affair. To my amazement this story was accepted in the pulp market. New York was certainly a city of varied possibilities.

The pulp market led me to visit various offices, and this in turn led to a decent job with the editor and assistant editor of *Popular Publications*. It was a group of three magazines: *Adventure, Black Mask* and *Dime Detective*. The first was about fishing and shooting and mainly for men; the second two were trash but served as useful training, editorial work being the same whatever the printed page. The editor was called Kenneth White and the assistant Kenneth Goodwyn, in other words there were two Kens. Big Ken (the boss) was very small, lean and lightweight, with a kind, lined, good-looking face. Second Ken was younger, plump and shy and a giggler as I myself was. We used to get huge laughs out of our 'Ready For The Rackets Department' (a column where we reported tricksters and warned about fraud), or the horror side of *Black Mask* with blood dripping underneath a door.

Sometimes Big Ken would take us out to lunch. It would be a mood decision, for on most days we stayed in the office and had sandwiches and containers of 'cawfee' sent in. If the coffee is the worst in the world, the sandwiches are the best. They were mostly Club sandwiches with chicken and bacon and lettuce. But on the lunch days we would go to a restaurant – where tiny Ken used to drink a surprising number of martinis. Strangely, these did not prevent work going ahead afterwards, they seemed to inspire him. Deadlines were met with enthusiasm and we returned to the lay-out sheets with pictures of men hooking salmon in torrents of rain (*Adventure*) or girls being attacked (*Dime Detective*) and worked faster than ever. The two Kens loved their work, and though mocking it they got enormous pleasure from it and, rapidly, so did I. I particularly loved our threesome, working together in the little office on East 42nd Street where I first learned the editing profession and I never forgot the tremendous time we had together. The quality of the prose may have been a joke, but the job was well-paid and serious. (Tiny Ken graduated later to *Esquire*, and later still started his own magazine, where he offered me the chance of joining him.)

Vsevolod and I left our brownstone and acquired a two-room flat.

In the red and yellow American fall my parents moved back to their apartment. I went to visit them and see Stephen. The fact that they were in the place of my childhood gave a feeling of solidity and safety. The Charles River . . . Harvard . . . all the old memories: the police searching for a skunk in a neighbour's garden; a grey caterpillar's nest being hit down from a tree by the seven-year-old boy next door who was also first to propose marriage; my parents going out to dinner one snowy, Christmas night (it always snowed for Christmas) and my sister wheeling me at top speed in our doll's pram round the block with me squealing my head off; being threatened at the age of six by a dirty old man at the time of the Lindbergh case with the terrifying joke: 'I'll kidnap ye!' and rushing home in a taxi. The memories were not all reassuring by any means, but they formed part of the tapestry.

That Stephen was here where it had all begun seemed to round off that circle. I walked with him by the riverside and we fed the ducks. His hair was gold in the sunlight, and I remembered the train journey in Spain when the old German Jewish refugee lady had called him Goldich – and here he was, after the long trek through France, alive and growing strong.

Then Vsevolod lost his job. He was not upset, he had gained confidence and was sure something else would appear. He had made a world of new friends at the OWI, including Karel Pusta, an Estonian, who had siestas in my bed after broadcasting at night. He asked if he could lie in my sheets and from then on seemed to have a fixation with the idea. He was very tall with a moon face and high cheekbones. Though we had only two rooms, people came and went the whole time as they had done in our Paris house; it was Vsevolod's way. We took it in shifts. Some of our visitors were night workers, some had day jobs like me. Karel had the decency to vacate my bed when I got into it. There was something disturbing about him, but something likeable and at the same time reassuring; he was huge and strong, and if I had clasped him round the waist my head would not even have reached his chest.

I saw less of Vsevolod now. He was always out somewhere, waiting for another job to drop out of the New York sky with unpredictable suddenness, but the wait grew long . . .

At this period I met the painter Kisling who was probably about fifty at the time. I had no idea who he was and knew nothing of his exhibitions or his fame in France, nor his wild beginnings in Montparnasse with Juan Gris and Derain. He had reached the summit of success and had been asked to go to Hollywood to paint Artur Rubinstein and his family. 'Meet Kiki,' said someone, and there he was – a warm, somewhat bulky (though not fat) figure slopping around his studio in espadrilles. The feeling of bulk came perhaps from the aura of generosity and largesse surrounding him. His eyes beamed with piercing keenness.

His studio was like a post office – stacked with parcels, packages of tea, dried milk, dried bananas and chocolate that he sent to Europe, not only to people he knew, but to anyone whose name he merely heard of. He appeared to spend all his money on other people and he entertained lavishly. His conversation was both funny and completely direct with never a trace of pretence. Anyone with a sign of humbug or hypocrisy (even in the name of politeness) would be shown the door. He was a man of contrast: very kind, yet very firm. His painting was lucid and strong, thick and bright – almost like sculpture, which in fact had interested him first.

On Wednesdays, women came to lunch. He did not need advance notice of how many there would be since there was always plenty to eat. He sat at the head of his table like a pasha. He loved women of all ages and types, not only because he was a sensual man, but also with his large heart he understood them. He painted women in preference to men though there exist many fine portraits of men and boys by Kisling. He had a quality which took away the defensiveness women often had with each other. New acquaintances were pleased to meet and there was no suspicious feminine approach at his lunches. On these Wednesday evenings the open house continued and included men, and any friends of their friends, so that it grew into a party of usually about fifty or sixty people. Kisling was not a recluse; he worked hard all week but he needed human beings. The windows of his studio opened on to green treetops in Central Park South. He mixed Manhattans (his favourite cocktail) and smiled and laughed. As I got to know him I sometimes sensed behind this laugh a lingering sad look that did not match the exterior; perhaps it was an underlying violence, perhaps his sexuality, or maybe a sense of the tragedy of life. One felt he might be furious if required. He remains the most generous person I have ever met, both in his views as well as his hospitality. During the parties his unfinished canvases would be turned to the wall; no one was allowed to see work half done. His obituary was surprisingly pinned to the clipping board; it had appeared after a mistaken announcement of his death.

The best times were those spent alone with him because then he would talk. He was Parisian, Polish, Jewish and his Christian name was Moses. Born in Cracow, the son of a tailor, (like Anouilh, and Robert Capa, sons of tailors too), he acquired French nationality after being wounded at Carency in the Great War, when he was in the Foreign Legion. Though America was now involved in the war, he was maddened by what he considered lack of enough action against Nazism; he found too much passivity and people who did not believe concentration camps were true. I remembered this from our Moore McCormack trip and we would fume and stamp together. He used to talk of his beloved Provence where he had a farm, and frequently mentioned also a friend called Modi; once when they were both broke they sold a batch of twenty of their mixed paintings to a dealer for 2,000 francs (twenty francs now). Only years later did I realize that this friend was the painter Modigliani. In the days of Montparnasse, none of them had made money except Picasso.

He also told me more recent stories. One was about a model whom he had painted in his studio in the rue Val de Grace in Paris, just before leaving for America. On discovering that she was pro-Nazi, he had gone wild, scratched her nude body all over and thrown her out and down the stairs, without her clothes which he flung out of the window. She screamed from the staircase, 'What will the neighbours think?' and he screamed back, '*Merde* for what they think, I'll have no Nazis here.' She found her clothes in the garden and dressed in front of the faces that were nodding from their windows, 'We always knew he was no good . . .' So here was the violence I had suspected.

He painted my portrait. It was not a nude, to my slight

feeling of sheepishness. '*Un beau nu!*' he would exclaim with enthusiasm; he loved to paint nudes apart from any sexual desire. They were *objets d'art*: the light on the skin, shadows on the thighs. He took pleasure in the human body as an aesthetic object and painted it with the same strength as he painted flowers. Again it was his strange latent violence that made his flowers and everything else he painted seem strong – a strength mixed with laughter and kindness that ran through all he did. I had not learned to appreciate nudes in his way, and found paintings of bodies a bore. I didn't feel like undressing and so was painted in a black dress with a white – almost sculpted – lace collar. '*La jeune fille au pensionnat,*' he said, teasing.

On St Patrick's Day bilious green shamrock cakes appeared in the pastry shop windows, with green carnations. Irish and more Irish poured down Fifth Avenue in the parade. It was impossible to cross the street east to west before 6 p.m., the city was blocked. It was astonishing how many Irish there were, and the fact that the blockage was allowed; they seemed to be loved. The Boston police were reputed to be mainly Irish. (When my mother in Cambridge asked her cleaning woman her nationality, she answered, 'Me and me husband's Italian, but of course the children are Irish.')

One night after dinner an Irishman called Arthur O'Neill took me to a Harlem nightclub that did not open until 2 a.m. It was filled with reefer smoke, as it was then called, and a Negress was playing blues on an organ. After a while I tried to go home but he would not have it. We finally left the place at ten in the morning by which time it was too late to change my clothes so I arrived very late at the office in a black sheath dress with bare arms. But the Kens did not mind. They laughed, and Big Ken took me straight out to brunch, and that afternoon we started an idea for a new magazine, not another 'popular', but completely different. This was Big Ken's dream and one that he realized much later. It started its first growth that day. 'I don't care what time you get here,' he said, 'it's the result that matters.'

No one in New York ever seemed tired, nor did they ever seem to stop. There were fewer tired people in those days than I remember anywhere since. Birdland, the Downbeat Club – the jazz was stupendous. Sounds of a piano coming out of a bar in

West 52nd Street sounded like Earl Hines – just anyone played well – anyone danced beautifully. It seemed natural and easy, like walking. I hardly ever saw Vsevolod now. He had made many more new friends but still had no job; he had time and I was busy.

On the following Saturday I took a plane to Washington to see the Goulds who had moved there. It was the first time I had been in an aeroplane; I was alone and felt very daring.

Washington was leafy and full of trees, unlike New York's cliffs of cement. There were gardens, but their owners did not know the names of their plants. The tempo here felt nearer to that of the South. Serene blacks sat about outside ramshackle wooden houses, looking fatalistic and unrebellious. We visited Bob Harbach (whose father wrote 'Tea for Two' and 'I Want to Be Happy') who lived in one room with large abstract paintings. He was learning Arabic for a State Department job. We ate in an Italian restaurant with vines hanging overhead, then went to a party where the host wore no shoes and spoke fluent Portuguese to his Brazilian guests. Washington was on a different wavelength; America was indeed exciting and unpredictable. But on the return journey in the train two people fought drearily, explaining the obvious as if it were a discovery; they were intense, earnest and humourless, and their children had cat-gut voices. Like a thermometer in a heat wave, the temperature could rise in a high crescendo, and sink just as quickly to unredeemable boredom. Country of contrasts . . .

Vsevolod met my train as we had arranged he would. He had borrowed a car in order to take me to meet a girl who lived in New Jersey. We became stuck in a jam in the Lincoln Tunnel; it was claustrophobic, it seemed to be full of fog, and I feared the river would come bursting through the roof. What *would* happen if a real crisis came, not just 'overseas' but within America's shores? There had been a practice air-raid alarm recently which had caused panic and hysteria.

We met Vsevolod's girl who was called Jean. She was handsome with strong bones and long hair; I liked her at once. She admired Vsevolod immensely and was carried away by his being European and Russian and having a glamour she had not known until then in her boyfriends. She also seemed motherly and kind. She was art director of Bloomingdale's. He still had not found a job.

Notorious figures abounded with a certain picturesqueness. Serge Rubenstein was one. He lived in a large mansion on Fifth Avenue filled with Impressionist paintings. He was given to clapping his rather pudgy toad's hands when summoning a waiter. Karel Pusta and company found him repulsive and mildly reptilian, yet fascinating enough to be discussed, because of the empire he had somehow achieved by self-made invisible means. Money could be a dirty word. He had bought a Portuguese title, de Rovero. He had a sensual intelligent face, too fat, but with soft brown eyes and a beautiful Dürer mouth.

One day he asked me to lunch at Le Pavilion, one of the best French restaurants. I accepted, vaguely curious; we had a succulent meal. His lawyer came too, I thought as a friend, but it turned out that this was a business lunch and the lawyer was there to note a formal proposition, with a contract to sign if I accepted. An astonishing suggestion – I thought – from a near stranger; was it because America was in some ways such a tough place that an agreement had to be signed? Or was this just Serge Rubenstein de Rovero's personal guarantee? When I declined they were both surprised. No bank account and mink coat? Mink, the status aim, the sign of arrival, the great American dream. No chauffered car? But how was I going to get on?

After lunch I went back to 42nd Street. 'What a weird rapid town,' I said to the Kenneths.

'You mean what a weird rapid creep,' said Ken the Second. 'We'll string him up in the rackets department.'

'Why? It wasn't dishonest.'

'That's true. An offer. Think what you could have got. All the same he's a creep.'

'He's just calculating and organized. The contract idea was like real security – quite *sympathique*.'

'A compensation for losing your reputation. He's married.'

Yet something must have been dishonest. Ten years later when I was in Madrid, I read in *Time* magazine that Serge Rubenstein had been murdered by a taxi-driver who had followed him into his house. He was found dead, wearing black pyjamas. (Incredibly like *Black Mask* magazine.) Motive unknown. The government had always watched him, suspected him, but had never been able to pin more on to him than draft-dodging.

12

Vsevolod brought a young man to meet me whom he had met at the OWI where he still dropped in frequently when he was at a loose end. He introduced him as '*un genre de jeune maréchal de France*'.

He had a Latin appearance with dark hair. Though not more than about twenty-three, he had been awarded the *Croix de Guerre* which was given only for bravery. After the fall of France he had come to America and volunteered for the American Army, but he was due to return to Europe. Meeting him caused a great, exciting revival of my feeling for the Cause, for our war, which was still being fought, and for whatever bravery had given him his decoration. At the time I had just finished a Red Cross course giving me a diploma in home-nursing – having foreseen a possibility of driving ambulances should I return to France. I was also a blood donor.

'*Here* is the man for you,' Vsevolod said. 'I showed him your photograph and he said, "That is the girl I will marry." How do you like that? I said you were my wife, but he is really your type and I am not.'

Everything seemed to break up around us, producing an odd pattern. Vsevolod was joking and yet was not; I felt an immense shock. We all three went off to dinner. The *maréchal* walked down Madison Avenue doing a ballet step on the edge of the pavement, one foot in the street as if he had a shorter leg, leaping from time to time into an *entrechat*; he was a comedian, too, a joker like Red Skelton, only good-looking.

At this time I was working on a book. Big Ken had shown my war-diary to John McCaffery, an editor for Doubleday-Doran, who had given me a contract to publish, providing I turned it into a novel. It was a mistake, it would have been better left as a diary. I invented people quickly who were unconvincing because I was not convinced. Yet when the *maréchal* appeared I had been re-thinking the war through this book, and feeling perhaps rather restless. Though America was at war it did not really feel like it; the war was far away somewhere else. People complained of sugar-rationing but the amount allowed was so vast I had not noticed the difference. The *maréchal* was fighting our fight, con-tinuing our belief. He also gave out a great sexual warmth. How peculiar that on seeing a passport photograph he had said we would marry . . . a fairy story. My parents had married after only three weeks.

We went out together every day. I finished my book in a hurried skirmish, telescoping it, less inclined than ever to turn it into a novel, but there was now a deadline. It was delivered on time and I received $1,000 which seemed at the time like a large sum indeed. (My father was pleased and very amused when this novel came out.) Vsevolod wanted to marry Jean; we got a Mexican Correspondence divorce without going there. The *maréchal* and I were married in an office in New Jersey where paper divorces were respected. (This was not so in New York.) There is a photograph of us standing in front of a church with his family, though I am not sure what part this really played. What was certain reality were the flowers, the affinities of belonging to France, to the Cause and to each other . . . or was it illusion? At the time it was very real. My father had a hernia so my parents did not come to the wedding, but the *maréchal*'s parents organized a reception at a house in Scarsdale; it was a rushed party because he was due to finish his training at a camp in Georgia. Kisling came to the reception, his dear face standing out in the rainbow haze looking rather grave. He gave me my portrait as a present which was typical of his generosity, since he had paid me to sit. He had written across the bottom of the canvas: '*A Gael avec mes souhaits de bonheur*'. But he looked sad. Was he not glad for me? (Was I not to have a real husband, a warm husband, like others did?) He never pretended, so why was his smile forced and faint? It had all been so fast, he said. '*Bonheur*, what is it? Shall I underline the word in my *dedicace* to give it strength? I do wish it for you.' He repeated the word '*bonheur*', in the way *malheur* could be used in French simply as an exclamation. He was an ambiguous guest. The wedding was a whirlwind, with the army camp waiting; but it was sincere and filled with hope.

Vsevolod married his New Jersey girl Jean and moved into her house; we gave up our flat. That he should have married felt somehow like an achievement; perhaps she had been waiting all this time, she had been the reason for my mission, for the fluke I had been for him. A double wedding like the end of an operetta.

The *maréchal* took me to Fort Benning, Georgia; we found a room in Columbus, in the usual wooden clapboard house with a pecan tree outside. The landlady was called Miss Della Bise and she rocked on her chair on the veranda most of the cloying sultry afternoons, talking in her sing-song southern voice that swung like a hammock.

'Lawd's sakes I do declare honey, that Hitler really is the Devil and no human man, hear?' Hear was pronounced haiyar and man was mayan. I was darlin. And she was the first person in all this time I had been in America who seemed fully to believe that Hitler was all we knew him to be.

The heat was fierce, with a humidity of ninety-five percent. It was best not to move fast, so as to avoid breaking into an even greater sweat than the normal, permanent, wetness covering one's body. There was no frigidaire, only an icebox, and large cockroaches swarmed round the water cooler. At night when thirst was greatest, there were three times as many cockroaches. I stood on the screened porch, debating which was greater, thirst, or disgust at the horror of stepping over the beetle river and the possibility of their crawling up my legs.

Twice a week a large steam engine came down the middle of the street. It was a residential district, the tracks were fairly flat and unobtrusive, so that when the monster came it was a surprise. On steam engine days Miss Della Bise stayed hidden in her room with a supply of bourbon. Several bottles stuck up out of the garbage can the next morning. The heat throbbed on.

I can't remember why we had no money since the *maréchal* must have had some kind of army pay. We lived on cakes, which were cheap and filling but did not sustain; a hollow unsatisfied place remained in our stomachs. My soldier spent most days training at the camp, or sometimes going away on manoeuvres. When he was 'home' he often went out at night in gym shoes, saying he liked prowling round the town. The engine, the heat, the large beautiful pecan tree . . . it was all somehow peculiar. When the *maréchal* was away I wandered about alone wondering what I was doing in Columbus. I was given a driving licence without a test because they said, 'You look honest darlin', hear?' I had the idea of hiring a car to discover America, but there was no money. There were GIs who got barbarically drunk and would fight, lying on top of one another on the stone pavements, smashing each others' heads on the concrete enough to break their skulls. It was horrific, but no one tried to stop them. Negroes loped along not noticing or caring, like indifferent panthers. They were superb-looking, long black pencil strokes I wished I could draw. The black people had a craze for colour, and even the vastly fat women dressed in tight purple satin. Their laughter had a music of its own unlike any other, and was infectious; hearing it made a person happy. Twenty years later I heard a laugh in a cafe in Dijon and said to the companion I was with: 'There's an American Negro in here.' He did not believe me till we looked around and found that in fact there was. The impact of the South was singing, swinging, gurgling and very soft – the North seemed hard and harsh by comparison.

In the bus whites and blacks sat on separate sides. I ignored this, because I did not approve, but was stared into retreat by both sides and slunk back to my white seat, feeling flat as a sole on the sea bottom. I spent most of my time alone. Gardenias on rambling, unpruned bushes gave out a heady, exotic, voluptuous scent, but there was also squalor; rubbish and old bottles thrown anywhere.

'How's that chile, what you doin'?'

'I'se on my honeymoon,' starting to talk the same way.

'All alone darlin'? Where's yo man then?'

'He's a soldier.'

At least there was sumpthin splendid about that, hear? In order to go to Fort Benning, where I had tennis lessons and swam in a tepid pool, and sometimes had dinner in the officers' club with my *maréchal*, there was a ride of about fifteen miles on an army bus. This went through the poor white trash district. There were wooden huts in tall grassy mosquito-marshes, with broken pieces of jagged mirror nailed on to their outside walls and tin basins underneath. Lean, rather wild white faces stared at the bus out of their lice and stench, out of the miasma.

We never saw the beautiful parts of Georgia like St Augustine or Sea Island, but we did cross into Alabama once. No stars fell there either, just squalor and sweat. In Phoenix City there were red neon lights with 'Jesus Saves' hanging over small wooden chapels which looked more like brothels than houses of prayer.

At Fort Benning a small group of Frenchmen (and one Russian, Moraviev) trained to return to France. The day this contingent left I returned to New York, wondering what had hit me. Back to 42nd Street . . . waking from a sleep. The Kens were welcoming, but I had to quit again a few months later to have a baby. Big Ken also left at this time to join *Esquire*. He said I had a great career ahead as an executive and that if I wanted to go with him we would start his magazine together in a few years. Did I want to be an executive? I didn't know. It was confusing. First of all, in spite of the war – perhaps because of the war – I wanted to return to Europe, to join my stranger-husband, to see my sister; I wanted to sort something out. I had only known my husband a few weeks and most of that time he had been away.

It felt lonely now – there was no longer the little two-room flat full of friends to go home to. I lived in a cheap hotel overlooking the East River and I saw the ferry and cargo ships going up and down from my window. I applied for passage on a convoy back to Europe. Civilians could not travel during the war, but I had an English passport and was allowed to 'return home' – though I was told there would be a wait of several months before this could be finalized. It turned out to be nearly a year.

My parents were growing old and Stephen was a problem. My parents loved him dearly ('We are the boys of the family,' he would say to Elton Mayo), but my father was planning to retire – probably to England. They were tired. My job had been supposed to produce security and a home for Stephen; I had been granted custody after the divorce (which, though a Mexican

Correspondence one, had red seals and fourteen clauses), and it was understood he would live with me. The *maréchal* loved children and liked the idea of a son, but with him in France, the idea was impractical. And Vsevolod certainly had no plan or desire to return to Europe. He was living happily in Jean's home in Montclair. Jean had roots, she was American-born and integrated into the elm trees and unfenced gardens and all the things Vsevolod had always needed.

They fetched Stephen who went to live with them in their large wooden house. I used to visit often. Jean and I grew very fond of each other and though only a few years older, she was motherly to me too. In a way I wished I could live in the house in the tall trees with them, instead of alone in the bleak hotel with the ships' funnels wailing in the *weltschmerz* night. In Russian tradition many wives and ex-wives often lived together; Vsevolod did not mind how many women there were. This year of visiting them and being together with them and Stephen was completely happy. He now had all I had wanted for him – all I had wanted for myself – a home. Safety. A dog and a piano. My sister and I had not only lacked parents, but also animals, and in my case a musical instrument.

My baby was born on the hottest day of August. My mother loyally came to stay with me beforehand but she had high blood-pressure and the great heat made her ill, so she had to leave. New York City was deserted in the stifling, sweaty summer, and I knew no one there except Kisling. He came to see me every day and he chose the name Guislaine for my little girl. I was out of touch with her father who was probably with Patton's army in Italy. A cable did arrive eventually but Columbus was a place of the past. Kisling and I sat together in Leroy Sanitarium and talked of Europe. I could feel he too was growing restless and wanted to be back there. He told me of Sanary, his goats, his parrot – and rather unexpectedly – his wife. He had not given the impression of having one.

Before leaving America I had an argument with Vsevolod. I had thought, possibly in some confused way, that Stephen would be coming with me. I could not conceive of leaving him behind, he had always been with me, clutched across the German lines, even against Fevzi's advice. It seemed physically impossible to leave him now, and I had never intended to do so.

Perhaps I had not faced what was really happening. I was fuddled, leaving on a convoy, yet wanting to stay in the house in New Jersey too.

'Not the war,' Vsevolod said. 'Not back to the war again after all the trouble we had getting out of it. He is safe now, he must stay here.'

Of course. They were both safe with Jean in her protective house. Should I stay then too? But the new baby was going to its father. I had not seen my husband for a year. Young children should be with their mothers. But there were two mothers and two fathers and two babies.

'Then I will come back soon,' I said, contained inside the shape of events that had formed outside our control.

When they saw me off on the steamer, the three of us looked at each other on a dimension of paradox, as if the Planner behind things were mad.

'*You* told me to marry him,' I said to Vsevolod. '*You* found him for me in the wise maturity I thought you had,' I repeated fatuously, and I walked up the gangplank clutching the warm bundle that was Guislaine this time, inside her shawls; wanting her father to see her but wanting Stephen with us too, yet wanting his safety, then shaken by the funnel's blast and the swerving gulls wailing and wailing forlorn. Vsevolod had taught Jean to be Russian already, so she had absolutely no bourgeois feelings about me; we waved goodbye as the steamer moved off and she cried to see us leave. Perhaps he had not taught her anything, and she had been that way all along; perhaps she would be the teacher. It was December 1944 when our convoy sailed.

There were fifty ships, like a forest of trees moving across the waters at an equal distance from each other. Alexander Fleming, who had just discovered penicillin, was on board with us. Ours was the only passenger ship; the others were tankers and men-of-war.

After three weeks, during which people complained of discomfort (but remembering the hold of the *Cabo de Buena Esperanza*, I thought we were in luxury: only six to a cabin and bunks with sheets), we reached the Irish Channel. Here the convoy divided. Forty ships split from us and continued eastward to France. The ten that were left started north toward Liverpool. We were vulnerable since the Irish had an agreement with the Germans and sheltered submarines in their waters. Depth charges boomed frequently. On the last day we were ordered to remain on deck and we stayed there all day. Guislaine had her father's letters strapped on to her back like the cushion of a kimono. When a depth charge sounded, the whole boat shook; once someone screamed, thinking we had hit a mine or been torpedoed. Some people played poker.

The blitz was over but now London was being bombed by V1s and V2s. We stayed with my sister and her husband near Russell Square. There was no warning of the V2s. To hear them meant it was over and you knew you weren't dead; an entire block of buildings would have crashed, leaving a deep crater. But the V1s had a warning siren which made things worse – one waited in suspense, counting one, two, three . . .

Londoners were patient, standing in long queues for food. Here the rationing worked; everyone got the same amount and Guislaine had orange juice and blackcurrant purée. The fairness was an amazing contrast to France where the ration tickets had been dud paper and the Germans had anyway taken all. Poor France – Jerusalem artichokes and no salt and our one piece of black market meat crawling with maggots. Each to his own and no team spirit (except for the Resistance which in spite of its splendour was a small percentage of the whole).

During this time my mother had corresponded with her sisters and her family in Australia, and as a result they knew all about us. One day a parcel arrived from the northern bush of unexplored Queensland. It contained a little hand-knitted white coat, bonnet and mittens for Guislaine, a present from our aunt, Ursula McConnel, the anthropologist who lived in a black man's camp. She was admired by Claude Lévi-Strauss for her writing, as well as being the only person to have explored so far into the unmapped Outback territory. She lived with the aborigines, a nomad like them. Knitting was a left-over from a life left behind. The little white coat seemed miraculous.

On VE Day Guislaine and I crossed the Channel on the first ship to take civilians. This time we were allowed, not because of an English passport, but because we were going to join the child's father. It was incredible to think we were to see the *maréchal* again . . . after a year . . .

The rejoicing in Paris was wild. Strangers kissed and squeezed and grabbed each other in vast bear-hugs. The war was over. We had won. Now man would be FREE. The tyrant was overthrown. Freedom – that recurring lantern of light, the will o' the wisp on the marshes, had now become a brilliant beam, celestial, shining.

In 1945 Paris was still the city of trees and cafes where people could sit and talk. The noise and stench of traffic had not yet come. There were new ideas after the war: existentialism, Sartre, people living and planning again, couturiers, the New Look . . . and dancing. The release and joy of victory seemed to burst out in dancing. Aimé Barelli, the Swing Club, St Germain des Prés, and Moustache with his orchestra. The jitterbug dancing was wild. People were made of elastic, or as if they had in-built springs. The twirling round and winding up of each other was also done in America – but the rapid spring-steps and curious bounce of the zigzag feet was a special Parisian feat.

But where had the *maréchal* gone? The young man who had read history with such passion, who had believed fervently in the great fight he was embarked upon? He had been very pleased to meet his daughter and had even changed her nappies and powdered her bottom endearingly, but . . . in his speech and attitude, who was this new cynical fellow with rather sinister plans to get rich quick in peacetime? At first it was too close and too upsetting to understand the reason, but I knew later: my soldier simply did not like peace. He could not adapt; he was bored without action. Yet even that could not explain his occasional cold brutality when he had been so warm. Could it be the head wound he had received while with General Patton? Or had he been disguised all along by uniform and the Cause? Where was our lovely love? The warm husband I had travelled all this way to find? He was a complete stranger. The unreality of it and the disappointment were awesome.

It had been a long trip across the Atlantic, touching wood in fear of submarines, looking forward so entirely to seeing him again. But after six months I went back across the old, grey ocean on a troopship with Guislaine, aged two.

13

Maybe every person carries their own touch-wood place inside, their talisman, their formula or recipe to hold on to when in need. I called mine Brattle Street: the generous avenues and white clapboard American houses where people did not lock their doors: this brought safety. America altogether seemed to bring safety, in spite of the paradox of gangsters and toughness; in America, there was a chance. Given hard work, one might get somewhere. The sky was wide.

We went first to Cambridge Mass., not to a house but to a flat where my parents were now fairly unsettled. They were preparing to leave America within the year. Two failed marriages hung between us and I was only twenty-four, though this was unspoken. Fortunately this was no Latin family that shouted abuse. Instead there was a dignified silence on the subject, kindness on all others, and a glow of arrival. But I knew what they thought, their perplexity and anxiety. Yet I believed in ideal marriage – one husband only – and did not believe in divorce! Try and explain that . . . Now if I had been allowed to marry Paolo . . .

In the meantime my parents' home was about to dissolve, and like the old movie seen before, I went back to New York to look for a job, but this time did not leave my child behind.

It was a very different New York. Jobs were not easy to find.

Perhaps it was because of the aftermath of war or because I had a baby to look after. I grew to know the pawnshops of Sixth Avenue where many White Russians seemed to be pawning the Crown Jewels. These people weren't the glamorous sort I had known previously and there were remarkable numbers of Crown Jewels.

Vsevolod and Jean also had a daughter; Stephen was six. He had his own dog which peed on the same tree each day while Stephen went down the same street to the same school. He was growing positive roots; he had a group of friends, habits, landmarks. The dog was called Bugle and there was a rough-tempered tomcat called Jake. Guislaine and I spent the weekend frequently in New Jersey; children of all ages came and went in and out of each others' houses, living the whole network of their lives on another level. In Europe children had had to be driven to schools or parties and fetched later.

Vsevolod had started an agency for commercial artists. He only had four or five of them but one was Bebe Berard who designed for *Vogue*. He found a job for me, decorating shop windows with a French painter called Mimouka Nebel.

Guislaine and I settled into another brownstone rooming house and she went to nursery school. Nebel was a fatherly man, simple and *bon vivant*, a Mediterranean Raimu in appearance. He cooked lunch for himself each day in his flat on West 57th street, which was conveniently near the shops where we worked. He produced *porc aux lentilles, canard aux olives* – no nonsense about a snack. He had time to talk and was not in a hurry like other people. We could have been in a provincial city of France, having lunch in a back street in Anger, unless you happened to look out at the view. We decorated the windows of Bonwit Teller and Bergdorf Goodman, treating them like stage sets.

The room where I lived with Guislaine was bare. We had a box spring bed and took the mattress off each night and put it on the floor, so as to make two beds; outside there was a square roof terrace where we could sit in the sun. Downstairs the janitor, known as the Supe, (short for superintendent) found some wooden boxes and sawed them to size for us to use for flowers. He had a hare lip and looked as if he came from a wet wood. He knew all about plants and when spring came he brought us geraniums and heliotrope and white flowers he called sailor's stars. We had no bath, but a shower and a small kitchen. There was no furniture apart from a record-player; we went to sleep each night listening to *Otello* until we got a few more records.

The Goulds returned sometimes to New York and stayed with their painter friend, Joan Higgins. When Maughan took us to lunch one day with his aunt, the Duchesse de Talleyrand, who lived in Westchester County, it was a funny feeling to sit penniless at the table and find a present from Cartier beside each plate. 'You can always hock it,' said Maughan later, and laughed. He and Suky had a small allowance only and he had a dull office job. Children of the American rich were brought up the hard way – the end of their month was like that of many others; only the distant horizon was rose-coloured.

The *maréchal* made a brief appearance as a sleek civilian accompanied by a caddish-looking friend whose plans for the future sounded alarming. They called on us in a car called a Cisitalia. The FBI had a special bureau for the denunciation of French by other French. Now that the war was over people sought petty revenge, though one would have expected the opposite. Since we had won the war, was it not now the time to show our ideals? According to Karel Pusta whom I met one day in a drug store there were roughly two thousand French people living in New York at this time and two thousand denunciations equally.

Kisling had decided to leave America so I went to see him to say goodbye. He lit a small thin cigar and we sat staring at the sky above Central Park, as if a shape like in a crystal ball would appear in it. He talked for the hundredth time about his beloved southern coast of France where he was returning at last – though now he was no longer wistful but eager. He told me of the colour of the sea, indigo with acquamarine patches, the white dusty roads with forests of eucalyptus and parasol pines, (the concrete blocks had not yet arrived). The light was 'sharp with accurate black shadows like concise drawings', he said, getting up and starting to walk up and down. I closed my eyes and listened to him tell of the midday heat (that I knew so well and remembered) when the animals lay under the trees and the villages were deserted – and then in the late afternoon the old women in black would put on their straw hats and return to the fields, after the rest inside their cool stone houses. As he went on walking about and talking, I half listened and half just thought about Europe

. . . the thick bougainvillaea on the terrace in St Tropez that summer, making shadows like ink, while we sat and ate shellfish for lunch after the long swim; the cicadas' continual clacking on and on like the pulse of the heat beating; coolness coming from the shade of the leaves and the stone of the walls. Another summer in Austria, when my sister and I were on holiday with our parents, we ate blue trout and did not understand the import of the first sign of Fascism when Dolfuss was murdered . . . There were cowbells ringing in the larch meadows where the grass was pale green and smooth like silky fur, and it was full of wild carnations. A chimney-sweep, a blond boy with a top hat, came to our inn . . . a mountain in the Bernese Oberland called the Wildhorn . . . the complete silence in the high snow valleys where only foxes and white hares left footprints . . .

When I opened my eyes Kisling was saying, 'Provence smells like a wild garden, you don't need to plant one, the maquis is broom, thyme, jasmine . . .'

We were in a tall cement building with a smell of car exhaust outside. I was glad for him to go back but depressed to be left behind. This time in New York had not worked out as before – the only good part was seeing Stephen. Nearly two years had passed getting nowhere . . .

I hugged Kisling and cried. When would I see him again? We were losing our friend.

'You should leave too,' said Kiki, wiping my face on his painting rag.

'We can't keep crossing the ocean like commuters to Scarsdale.'

'You should not have come back. Why did you?'

'I bolted from a mess. I thought there was a sort of life to return to in New York, that it would pick up again – I had had jobs and there were friends. You were here, and my parents.'

'I am leaving tomorrow, and your parents are leaving too.' He squashed the remains of his cigar into one of his many pipes, and lit it, saying, 'You should paint.'

It was a big statement, coming from him, but I only felt I was losing a father and I continued to cry. I wished we could go with him. New York would be so empty now.

'I know you should paint and I tell you to do so,' he said again. 'And don't waste time going to art schools. They just teach you rules and put you in prison. Work and discover. You'll get there. I knew it the first time I saw those water-colours you did to hide the walls. They call it in France a *tempérament de peintre*. It takes longer alone, but you'll get there.'

Kisling never returned to America.

14

My parents retired to England, their furniture and books being shipped after them. My mother wrote to tell me they were living in a flat in Polesden Lacey while deciding where to look for their own small house and garden at last. My father had started work on his third book, *The Political Problems of an Industrial Civilization*, and was going to meetings. His post-retirement activity sounded promising. They went to dinners together in London and afterwards a car was provided to escort them back to Surrey.

Guislaine and I left America again too, following Kisling's advice and the general movement together with the feeling that my family were all in Europe. My sister was remarried to Dunstan Curtis who was in the British European Movement and she was head of the field research group of the British Institute of Management.

Our ship docked at Le Havre; we went to Paris by train, crossing fields of apple blossom and very straight poplars that made shadows like the teeth of a comb. Guislaine was excited when we reached Paris. Hundreds of chestnut trees were in flower in the Cours La Reine; our taxi-driver had a black dog and called us *mes petites poulettes*; small familiar things like the smell of Gitanes, croissants, strong (real) coffee made it feel like home. Anywhere in Europe would probably have seemed like home.

That weekend my sister and Dunstan were in Paris. My reunion with her was delirious and her husband seemed immediately like a brother. We celebrated by going to Jimmy's nightclub and kept bursting into tears, to the mild surprise of other customers.

But by the time we reached England my father had had a mild stroke: officially he had recovered, but he had put off his writing. His energy was diminished, and instead of working he sat on a bench in the remarkable garden at Polesden and chatted with Robin Fedden, the curator and our friend, mainly about birds. *The Political Problems* remained a pamphlet. My mother fretted and tried to encourage him to go for walks, to regain vigour. The meetings in London had been expected to lead to new ideas; he was needed. But he took pleasure now in recalling the past. We sat in the garden while Guislaine climbed trees with Fedden's daughter, and he told me of the South Australian beaches, of the moonlight that was clear enough to read by; he reflected on the 'dreaming' of the aborigines and how they were freed from time, their only reality being the present tense – the past and future both being the same; he talked of his father, Old George, and the garden they had had in Adelaide full of peaches and the famous Australian fruit.

My mother's garden receded even further. The flat in Polesden Lacey was beautiful but it was not theirs and they still did not have their own home. According to Browning (whom my father often quoted) the last part of life was supposed to be the best, it was what the first part was made for. But was this so suddenly and already the last part? Old age had come upon my father prematurely. He was still only in his sixties, and, before his stroke, his mind had been at its most productive. But now he was tired. He did not like what the world had become, he felt disgust, he said, at its vulgarians and its paranoid politicians.

It was a shock to find him seeming so much older than he was – and though he did not need the world, it still needed him, and so did my mother. He and I had missed the grand tour together, but now we were very close in a timeless way. We called each other Tegumai and Taffy, from Kipling's *How the Alphabet Was Made*, which I read aloud to Guislaine at night. I embroidered T on his handkerchiefs. He had quoted poetry all his life. His voice was deep, clear, and moving; the sound of it was arresting and would cause people to stop and listen. 'And then I saw the Congo cutting through the black,' he would say, reflectively, in a moment of quiet . . . At this time it was invariably Kipling he quoted. 'When earth's last picture is painted, and the oldest critic has died . . .' his strong yet soft voice would say, 'we shall rest, and faith, we shall need it – lie down for an aeon or two . . .'

Long ago in Philadelphia a black cleaning woman had apparently been left alone all summer dusting an empty house while the family was on holiday. On return, my mother had asked, 'Were you lonely, Delilah?' And the answer came, 'Well now, sometimes I was, then I would say to myself, "Dorothea dear," and hear his voice, and it would pass.'

This voice now recited:

> There runs a road by Merrow Down
> A grassy track today it is
> An hour out of Guildford town
> Beside the river Wey it is

Guildford was in fact their nearest town. Elton Mayo was a classical scholar, sometimes nearing genius intellectually, but he liked simple poetry, light music, Chesterton, H. G. Wells, and after hard work, detective stories.

> For far oh very far behind,
> So far she cannot call to him
> Comes Tegumai alone to find
> The daughter that was all to him

His voice reciting these lines filled me with fear and sadness and made me cry; it was the twilight of his life. I felt immense love for him and immense pity for my mother, who had longed all through their years in America for this part that lay ahead. From an energetic visionary, he had turned into a shaky old man. And as he recalled the Australian moonlight, it grew ever clearer in his memory – first it had been light enough to read by, now it seemed they could even have played cricket by night. And remembering this ghostly game, he would walk slowly, with his stick, along the herbaceous border to the house where 'Dorothea was waiting'.

Dorothea's hair was now white, but her energy had not faded. They had married when they were over thirty, so it may have seemed a short time to her since their meeting at Cressbrook, where he had called her his 'gracious lady' in his letters. I have a switch of my mother's famous hair that she cut off once in Paris when she had a fever; it is a gold, slightly reddish Titian colour and still amazingly full of light. Whether or not the time seemed short, this period of wondering and hope during what was to have been their crowning summit certainly caused her great concern and distress. I wished Guislaine and I could stay, and live with them; London was only half an hour by train, should I have had a job. But my father said, 'Get on with it old lady. You must be off. Go and attend to your life.' So we went to London and just came back for weekends.

We found a mews house in Pavilion Road. It was called 'house', rather grandly, for in fact the front door opened on to a narrow staircase, leading to three rooms only, spread on to two rickety floors, but it had a curious atmosphere that we loved and we put bay trees in tubs on each side of the red front door. A 'distressed lady' came to live with us, so as to be there when I went out. She had a formidable face and we called her the dragon, but she was a nice dragon, in spite of seeming to live entirely on fish, which gave our tiny house a perpetual stink.

My sister and Dunstan were living in Hornton Street and owned a cat. On the opposite side of the street, bombs had fallen; the result was a land of hills with shrubs and creepers, full of other cats leading a jungle life. In the street beyond there was a pub where we went in the evenings sometimes. They owned a scratchy gramophone record of the Battle of Trafalgar. Dunstan, who had commanded the leading motor gunboat in the raid on St Nazaire, and been given the DSO, delighted in hearing what was the so-called voice of Nelson.

My sister's office was in Hill Street – I fetched her there at teatime – where she was usually involved in discussion of miners' strikes with various young men. She had trained with Elton Mayo in America and was following on his work. Sometimes we all went for the weekend to Polesden Lacey, where friends stayed with the Feddens and went pheasant-shooting: Renée Fedden, Robin's Egyptian wife, produced delicious game pâtés. Elton Mayo made a slight recovery and started writing again. The grounds at Polesden were unusual: they were laid out on the edge of a steep valley, with a hill covered with bracken rising on the opposite side, and sheep grazing the turf patches. The view was as wild as Scotland; one could forget that somewhere beyond lay the tamed county of Surrey.

The garden itself was a mixture of lawns, flowers, and a walled vegetable garden. There was a long slightly creepy walk beside a wood which had been laid out by the wife of the playwright Sheridan when they had lived in the house. A sundial read: 'Haste thou traveller, the sun is sinking low – it shall return, but never thou.' A tunnel of yew trees led away at the bottom of the hill into the woods so that there was an area of formal gardens with a contrast of wild and even rather witchy land beyond. Though it was a National Trust house, there were few visitors. Today I believe there are coaches and busloads – but in those days it was solitary and magic.

In London I finally got my first assignment with *Picture Post*. A friend took Guislaine to her first ballet. The efforts were bearing result, we were growing organized, we were happy.

In the winter Robin Fedden invited us to go skiing. He was perhaps one of the best skiers in Europe, but not the obvious sort; he would soar the high routes of the Alps, from Italy through Switzerland, not needing *pistes* – often entirely alone like an eagle that changes its feathers to white in winter. Fedden loved the mountains in all seasons – they were a great part of his life. He had spent six months in the Andes with his wife, his dream being eventually to climb the Himalayas. Later he was to write of the Pyrenees: 'I think of these mountains as friends for whom feeling cannot change. Sabouredo. Gran Pequera. One wears a regal toque of snow, another an iron helmet, another a skirt of green trees and a girdle of black shale – another (perhaps the best), a vein of white quartz across its breast like the ribbon of the Saint Esprit.'

To ski with this teacher would not just be learning, it would be knowing the mountains, the special routes, sleeping in huts and shelters far from the ski-lift crowds, hearing just the faint swish of skis and the plop of snow falling from fir branches. I had only skied twice before in my life but each time found an affinity I longed to pursue. The first time had been at school in Switzerland when we were taken to Grindelwald for one week. Being foolish, young and carried away with enthusiasm, I entered a race and by some miracle arrived third. The second time was with the Goulds when we left New York and went to Stowe for the weekend – there had been a yodelling Frenchman who filled us with amusement and again led me to think it would be a future achievement. Now this rather vague and distant lure was suddenly on the front of the stage. Guislaine was to have her first lessons with Katherine Fedden – we were both mad with excitement, joy, fear, apprehension and pleasure.

Two days before we were due to leave, Guislaine's father appeared to our complete surprise; since we had not seen him for so long he looked slightly unreal. However: good morning. He would take Guislaine to the cinema, he suggested, and they would eat cakes. Very splendid – and quite a normal outing.

They did not come back. I waited by the telephone. I rang the police. I grew frantic. Finally, as the wait was prolonged into a shivery night, I guessed. When the message came from France it was what by now I already dreaded: they had gone. They were in Paris. When I asked about her passport, he laughed. 'Easy,' he said, 'I found it in your desk.'

But I had only left the room for two minutes, when he was making funny faces endearingly and she was laughing; how had he been so quick, or known where the passport would be, or was the desk an obvious place, so it was just another fluke? What must she be thinking now, this little girl who was so quiet and trusting, excitable and funny at times but usually secretive? What could she understand, at five, of grown-up behaviour? And it was not grown-up behaviour.

I went to Paris and the new organization of our life completely collapsed. After two weeks of talks, drinks and dinners – all paradoxically friendly – he returned her to live with me. Once the act had grown stale he did not know how to cope. He loved children, yet also led a great night-life and slept most of the day. He did not conceive of down-to-earth and rather tedious things like the importance of going to school and having a stable routine. The whole action had been a whim.

He said that when he heard we were going skiing he had decided to put a stop to it. Why? And how had he heard, since I saw no one he knew? It was eerie.

He asked merely that we stay in France so he could see his

daughter sometimes, since he was now living in Paris. Quite a reasonable request. If only, I thought, squeezing hard the insides of my coat pockets as I set off again to look for a place to live. I thought, but did not want to think: how *mean*, the method. If only there had been another way. Now we had lost the high routes of the Alps; we were surely on the low routes and the petty lanes. Goodbye dragon lady, please pay the rent and close the house. Please telephone *Picture Post . . .*

We started again in the Cayré Hotel in one of the cheapest rooms on the top floor, head to toe in a single bed. The philosophy required by life seemed to be to plod on and not think about the alternative. 'This is the way it's written, this is what we have to do, so don't question it.' I tried to switch off remembering the new life that had been beginning in London – and in this I was helped by the next events.

I found a school for Guislaine, Frederic Le Play, which was fairly near. We ate picnic meals in our bedroom at night. The Cayré was small and modest in those days, and the porter occasionally fetched Guislaine from school. Very fortunately my *Picture Post* job followed me; it was to write a story about Menton (a ghost town at the time) with a photographer called David Seymour who belonged to Magnum. And so I met him, and with him I met Capa – Robert Capa (really André Friedmann) who had invented himself by pretending that the first photos he had sold had been taken by a rich American whom he represented. He had been caught out and then taken up by Lucien Vogel, editor of *Vu* just before the Spanish Civil War. He had then become famous overnight for his photo, taken from a trench, of a man in the act of falling dead: a 'fanatical, ignorant, brave republican volunteer'. By the time I met Capa he was legendary in his own lifetime for his war photos, for being in the battlefield himself as if he were somehow in the armies of the world, wherever the fighting took place: in Normandy, in North Africa, in London during the air-raids, where he had jumped as a parachutist. He hated war and so had to be where it happened; his photos were records of protest, documentaries.

It is important to remember that there was no television then. It existed perhaps, but no one owned a set nor were there any visual images of the world except through illustrated magazines.

Therefore *Match, Picture Post, Epoca, Holiday, Vu* etc. were far more important than can be imagined now. The first war photographs had been 'shocking novelties' (taken by Capa, and also David Seymour in Spain – civilians under fire in Barcelona in 1938). All photos through the forties and into the fifties were amazing, exciting – and essential for knowledge. By the time Magnum was founded, the work was also essential in order to live.

In Paris when I met Capa, he was the catalyst behind Magnum, which was still in its first stage. What was it, apart from being known as Magnum Photographers, a group of eight men who reported the world? It was founded in 1946 by Capa, David Seymour, Henri Cartier-Bresson and George Rodger – and four other photographers. Capa gathered people round him, encouraged them, taught them, sometimes feeding and clothing them. A special quality of skill grew into their work – yet Capa himself appeared to be a wild, good-time, laughing, drinking man. He was sturdy and dark, with a warm, animal attraction, and was much deeper than he seemed. After inventing himself, by creating the imaginary photographer Capa who became true – he also invented the spirit of Magnum, that drew its group together and it was he who thought up most of the story ideas.

David Seymour, who was known as Chim, was completely different; quiet, small, owlish with thick glasses, clever, funny but pessimistic. There was something very endearing about him and Capa obviously loved him. 'Chim' derived from Szymin, his real name – it was pronounced with a soft S like Shim, and suited his compassionate gentleness. He loved children and at this time had photographed the poor and underfed ones for UNICEF and UNESCO. He anglicized his name to Seymour after being in the American Army for which he volunteered. Due to bad eyesight he was put into intelligence and was awarded the Bronze Star when he worked as a photo-interpreter with General Bradley's 12th Group. Whereas Capa was open and hard living, Chim was quietly intelligent, almost like a professor.

Out of the eight photographers that formed Magnum, I knew and worked with only three of them: Chim, Capa and Cartier-Bresson. In the end, Chim was my partner. I did the research and the interviews for him, wrote the captions and the story. For Cartier, I did mainly the arranging, interviews and some notes.

Capa worked alone but organized us all. When I occasionally met the other photographers (like Ernst Haas, for instance – a good-looking Austrian) in the office where Margot Shore kept dates and accounts, I would hail them with a feeling of belonging and the kindred feeling of a certain pleasure about the next job, and curiosity about the last one.

However in this first stage in Paris, while Guislaine and I were still camping out in the Cayré, the Menton story was delayed. Sitting with Capa and Chim in a restaurant, we pondered what to do as a fill-in. When we did not work, we did not eat – it was that simple. We had no state aid or unemployment money as there would be now – added to which the three of us were in any case freelance foreigners. A rest between jobs was useful for recovery from hard work, but we could not afford to stop for too long. Over the next years I remember most of our discussions took place over lunch in the cafe below the Magnum office, or often in Chim's favourite restaurant in the Avenue de la Tour-Maubourg where the cooking was Norman and rather rich. In London it was in the White Tower in Soho. Chim was a gourmet and very greedy: it was always he who ordered the food and wine, giving it much thought, while Capa sat with a cigarette stub in his mouth, looking into space to see a future story take shape: this was their usual pattern.

By the end of lunch on this particular day Capa decided that while waiting for Menton I would do a 'profile' of Anouilh with Cartier-Bresson. (Perhaps he was partly trying me out?) Chim was able to afford a short holiday and wanted to go to Greece to 'pursue some antiquities'.

Cartier-Bresson, who came from Normandy, was entirely different. Blond, with frank blue eyes looking candidly at the world almost like Peter Pan, he had a sort of purity. Already a great photographer since long before, he had probably joined Magnum because of the brotherhood, the intuition Capa was famous for, and for the way he knew when to push people and when to leave them alone. In Ernst Haas's words, 'he was the only master I ever respected'. Capa was a magnet.

People at that time were fascinated by Anouilh's degree of facelessness. No one had seen him. What did he look like? He hid from publicity – though his plays were famous, translated and staged in London – not even Parisians in France seemed to know anything about his personality.

At opening nights he would be incognito at the back of the theatre in the cheapest seats, hidden like a mole from the lights, looking rather like a mole too, with his rimless glasses and gentle blinking. What was the connection with the biting, scathing wit taking place on the stage? There was an undertone of despair in his funniest plays. He never took a bow, like some playwrights who appear at curtain fall. Before the end of the last act, his seat would be empty.

Yet when I met him he was easy to talk to. It was public recognition in the street that he recoiled from, and public knowledge of his private life. Once tracked down, I had several meetings with him, sitting in the Brasserie Lorraine in the Place des Ternes, which was near where he lived at the time – and then he would laugh and talk with no restriction at all. He said he did not like plays with a message. 'But you have a message, Monsieur Anouilh. All your plays say the world is a dirty place, that pure love will be hurt, that we must beware of the cynics who will be jealous and try to soil it. . .' Behind the glasses the small eyes were intense and piercing, then his whole face was changed by a smile. 'If there is a message, it is by mistake,' he said, and laughed.

He had taken a law degree and then worked in a publicity agency with Jacques Prévert. He despised publicity. Privacy was freedom. (At this time he was divorcing his actress wife, Monelle Valentin, which made matters worse.) He was born in Andorra, the apart-place, and he was an apart-person. He said everyone in his village was called Anouilh and his father was a tailor. So easy to talk to – so hard to have met. Yet on we chattered. He was not curious and did not travel. He had only been to Switzerland, England and Rome (where he visited the Sistine twelve times, but saw nothing else). He liked London and had obtained per-mission from the Office des Changes to buy a flat there. But when the red tape was finished there was no money left! English taxes took fifty percent of the profit and agent's fees the rest – he made a fiver on a hundred pounds. He had never been to Spain because, he said, it frightened him, it was too pure, too noble. 'It is easier to live among corrupt people,' he said. 'You know where you are then –' and again his laugh. 'France does not need to be governed,' he added thoughtfully.

The author aged eighteen

Elton Mayo, called 'The Philosopher of the Picket Line' by *Fortune Magazine*

A miniature of the author's mother,
Dorothea, painted in Paris

Dorothea in pre-revolutionary Russia

E.M. with the author's sister

Reugny, winner of the Grand
National, imported into Australia

Paolo, the husband who wasn't allowed, an anti-Fascist in spite of the uniform

The unknown father-in-law

iquième année. — N° 95.   Le Numéro : **25** centimes.   DIMANCHE 19 Septembre 19

LE MIROIR

LE MIROIR

L'ESCADRON HÉROIQUE DES "HUSSARDS PARTISANS

— **Après une reconnaissance à pied, les cavaliers russes chargent sur leurs chevaux** —

Parmi les engagés volontaires de l'armée russe, l'escadron des « hussards partisans » mérite une mention spéciale. Partis cent vingt au mois de novembre, ils n'étaient plus que soixante

rangs de ces braves dont beaucoup portent les quatre grades de l'ordre de Saint-Georges. Leur commandant W. de Schneeobé les a conduits jusqu'à Dorna-Watra en Bukovine. Ils ont combattu

A newspaper clipping showing the father-in-law among the charging hussars

Vsevolod, the husband by mistake

The author aged nineteen

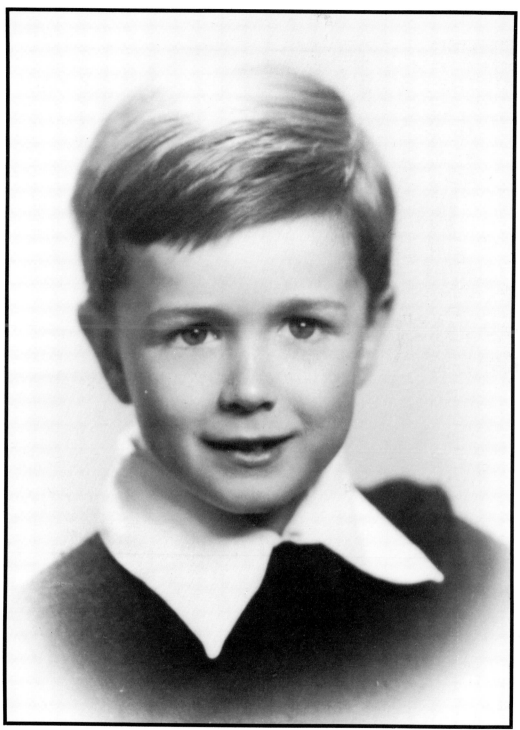

Stephen aged five

The author, portrait by Kisling

Self-portrait by Kisling

Robert Capa, founder of Magnum photographers, 'the man who invented himself'
(Carl Perrutz photograph)

The author with Jean Anouilh – the playwright invisible on opening nights

David Seymour, 'Chim', who hated
violence and who died a violent death
(Judith Friedman photograph)

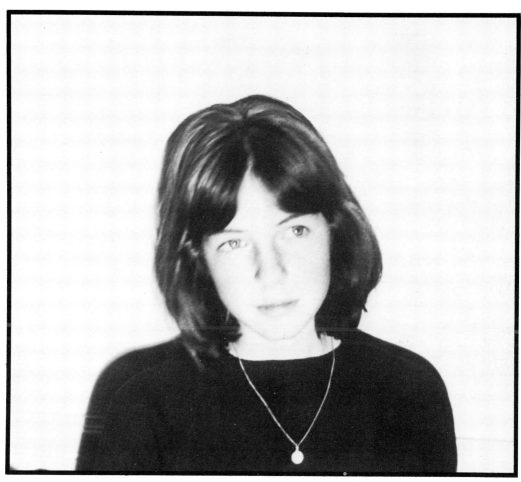

Guislaine aged twelve

The author with Guislaine in Spain

ALVARO

The author aged thirty (Michael Wickham photograph)

Asolo, returning to the dream

The author with Antonio Bienvenida
– 'the bulls were his brothers'

The author at her first exhibition,
photographed by Baron for *Tatler*

The author with her sister

Georgia aged six, off to school in
Walton Street

Georgia aged twelve

The lost chateau

The author with Georgia, 1981

With Cartier–Bresson we were permitted for the first time ever into one of his rehearsals. The play was *Colombe* at the Théatre de l'Atelier and we were allowed to take photographs. It was an achievement and an honour, simply attained – due merely to talking as from one human being to another, and convincing him nothing would be published of which he did not approve. He had become my friend: a Beatrix Potter mouse with glasses.

This method, which had not been a method at all but was just 'being myself', later turned into our system with Chim. 'Go in there and get the doors open for me,' he would say, smiling his secretive, shy smile. He made me conscious of something that had been unconscious, he used it as a quality and was the nearest I ever got to having a manager.

Chim and the Menton story were now the next job.

Guislaine's father had left Paris and gone to live in America. Since assignments meant going away, she changed schools again and boarded at Dupanloup. Whenever I returned, she came back to me and attended as a day-girl. The system was the best we could do in the circumstances and it was a pleasant change to earn the money to pay the school without all the *angst* in the small hours – that old waking at three a.m. and thinking: what now?

15

We went to Menton on the Blue Train. First we ate our dinner in the restaurant car where Chim carefully ordered an excellent claret. We were relishing not just our meal but the rather intriguing job ahead. We rocked through the night in the wagons-lits and woke in sunlight, looking out at mimosa as we ate croissants and drank coffee. Three weeks with all expenses paid stretched ahead during which we would portray Menton, a haunt of old, secluded people who were almost in hiding; it would mean gaining entry into secret gardens.

The job was subtle, the work hard, and it took all the time we had. I suppose we must have slept but the job seemed to take twenty-four hours a day – though we did not mind; we were absorbed.

Menton was nearly dead thirty years ago. It is hard to conceive now, since the population has grown so much, buildings have been built along the entire length of the coast and the world has changed in a shorter time than ever before. But when our assignment took place, it was because *Picture Post* was interested in Menton as a strange phenomenon – a retreat for ex-patriates, mainly geriatric. We managed not to frighten them, and were allowed into their gardens, though some were poor and did not have gardens. There was a chorus-girl of eighty who stood up and danced in the cafe where she went to drink pastis with the 'respectable' man she had married. But the gardens were the miracle, the capacity of the English applied in a hot climate. The Garavan district was balmy and protected from the mistral by the curve of the hill towards Italy. The Waterfield garden was the most beautiful – and beyond and above it, the Russian cemetery high above the sea, for many Russians had also gone to Menton to die.

We called our story 'City of Unburied Dead'. But they are buried and gone now – and their eerie, exotic lawns with the long purple shadows have been bulldozed in order to erect concrete blocks. The time-change can perhaps be felt in the first two paragraphs of the article:

There should be a boundary line on the road outside Menton with a notice warning you it is disturbing to enter the town. When you leave you will be haunted by shadow-people who wear lavender and grey, who are pear-shaped, whose skins are fine parchment. The colours of the picture are dim rose and silver like pot-pourri in bowls, the textures are of lace; this is the last moment before the rainbow dissolves.

These were the golden days before the First World War when the English were the most powerful nation in the world and, abroad, took it for granted that they would be treated as such; when *The Times* was still known as the Thunderer and income tax ranged between fivepence and a shilling in the pound – the quiet, respectable members of the upper and middle classes, who spent their lives keeping the whole splendid edifice in being, came to Menton to end their days in honourable retirement. As late as 1939 the English owned eighty percent of the villas . . . where today a stray goat wanders . . .

It was already derelict and haunted while it was still lived in by these old people with their ancient mariner faces and stories to tell. One of them remembered Queen Victoria's visit – her statue was later smashed off its pedestal and thrown into the sea by the Germans.

We returned to Paris, Chim feeling gloomy about the result. For Magnum it was an off-beat type of job; was it really a story at all? The photographs were superb: a broken bench, the

119

eighty-year-old crone dancing, the empty pedestal . . . the little cemetery with all the gravestones inscribed in Russian . . .

When we sat again in the Tour-Maubourg restaurant with Capa, Chim spoke of his misgivings. He looked so gloomy as he ordered the wine that Capa and I laughed. Capa said he was known for his dim view; we said we would call this the 'Lamentations of Chim', which had a biblical sound and made him laugh too, so then his gourmet's delight took over and we settled back into the importance of food.

Chim was always carefully dressed, always with a black, knitted tie – Capa wore any old thing, usually a black sweater, and did not care about his clothes. Chim read and had a rare collection of books in a large suitcase that he hoped to house one day in a proper flat with a library. Capa read detective stories and lived on action. He was Hungarian, had studied political science at Berlin University in 1932 and later became involved in a student's skirmish and was helped to escape from Budapest by his very kind father. Chim was the Polish son of a Yiddish publisher; he was an intellectual with a reflective, careful mind. He worked always with three cameras round his neck: a Leica for speed, a Rolleiflex for portraits, and a second Leica for colour. They became like my older brothers. Not 'brothers of the road' as Vsevolod had been, although the road may have been our life – but in a strange way we loved each other. They were family.

Capa told me to get ready to go to England with Henri Cartier-Bresson to do 'Generation X' with him. This was a compliment, it meant he was pleased with me, because Generation X was so far one of Capa's biggest ideas, his child. It was the name given to the unknown generation, those who were twenty after the war, and in the middle of a century. He wanted to choose a young man and young girl in each of twelve countries and five continents, examine their way of life, and find out what they were doing, thinking and hoping for the future.

On the night before I left, Capa said he would take me to dinner but that he had to look after a friend who had the blues, so we would join him. The friend turned out to be Joseph Kessel, who was completely drunk. He was in the mood where he smashed glasses and then swallowed down the broken glass. It was quite a feat, but monotonous. The dinner was in the Ritz and the other diners were watching with glazed dignity. Kessel, who was considered to be a great writer, looked like a wonderful lion with a mane of unruly hair. I wondered why he could feel so desperate when he had all that most of us wanted. His Irish wife was greatly distraught, and in the middle of dinner she decided to leave him permanently and forever. She stood up and left, with tears and mascara streaking her face, dashing through the hushed and somewhat dumbfounded room and along the corridor where Louis XV chairs were placed in correct positions, like judges.

Capa and I somehow managed to get Kessel up and out of there, staggering through the increasingly disapproving silence with his burly frame propped between us, like three wild bears. The cool air in the Place Vendome was calming. We got him into a taxi and drove him home. 'He often does this,' said Capa, calmly and unperturbed. 'It's one of his tricks, swallowing glass.' So Capa was Kessel's nanny – and here was again another side to this man who at first meeting would seem to be a hard-drinking, sexy, immensely physically attractive good-timer. But in reality he could drink and never get drunk, and was usually looking after a friend, or working out a new idea, or, now that the world war was over, due to leave for a local battlefield he had just heard of. There was nobody like him.

For Generation X, Cartier-Bresson chose two young people in opposite circumstances – one town, one country – one a bus clippie, the other a gentleman farmer. I drove Henri's Volkswagen down Regent Street with the roof open, while he stood up as we followed the bus, taking photographs of the clippie standing on the back step. We had high tea with her family at Hendon (Henri loved cream buns). He photogaphed the mother pouring tea from a brown pot with the spout sticking out like a nose from a home-knitted cosy, the father, the brother, the baked beans and bacon, then our yellow-haired clippie girl walking to the terminal depot where the buses were lined up like red monsters in a stable.

The part in the country took longer. We stayed in a pub near Upton, Hampshire, and settled for an indefinite time. The young man was Andrew Heath, engaged to Harold MacMillan's daughter. Geese wandered through the village, the pub-keeper mowed his lawn, creating the unforgettable smell of fresh green always associated with England. There were primroses, and

April was 'stirring dull roots with spring rain, breeding lilacs out of dead land' and truly it did 'stir memory with desire'. I wished we could stay forever; it seemed like some life of origin that had got lost somewhere and now been refound. Home, wherever that was. Each day we drove the few miles to Andrew's cottage and his farm, in Henri's little car.

While Henri took endless photographs Andrew taught me to shampoo heifers with him, to rid them of their warble flies. One heifer craned her neck in pleasure as if she were having an Arden massage; I grew fond of her and called her Daisy. More photos of Andrew Heath on his tractor and Sarah MacMillan arriving in a cloak and sitting by the fire. It was endearing the way Henri loved muffins, buns, toasted tea-cakes and never seemed to miss the excellence of French cooking. (In London we spent much time in Lyons.) Andrew told us that Weyhill, one of the nearby villages, used to have the biggest sheep market in England. The hills surrounding his house folded peacefully into each other, and lay together, and gradually while we were there the country bloomed; wild anemones in the woods, violets and cowslips in the fields.

There was so much material for Henri on this job that he sent for his wife to join us. When she arrived the pub-keeper took a dim view, saying that she had a rather dark skin. Liberation had not yet been achieved in 1949. We explained that she was an Indonesian princess and had been a dancer and that they were very lucky to have such a person to stay. They looked at the world through lace curtains and did not like the smell of joss sticks.

When the job was finished we stayed in London to make final notes. We usually had dinner in the little Italian restaurant in Curzon Street that is still there today and has not changed. It is run by what seems to be a family of waiters; it feels more like being in the old part of Bergamo on the hill, than being in the centre of London. Henri's wife left and we visited my parents. We also went to Winchester where he was indignant at the Wykehamist motto: 'Manners Maketh Man', which he said was English hypocrisy.

He was always anxious. He would telephone my room at seven in the morning to go over what we had already agreed on the night before; we lived on nerves at the end of the job. At the same time he was funny, appreciative and tender. When all went well, he used to sing a song: '*Ah, je l'aimais tant, je l'aimais tant mon barbot de St Jean . . .*' which is still in my head and has always remained associated with that time. It was incredible to be highly paid simply to lead one's natural life. This was especially true of the part that had been in the country, where we woke up to rooks flapping, wet earth giving out its leaf-mould smell, and birds deafening in the first light. When Henri sang his song it meant he was relaxed and satisfied that all was in order . . . and so we would go out to dinner. But was it relaxed? We took the Leica, just in case. One never knew what one might miss. It could not be left behind, it was part of his person.

Unexpectedly, disaster struck Generation X. Thousands of dollars and months of shooting and research had been invested in it, but according to John G. Morris, in his article published in 1974, this child of Capa almost died, 'killing with it Magnum's future'. The reason was that the magazine that had originally agreed to back it wanted to make radical cuts. Capa did not agree, and since he was not one to be pushed around, he withdrew it from them. It was not until six months later that disaster was averted, Capa sold it to *Holiday* – and Magnum's momentary fragility was overcome. It grew its true strength from that time on.

Holiday called it 'Youth of the World'. Our story was the lead in three issues. I can't remember where I was six months later, but I never saw it. I was told an abbreviated version appeared in *Picture Post*. I was also told much later that Andrew Heath's girl had committed suicide.

We returned to Paris. Guislaine ceased to board and for a while I did not work, but rested, and we lived in the Hotel St Thomas d'Aquin. A friend gave us a Siamese cat. Guislaine put her doll's straw hat on it, which it did not mind – but when we tried to teach it to walk on a leash, it walked only backwards. So in the rue St Thomas d'Aquin there could sometimes be seen a cat in a straw hat in reverse gear.

16

Paris was at its height at this time: Philip Toynbee and Robert Kee could be seen talking on the terrace of the Deux Magots; Gene Kelly was making his film *An American in Paris*, and Litvak, who had made *The Snake Pit*, was filming a Sagan story called *Aimez-Vous Brahms* with Ingrid Bergman. Irwin Shaw had a flat with his wife and son in the rue du Boccador, but went away alone to the Hotel d'Iena in order to write in peace. It was here that he wrote *Two Weeks in Another Town*. Paris was buzzing. All these people live elsewhere now, and some have died – but then it was like an aftermath of the days of Gertrude Stein and Scott Fitzgerald – foreigners could be Parisians.

There were gala evenings at Deauville, where Litvak, Selznick and Zanuck often spent their weekends. The gambling was tremendous. They would stay at *chemin de fer* till dawn came over the sea outside. I remember once hearing them betting their film rights. Women wore dresses by Piguet or Rochas or Balenciaga, couturiers were still 'great' then, clothes had a magic. After elegant lunches, women with nothing to do went together to the collections. The new season's clothes were secret till the last moment, and invitation cards were necessary to be allowed to see them. Mrs Snow, of *Harper's Bazaar*, wrote her 'Letter from Paris' letting the first news out of the bag. She did this mostly from her bed in the St Regis Hotel, wearing a glamorous negligée. I sometimes worked on it with her.

One day, when Gene Kelly gave a party at the George V where he was staying, the police arrived. Gene, always hospitable, opened the door with a big, wide smile and welcomed them in, offering them champagne. An American standing beside me said, 'I understand they are looking for a black marketeer who was here. Do you know who it was?'

'It was my husband,' I said, though I had not known he was in Paris. The American did not find it funny and edged away, but Chim, standing small and quiet on my other side, laughed and laughed.

'Well I won't disown him,' I said, 'we must be loyal.'

The next day he found us (through the Magnum office) and appeared in a superb Delahaye; we drove about Paris with Guislaine and had a succulent tea at Rumpelmayer's – he had always been rather keen on cakes. He was most generous in his invitations, but never had any cash. He was so friendly and funny, perhaps the police had made a mistake. He was due to leave for Guyana where he told us he was prospecting for gold. Always glamorous, never small-time.

The next day I took Guislaine to lunch at the house of Marcel Rochas in the country outside Paris, near Villennes. It was interesting that he was the only couturier who was not homosexual; this must surely have made a difference to the clothes. Presumably a homosexual would design clothes as for his sisters – but Marcel Rochas conceived clothes with desire, all the more so as he was a virile man, greedy about his food, liking the good things, loving beautiful women. He would visualize and design feminine clothes for them, as seen from the masculine man. There is no disparagement intended here about the others, who also made extraordinary clothes. One might say equally that homosexuals would have better understanding of the femininity of women and what they wanted for themselves. This bears no judgement. It is just an oddity worth mentioning, that Rochas was unique of his kind.

His second wife was called Helene. He had found her as a young girl running round St Germain des Prés in any old sweater. She was already beautiful but he groomed her and made her elegant, giving her a personality – he was her Pygmalion. She was painted with their two children by Leonor Fini – not conventionally – but looking like a blonde gypsy with her two leprechauns.

For lunch we ate *boudin*, entrecôte with baked potatoes, salad, and a frangipane cake. Marcel repeated many times that it was a *déjeuner de campagne*. An Italian couple served the meal; the man wore his beret, the woman had big bones like a carthorse. When she brought the coffee she announced that she was from the *pays de Mussolini* but had turned her coat round.

We walked in wet woods, with Guislaine disappearing through the trees and hiding like Indians with François and Sophie, children her own age. The boy was dark like his father, the girl blonde like her mother – it was almost impossibly perfect. There was a woman called Perla with her Polish lover who walked on alone; there was the Prince de Beauvau who talked a lot and did not notice the view. Marcel talked to me entirely about himself but with clever asides. He was most handsome – he knew it but he laughed. His hair was black; he had that very swarthy complexion of the people from Auvergne (the origin of the Auvergnats seems to be unknown). He was a sensual man, even to the point of explaining that he liked his women to have their own smell on all parts of their bodies. He did not appreciate too much washing or American hygiene. He said this not on our country walk but one evening before, when we were sitting at his elegant dinner table in Paris, with the *valet de chambre* passing *fraises des bois* in a silver dish. His remark that he liked his women 'high' seemed the more striking among the cut-glass goblets and chandeliers.

He suggested making me some clothes at a 'friend's price' – but I said vaguely: some time later when I had a job. 'Or a man?' he said, 'Why not a man to pay? It's ridiculous.' We were good friends but I knew he thought me hopeless in some ways, and did not see the point of Magnum. In this zenith of the Parisian era, or perhaps its sunset, there was something wrong with a woman who did not take great care with her dress. He subsequently made me three dresses: one in heavy Ottoman grosgrain silk, another in taffeta, and a white brocade ball gown with silver leaves faintly imprinted all over it. I wore the last one to a gala in the Monte Carlo casino where I was taken by Litvak. Larry Adler played the harmonica and Litvak played baccarat. In my beautiful dress I felt empty.

This was very fine, but time had elapsed now since the last job and I needed to work. Chim was away, he had gone to investigate a palazzo in Rome where he hoped to acquire a flat that would be his home later. Chim, who lived in a suitcase, longed to unpack his books and treasures. Capa, who lived in any small room anywhere, did not mind.

One day, drifting down the Champs-Elysées wondering this and that, a job dropped out of the sky. I ran into André Ostier, the *Vogue* photographer I had not seen since Cannes during the war. We exclaimed at seeing each other and sat down in Fouquets to hear the mutual news. He told me he was leaving for Venice where he was to photograph a big wedding and asked if I would like to go with him.

Guislaine went back to Dupanloup. She did not seem to mind, she was fond of one of the nuns who used to take off her coif and let her long hair down and brush it, like Rapunzel. She probably did mind inside, and I was certainly wistful for a settled place, like the one we had briefly had in London, with Guislaine at home every night in her fuzzy dressing-gown.

In Venice, we waited. The wedding, which was to be a social event, was postponed. We sat in Harry's bar in uncertainty, we ate raspberries in the Fenice, and still the wedding was postponed. We dined with Arthur Jeffress, who lived in Venice in summer; the street leading to his house was dark and narrow, even slightly alarming – but when his front door opened it was on to the Arabian Nights. The door closed behind us and we were in a patio with orange trees – beyond there was a dining-room shining with lapis lazuli and gilt, and Peggy Guggenheim was sitting at one end of a long marble table.

The next morning the wedding was cancelled altogether; the couple had quarreled irrevocably. The only certain thing was our hotel bill.

After his first consternation, André said, 'Since we are here, let us stay – we may think of something.' So that day we joined Arthur Jeffress who had again invited us to the Lido where he had his usual picnic lunch – usual for him, that is – but to us quite Edwardian: it was spread on a damask tablecloth; prawns, seafood, peaches, figs and champagne.

When we returned to Venice, we walked by the canals with

their damp, mossy darkness and their hollow sound of water lapping, hearing the warning cry of the gondolier as his prow rounded the corner ahead of him. I listened to the Venetian dialect – and thought of the summer ten years ago, and Paolo. I told André about Asolo, the hill town where Eleonora Duse had lived, where her clothes still hung in the musuem – where Katherine Cornaro, Queen of Cyprus had been exiled, where Browning had stayed and his son had built a house . . . about the strange Palladian villa with a tunnel that led through the hill behind into another house – the ancient Etruscan ruin on the summit with ivy growing up it in the shape of a hand . . . and André listened to all this, and nodded, and said it was very well and we would do a story about the place. We were not let down by the wedding after all, this was better.

So we arranged to go there, and as I thought of the arcaded streets, the bumpy green hills behind the little town and the blue Veneto plain stretching away in front – so hazy, so flat, it looked like the sea – I wondered if there was still a Topolino swerving to a stop in front of the cafe. Would he still be there? Would he be married? Would he remember?

The roads had been tarred and there were several cars. It was less dusty and there were no more donkey carts, but there were still roses everywhere. Where was La Nina who had fried melon flowers with the chicken? There was still that extraordinary Englishman who floated, lank and wilting, through the street in a white silk suit like Blithe Spirit (I remembered Paolo telling me the Asolani thought all English were weirdos because of him). I proudly showed André everything as if I belonged. The Palladians had described Asolo as being inexplicably related to the inner reason for things. I grew feverish, wondering who we might see at the next corner. (Was it longing or dreading? He might be with his wife.) We saw the Duse's dresses for Cosi Sia and Francesca da Rimini, hanging in their glass wardrobe, as if she might return and put them on – an *apparizione melodiosa*, as she was called on her tombstone . . . we saw the bust of the lonely exiled queen, Katterina Regina Aliensis – who died, as the Asolo poet said, 'as clouds disperse in the mountains, without royal magnificence, having outlived tribute'.

There was much to photograph. We stayed in the Albergo del

Sole, going into the kitchen in the evening to choose our dinner from whatever looked most appetizing in the black frying pans on the huge old stove, where the father of the family was cook. We ate on the wide stone terrace, overlooking the piazza below, with the tallest hollyhocks in Europe, the tallest campanile ringing its resounding bells whose chimes rolled through the streets like a hoop. No Topolino drove swerving to a stop, however. Nor did I recognize anyone from the summer that had grown into me ever since, as part of my insides. Neither – sadly – did anyone seem to recognize me.

When the photographs were finished André suggested I stay and write the story while I was still there, in case I needed to check anything – and then he left, saying he would see me in Paris. I stayed on in Asolo and wondered – and then, somewhat apprehensively, I telephoned Paolo's number. A man's voice answered. I asked if Paolo were there.

'*E morto*,' said the voice.

Dead. How could he be dead? The voice was his half brother who told me he had died from a heart attack, while walking in the piazza, still only twenty-five. He had passed his law degree. He had lived in their palazzo in Venice and had come to Asolo in summer. He had not married. He remembered, yes indeed the brother remembered who I was, though we had not met.

So now the light went grey and the day looked like empty glass. Was it true? Or could he have been killed because he was an anti-Fascist?

The brother asked me out to dinner. He was dark and fat and bore no resemblance to Paolo except for his voice. He was dull and probably I was too. Driving through the green hills I fell asleep – mortifyingly. When I woke the mountain breeze was blowing from the Dolomites on this road where the children used to throw cyclamen at our car. I could not wait to leave.

The next morning the brother kindly drove me to a train which was quite a long way. A plume of dust rose from the Veneto, like the white smoke of some old hope dying. He was not my brother-in-law as he would have been, and I did not have a house here. Nor did I have any money; he lent me the amount for the ticket. I was just a foreigner who could not pay her hotel. It was long ago, that summer when I could not marry. I did not look for La Nina as I had originally planned, for it was she who, when I left that other time, had said, '*Coragio Signorina,*' and I did not want her to see me in tears and have to say it again.

Looking out of the train window, I cried for Paolo, for the life he had never lived, for the waste of his person and the waste of mine. I would have been an Italian widow but with children who had roots; Asolo would have been home. I could not quite believe the heart attack and wondered. It might have been different, I might not have been a widow – if we had married, and he had been happy, and I had looked after him, he might not have died . . . But anyway he had gone. He had not even lived to be thirty.

When I reached Paris there was a telegram: my father was dead too. He had had a third stroke. He had died in the hospital in 'Guildford town, beside the river Wey'.

Even apart from his strokes, which lowered him physically, I think my father's disillusionment with the world meant he did not really want to stay in it – he did not fight to live. A propos of an obituary in the *New York Times*, which had made much of a notorious character, he had said, 'Anyone would think he had been a great man, not just a successful one.' When Elton Mayo's friend and colleague Pierre Janet died, I said, 'I am so sorry Daddy, you will miss him.' And he had answered, almost angrily, 'When a man is eighty-six, he has a right to die. Let him go.'

Let him go. But the figures were reversed; Elton Mayo was only sixty-eight.

And now when I lie awake at night, I can always hear him slapping his hands together as he walked down the passage at Polesden. He had a very dry skin, prone to infections, so would use 'Hinds Honey and Almond Lotion' after washing – slapping them together, saying, 'Damn,' aloud as he bumped into the wall, not turning on the light at night so as not to wake the household. Sometimes he carried a flashlight in the house which was more alarming, if one met him, than having the light turned on. On to any skin blemish he put iodine, even on his nose – this gave him an odd appearance, as did also his hatred of flies, which caused him to hang a handkerchief from the inside of his hat on to the nape of his neck, like someone from the Foreign Legion. My old eccentric Daddy had no vanity at all.

And I hear again – and always will – his voice, so deep and soft, yet carrying so far, telling me of the superb, wide, vast, Southern Australian beaches where the rollers came in from miles out at sea – beaches that we have never seen – and they are our Dreaming as they were his last dream. Elton Mayo's life went out in brilliant Australian moonlight.

R. Tagore said: 'Death is not extinguishing the light, but putting out the lamp because dawn has come.'

A bereaved person holds on to the sayings of great thinkers, as on to a raft. Santayana wrote to Iris Origo, on the death of her young son, that she was closing a book she would keep on hand for another occasion. Time does not heal, in spite of the saying, but it produces acceptance.

Ever in my memory, I hear the last lines of my father's favourite Browning poem on Venice:

> Dear dead women, and what hair too
> What became of all the gold
> That used to hang and brush their bosoms?
> I feel chilly and grown old.

He felt chilly long before his time.

My mother lived on alone in an emptiness that was never filled – and she never got her garden. She had started life certainly in a very splendid one at Cressbrook, but it was ordered – there were relatives and guests and gardeners – it was not quite like the one she used to describe – 'I shall have just a *little* garden,' she used to say, 'when I grow old.' There was something tender and secret and private about it.

She retained her spirit of adventure and went to Denmark 'because she had never visited Scandinavia', and also briefly to Australia to see her remaining brother and sister and 'smell the flowers', then settled into her London life of music, painting, new ideas – but alone. She came to stay with me or my sister, but always independent, never for long. With old age she improved, like all true people; her anxieties faded, she was brave about illness, a good sport in discomfort, an appreciative guest, delighting in small things. But she told me she missed her husband every day, for all the rest of her life. Time did not heal.

Part Three

17

Many enigmas can be traced back to the things that came before, but even then, cannot always be explained. An Australian saga has run through my life and that of my sister – though we left in infancy by a decree not of our own. Some cousins we have met understand this; there are others, it would seem, who view us with irritation as absentees (as if it could have been our choice). No matter – that is the way of the world – the Dreaming still belongs to us all, as do some historical facts.

In 1840 David Cannon McConnel, who had studied natural science at Edinburgh, left his country in secret, posting goodbye letters for his family to receive after he had sailed. When the ship stopped at Plymouth, his brothers came on board and pleaded with him to give up his mad plan, but he continued on his way. He settled on the Brisbane River, built a house he named after the family one in Derbyshire – not in pseudo-Georgian style or any nostalgic copy of England, but in what might have been called native style, had there been one. The natives were in fact nomads. It was a long pagoda resembling nothing before or since and is classified today as the only one of its kind – an original idea of one of the first settlers.

He then built a forge, a school, a barn, stables and a chapel. Behind this settlement lay a chain of lagoons, covered with lilac-coloured lilies with gold centres, floating to the dark creek where the platypus lived.

His son, James Henry McConnel, continued: he imported Herefords into Australia for the first time, cross-breeding them with Shorthorn, to produce a breed for milk as well as meat. He imported Reugny, the winner of the Grand National, and also bred polo ponies and trotters; Harold was champion trotter for Australia. He built a factory for canning his milk which he later sold to Nestlé; he built the first stone house in Brisbane, a hundred miles away – to use as his town house – and a railway station two miles away – a distance adequate not to be disturbed by the noise of trains. It was a private railway station and the train only stopped if required. In later years, my father said my mother was always late for trains, and could never quite realize that they would not wait; she once expected him to hold the Rome-Paris Express, which he managed to do, in agony, for one whole minute. During her youth someone would 'just telephone the stationmaster' asking him to stop the train. Passengers would peer out to see what was happening in the middle of the vast bushland – and there would be the galloping carriage arriving with the Cressbrook girls waving their wonderful hair.

James Henry had ten children, the eldest being my mother. Each child had its own thoroughbred horse that no one else was allowed to ride; he said it gave a horse a hard mouth to have too many riders. There were general horses for guests – the guests who came from England and stayed six months. There was what amounted to a whole village of stockmen, overseers, butchers, carpenters etc.; it was an almost feudal establishment. The remarkable garden was laid out and planned by his wife, who had a special flair.

She brought up the first of her children very strictly, with an almost harsh severity, but with the best, puritanical Scot intentions. She was only nineteen when the first child was born. By the time of the last children she had grown softness. By then she had a small house in the garden where she used to retire and make drawings of flowers; she is remembered by some as being understanding, by others as frightening. My mother, Dorothea, certainly feared her. She was often put in charge of the younger children, which she hated, finding her sisters especially boring, with the exception of Barbara, the most beautiful. She loved her dearly and they later travelled to Russia together. The closest to her in age was her brother Hugh, her greatest friend and companion of wild escapades into the bushland; he died of diphtheria when at Harrow. (The sons were sent to England to school.) Her grief at his death was immense and everlasting. Later she cared greatly, but maternally, for her little brother Kenneth who was seventeen years younger.

When Dorothea was only twelve she was put in entire charge of the household during the great flood; her mother was away for the birth of the only one of her babies not born at home. Later in life she wrote this account in a letter:

The river was miles wide and lapping the edge of the veranda, and we had yet another eleven inches of rain by dawn. Father and the stockmen were out shifting the stud cattle – I was left to order the carpenter and gardeners to move everything possible into the loft. One servant had hysterics and another got drunk; I was terrified.

The water suddenly began to rise with a roaring sound – whole trees floated past – and high water started to come into the house. At the Cottage Granny and Uncle Ned's children sat on a table waiting for Father to take them away in a boat. We slept all together on the floor of the stud stable. Next day the water started to go down and we moved to the school house. There was no food. The river left inches of mud and got into the big underground tank so we had no clean water and none to drink. It was muggy and tropical; the children screamed. Mother counted on me to organize everything; I tried.

When the flood went down a cow was found in the slime on the sofa. The kookaburras shrieked with laughter in the bunya tree, eating fresh grubs. I lost a stone that week.

The granny she mentions in this letter was her Scottish granny she much loved – but from this account she was not a great help in the crisis.

My mother was an excellent rider, and the only person to tame a horse that had gone wild after being put out to pasture for a year after breaking a leg. It was rounded up and brought into the yard where it reared and snorted and no stockman could approach it.

My mother taught her horses the circus trick of shaking hands; she went up to this frantic animal, snapped her fingers and spoke its name. It quietened and raised its right front leg – she held its hock, stroked its mane and led it away. (As an elderly lady of fifty in Canada, she was terrified of farm dogs but the local, fearsome and frequently escaping bulls never worried her. Once I was walking with her in a wood and a bull stood in the middle of our path. I climbed a tree, but she advanced towards it opening and closing her parasol in its face. It veered away and disappeared. 'Silly old thing,' she said, 'I was brought up with stud bulls.') She crossed rivers with her brothers, on the backs of their horses, though they themselves never learned to swim.

At Shafston, the house in Brisbane, she entertained for her father. Grandmother was busy having babies and also apparently less sociable. A cousin in London, Jean Bruce-Lockhart, who is ninety this year, told me Grandfather always wore grey and was dressed by English tailors. His house in Brisbane shone with flowers, silver and conversation. There was a garden whose lawns swept down to the river; when the steamers passed the house they dipped their flags in salute. There was a Chinese gardener.

My mother's coming-out party was at Government House where the rooms were filled with white azaleas. It is hard to imagine loneliness or fear in this scene, yet they were there. The cousin tells that she was terrified of staying at Cressbrook, because of Grandmother. Yet it was to this same woman, in her later life, that young people went for advice about their love affairs . . .

When Barbara had problems, her right arm became stiff. Elton Mayo traced this back to her childhood, when as punishment for taking all her clothes off at night, her arms were strapped to her crib. My mother's constant fear was of responsibility beyond her strength. All her life, even as an old lady, she cringed at harsh words.

In spite of the forests of eucalyptus, the flocks of coloured parakeets flitting through the branches, the luxury, her father's love and her mother's admiration (she learned of this only later) – there was a queerness about Australia, my mother said, something vital was missing. She went to Russia with Barbara, who studied singing, fell in love despairingly with her teacher, subsequently continued her singing in America but died tragically and too soon. She went to Italy with her young brother Kenneth to the Palio, at Siena, and to Rome. He became an architect, a pioneer in certain types of construction, many of his buildings in Sydney being innovations of their time. Kenneth was shell-shocked at Verdun in the Great War when he was only eighteen – this trauma never left him, even 'forty years on'. They were a family of sensitive highly-strung people; the horror of Verdun was indelible. He had a huge sense of humour and great kindness – but during all his life there were moments when he required electro-shock treatment. Elton Mayo, who worked with shell-shocked soldiers in the war, also diagnosed Kenneth's depression, but it is impossible to erase a scar.

Luckily at Shafston they danced, for their empire was not to last. What became of all the gold? The Bunyip got it, that legendary Australian creature that aborigines say emerges out of the marshes, but is never seen – otherwise how could it all evaporate so entirely? For sure no one saw where the money went. By the time of the third generation there were one thousand square miles of land on which there were eight thousand head of cattle, not counting the horses. But by the fourth generation – it was all gone: there is nothing left now but the house of Cressbrook itself. Several factors can explain this, but none fully. A crooked trustee at the time of Grandfather absconded with fifty thousand pounds; the elder son, who became manager when his father died did not have a business sense and acquired thirty thousand pounds worth of debts. These were 'pardoned' and allowed to be written off the books by his sisters, for whom the estate was managed. Eighty thousand pounds in the years just before and after the Great War would represent a large sum now – but still, in an estate that remained the size of King Ranch Texas, it could normally have been rebalanced. James Henry McConnel's will was clever: it left land and property to the sons, income from the land to the daughters, the idea being that the daughters would marry and not want property. It was surely irritating for the brother to provide the income for his sisters when things went badly, and with so much truly bad luck.

My first cousin, his son, the present owner and ex-manager, inherited only redwater fever, drought, and outstanding debts

. . . Yet Australia is the land of the future, they say, and there are some who talk of booms.

Ursula McConnel, the anthropologist, was the only daughter to have a career. In her will she left her house on Mount Tambourine to the three of her nieces who worked for a living: my sister, myself, and our cousin Mary. We received the proceeds of the sale of the house but never the jewellery that was also to be divided. For sentimental reasons, this is sad; we both admired her tremendously.

Our relatives were great travellers, staying with each other in Scotland and Florence, and with us, so we knew them well.

The Eltons came from Somerset. Thackeray fell in love with an Elton when staying with them at Clevedon Court (which is full of his portraits still) and put her into his novel *Henry Esmond*.

The Mayos (the families intermarried) were less flamboyant, but there was a grandfather who left England at nineteen to join the McKinley expedition. This plan to explore the Western territory had been drawn up by a Scot with no notion of the climate or the vastness of the desert. Elton Mayo used to describe it with small fits of laughter: the men were stranded and had to eat their own horses; one of them lost his mind and stalked his own companions, taking them for enemies. Finally they reached a river and made a large raft on which to escape, but this raft took them shooting miles out to sea in the strong current . . .

The Mayos were men of science: a surgeon, a paediatrician, a Supreme Court judge. They were warm, balanced people with an immense degree of human kindness. Elton was the exceptional one, the outstanding one – and in many ways the misfit.

When my sister and I were closed away in boarding schools during our youth, or staying with strangers at times – always with a feeling of imprisonment in some institution – we recalled the tales of our mother's childhood and this was our Walter Mitty escape. Yet the tales were real, and she was the bird of paradise.

I dreamed of riding bareback across the moors. At school I was not allowed riding lessons because the horses were hacks. Indeed they were, as were all horses compared with Reugny . . . Also, riding was expensive. The Australian daylight was already fading, my mother having married a not-rich intellectual, and they had to make great efforts for our education.

There was evidently something wrong at the core of the Australian life, in spite of its glamour. My mother's own daughters, though she greatly loved us, may have seemed hard to cope with at times, stirring up her ancient dread that she could not analyse, though in her consciousness it had nothing to do with us; but it had something to do with my marriage to Vsevolod – the unfathomable illogic of which lies somewhere in the Australian saga.

My mother had a passionate nature, Elton Mayo said, and in her youth her beauty was transcendental. Peace came to her, with her own true character settling into place, only with age.

And so Cressbrook runs like a thread of bright gold through our tapestry, and has done so all our lives. Joey, the pet kangaroo, six feet tall, would hop into the house and filch the bread from the table just before lunch. There were twelve in the family, so an impromptu guest would make thirteen at the table for dinner; though traditionally feared, it was considered the Cressbrook lucky number. At my first exhibition I had thirteen paintings, by chance – but without fear; it was the Cressbrook lucky sign.

My sister recalls Grandmother in her garden. She knew her in her 'soft' time – when we left Australia my sister was eight, and can remember . . . Grandmother knew how to kill snakes with a stick, breaking their backs – but there were types she liked and left alone; they were good for the garden.

I am sorry for Grandfather, especially. He had such energy, such vision – it seems he was a complete man, physically active, intellectually entertaining. He would have been sad at the rip–off and wreckage, after all his planning to make something that would last. Whenever I see beautiful horses, or colts galloping wild, I think of him, and wish I had known him.

Our American home, though short-lived, was a true one: the doll's house in my room on Christmas morning; our parents the kindest and most patient. I recall my mother's hands, holding my hot forehead over the lavatory basin when I was frequently sick as a little girl and feared the vomiting with such unearthly terror – the hands were so infinitely soft, making me safe. Why on earth were we sent away – when they were so loving? It is a paradox that remains unanswerable.

18

In 1951 my sister and her husband were living in Strasbourg. People who put all their energies and their life-work into ideals and aims outside their own, immediate lives, are always admirable. A new Europe was being born, or trying to be born – and it was still at the stage of conception, when Churchill came to make his speech, true Europeans, like Robert Schumann, being among his listeners. In spite of what is said of the baseness of politicians, there are some who are sincere and disinterested; there are even some who love mankind – not with pretence, to get votes, but truly. They may be rare; perhaps a book could be written on the subject (Blum? Did Juarez really love the people?), but it is not the subject here, but that of Europe which was being reshaped as one of the fruits of our winning the war, and this by people who were true believers.

Dunstan Curtis was Deputy Secretary General of the Council of Europe, and so he and my sister belonged to, and entertained this world of planners and leaders at their dinner table, where ideas were sometimes heatedly discussed, along with the *lapin à la moutarde* and the Alsatian wine. On another parallel my sister managed to do her own work as a sociologist. The result of this was to come later – first with her book *The Making of a Criminal* and subsequently the study of separationist groups in another book: *The Roots of Identity* – but at this time it was still all in the making: her research and writing, the new Europe, their home which was first a flat but a little later a house where she made a garden in which all kinds of flowers seemed to grow together. My life was also growing definite: Chim had offered for me to be his permanent public relations partner; we had just been to Venice for the Biennale, and written about the two avant-garde painters Santomaso and Vedova for *Epoca* magazine.

Guislaine was to go to America, to spend a month of her holiday with her father, but first we went to stay with my sister and Dunstan in a farmhouse they had rented for the summer in the country outside Strasbourg. It had balconies of geraniums around the courtyard and was surrounded by vineyards. There was a stork's nest on the church steeple; one stork could be seen sitting, while the other circled, flying low enough to show the span of black and white of its wings, flapping lazily and low, the sheen of its feathers like green dust. Their cat, called Minch, had come with them from London. We swam in a disused quarry where the water was clear blue and cool, in the heavy Alsatian heat.

A friend and distant relation of Dunstan's was staying in Strasbourg then too. He was a political journalist and he became a great friend. Through the years that followed, though our lives ran separate courses (or perhaps because of this) we corresponded, and many letters accumulated. The other day, as I was writing this book in 1981, he moved out of a house in Sussex, and as he was throwing out rubbish, he found a grocer's bag full of old news; he came to call and presented it to me. Some of it has been useful for remembering dates and details, and later in this book I have quoted a few of the letters in full.

It was a peculiar affection we shared. Was he just a rather special friend to me? What on earth was I to him, since I did not belong to the group who ran the world, and it was the world's affairs that interested him most? Was it an *amitié-amoureuse*? He loved other women and attended all the balls or parties that were given, and spent much time talking with politicians for the writing of his weekly slasher – I say slasher because he had incisive vision and could cross-section events or show them in a new light. In any case we shared a friendship that for some reason made various people cross or jealous, probably because they could not fathom it, but neither could we, so what did it matter? I also led my own other life in a different world. But sometimes we would go off together – once it was on the road to Spain – he was at a loose end perhaps when he suggested it – no matter why – but we made one memorable trip to what Rose Macaulay then called the Fabled Shore; we saw the coast long before the concrete blocks sprang up. In Benidorm there was one *fonda* (with bed-bugs) and the most curious shells on its deserted beach. I remember one lurid conch like a red mouth; the creature that lived inside had come out like a wet smile in the surrealist sunset. (I hear that now Benidorm is a metropolis.) I never forgot that trip and felt it stirring inside me like something unfinished, and knew it was a place where I must return.

After leaving Strasbourg that summer, and while Guislaine was still away, I went to see my mother, and since she had no guest-room, I stayed with my new friend in his flat in Eaton Square. He was out most of the time leading his grand 'other life'. When not with my mother, I chattered with a South African tennis-player called Julian Lezard who lived in the same building. He was an excitable man, and fascinated by our mutual friend, to whom he referred as the professor; he used to spend a large part of his time in his dressing-gown, paying visits to the upstairs flat to discuss the philosophy of life, rather as they do in Russian novels. (He was by then an ex-tennis-player, retired.) This man turned rapidly from Lezard to Lizzie and became a friend one might have known since always. One of his games was the perpetual study of the professor's character (who feigned annoyance when he got home but was really quite amused). He also made my stay in London warm; he was always home in his dressing-gown when everyone else was out.

Randolph Churchill telephoned frequently. The professor appeared to be his nanny, rather like Capa was to Kessel. Randolph was a good journalist but a rude and difficult person after a few drinks. He was a sad, sometimes endearing, drop-out with a chip on his shoulder about his father who overshadowed him. He would ring up at night, wailing, and the professor, who was the kindest of men, would go off to see him and spiritually hold his hand.

A letter from Chim arrived saying that eventually he wanted to live in Rome, and though his base would still be Paris for the present, this was his definite future plan. Would I agree to live there too, since we would be working as partners? It delighted my mother, always anxious for me to settle; also she loved Rome. A solid shape was starting to grow.

Then the gong sounded again: a message came from the *maréchal* saying that Guislaine would not be returning; she would stay in America. Was it a coincidence, or was it purposely to disrupt the plans, just when all was going well? She would go to school in America, he said. He was successful now and would pay for it.

But paying was not the point, or not the only one, however much it mattered. To change her school again . . . and my job? I was staggered. I sat with Lizzie in awe. 'Why did she go in the first place?' he asked.

'Why? She had to. A child must see its father – and he loves her. She had a return ticket. Anyway, we agreed. He's away in Guyana most of the time – how could I have guessed . . .'

'Never trust a war hero.'

'My job, Lizzie. My beautiful, precious job . . .'

'You could stay here.'

With the message, a plane ticket had been included. I could be with Guislaine, but in America. She was eight. There was no decision to be made, no alternative. Her father appeared in London, and we had a brief interview. Guislaine had been left with his mother. For his own inscrutable and seemingly footling reason, he was annoyed that I was staying with 'this journalist fellow'. We had separated years earlier; our lives were no business of each other's.

'He's a professor,' I said. 'He gives lessons about life.' So he did, I thought then, and the name professor truly suited him, for he held definite views and had high standards about language and ways of expression. He could be a martinet and ticker-off with the best intentions, but to know him was educational. But the *maréchal* did not find it interesting, so I changed the subject.

'I have a job and don't want to lose it,' I said. 'It has taken long to achieve, but this time I am *there* and will never have to quit.'

Foolishly, I hoped for approval, even congratulations on any form of success, for it had been hard enough to reach. The cold hostility was frightening; it made me feel sick.

'You will have to quit, won't you, if you come to America? It's up to you.'

The ticket was for a sleeper on a Boeing Stratocruiser. He was generous at least. What a pity to change school again, when it was not necessary.

When I climbed into the huge plane, I was looking forward with panic and backward with despair. I was frantic to see Guislaine, who must surely be puzzled. Yet I knew it was the death of my job, which was about to make our real home. I had 'lost the north' as the French saying goes. We rose up into the night and I descended the spiral staircase to the small bar, where I had a double vodka. Then upstairs I got into my bunk and drew the curtains across the aisle. It was complete privacy, silent except for the humming engines. Through the porthole I could see the stars and the whole vast cosmos – there it lay, the constellations in the September night sky. There was Pegasus, Aquarius, Cassiopeia; there was the Milky Way, the Great Bear lying rather low, Cygnus, the swan of stars swimming . . . My bunk was on the right side of the plane so I was facing north, and there it spread before me, not lost but permanent. And gradually, flying smoothly across the universe in a bed with sheets, facing the north all night, not losing it after all but *holding on*, a great quietness came over me. Orion, the seven sisters . . . I thought of Saint-Exupéry who had disappeared in the air. It was not known where he had left earth, but one day he simply did not return: plane never found. We are tiny, our homes and jobs the size of ants. Only love cannot be measured, for it has no size. Strength came from the vastness of the sky, and the smallness of myself.

The war hero had an apartment on Park Avenue, with a butler, and still never any cash. But I had to admire him; the structure of his way of living really was done with mirrors, and it seemed to hold together. The rent must have been paid, I supposed, by a contract or some agreement in the business world – an abstract Einstein realm of high finance on another level, where trite necessities were not discussed. He was not mean; cash was just something that did not happen to him; he did not have any.

The sudden transition, the view and the way of seeing things, after Strasbourg and Capa and Lizzie and the professor, threw me off balance at first; it was so different. But then I found the old rut again: a walk-up flat in a brownstone, four floors this time. Guislaine spent her nights in either of our flats which were both

146

quite near her school. It was a good school but a complete change in type of teaching, which she found difficult. Her father was frequently away, so gradually she was with me again. A reheated New York life started, like a left-over meal. The last time here it had been a flop. I hoped just to get through the year. Surely after a year something could be arranged. 'Dear Chim,' I wrote, 'how long can you wait . . .?'

The positive side of this equation was seeing Stephen, who was twelve now. Guislaine doted on him and prepared her handbag with perfume when we went to visit. The bus-ride was horrific, queueing first with commuters, all chewing gum like cows on the cud, only not smelling of clover, but a rather stale spearmint halitosis. The terminus was ultra-modern but it made the new world seem grim. Vsevolod must have been very *apatride* not to mind this method of getting daily to New York to work, I thought. The bus stopped at places with names like Carlstadt and Edgware, even Verona. (Why not Warsaw, since that was where Chim was born? He was always on my mind.) The interesting faces were usually black. One Sunday there was a whole family in best clothes, with flashlight cameras, and their small picaninny girls with cherries bobbling on their hats. After the claustrophobic Lincoln Tunnel we reached the New Jersey flatlands, not unlike the approach to Venice; industrialized, drained marshes. And then – once in Montclair – the big relief: back to the talisman of wide avenues and wooden houses with their Mother's Days and white Christmases.

Vsevolod now had three other children who appeared and disappeared, in and out of each other's homes up and down the streets, and his house vibrated with guests from Europe.

'Custody?' he said to me. 'What nonsense! You don't need a divorce, you are still married to me,' and he roared with laughter, ho, ho, ho and my *angst* seemed absurd. (All the same, I knew there was a document about schools; custody and an agreement were necessary if there was to be any peace.)

A Fuller Brush man walked in once. The doors were always open so he did not need to ring the bell. He was suddenly there in the sitting-room with his free samples and sales-talk – except that Vsevolod gave him no chance. *He* did the talking, said he'd been champion dancer in Europe, whereupon he grabbed the fellow and made him dance. They twirled together all over the room, leaping once across the sofa like Rogers and Astaire. The man was pleased, and without unloading one brush from his wares box, he had a beer. Vsevolod was acting in *Bittersweet* at the local club. He had come a long way since his stateless days. It was smug of me but I felt some credit: I had saved him. It had worked . . . here was an integrated family man.

I heard Jean say to him once, 'I wish we weren't both so old. My whole lifetime is not long enough to be with you.' She was not yet thirty-five when she said this.

For a while the *maréchal* remained in New York, alternately charming or frightening, as if he held some power. He was unpredictable; there would be dark looks, causing an inner panic about what might happen next – then he would say kindly that I could use his account for theatre tickets. He lent me a Nash Rambler to get around in. I felt sorry for him. (*Why?*) But I could not make out what he wanted. One can hate a person for *not leaving you alone.* Through the years I discovered this is the hardest thing to obtain. The majority of people do not want to be alone and therefore cannot understand. After hate, comes guilt, then pity. His mother told me he had not learned to read until he was seven. He was born in Algiers and had spoken only Arabic at first. I found this romantic.

But I had lost the north again in spite of the promises to Cygnus and Orion. The needle of the compass was whizzing and I was afraid of losing something precious, of wasting time. Magnum had an office in New York where I hung around for a while. They seemed surprised to see me. I told them I worked with Chim (there had been no answer yet to my letter. Chim loved children, so he would understand, but could he wait?) One day Ernst Haas came in, which relieved the tension, since I knew him. He pointed out to me Fenno Jacobs (who I remembered Capa saying was a nymphomaniac) and Carl Perrutz, the 'spade-work photographer' who had just been sent to photograph the sports cars of a certain Mr X – who, it appeared, also raced, and was showing in the International Car Show (where there was a car called a Pierce, lined with wallpaper). Mr X turned out to be the *maréchal*.

Ernst Haas took me to the Alrae, where he usually went for drinks, since it was near the new Magnum office. Vsevolod was there with Mimouka Nebel, who was excited because Metro Goldwyn had offered him a Hollywood contract. He was spending the money in advance by asking us all to lunch, then said the contract might not work, because of the unions (there was a union he was expected to join and did not want to). I remembered that Elton Mayo had been offered a large sum by Sam Goldwyn, to discover the reason why certain stories appealed to the public, thereby guaranteeing success . . . He had refused; at the time he only told us he did not like Goldwyn's green suit, and did not explain further. I guessed E.M.'s dislike of some unnamed factor, and wondered if Mimouka would last.

'*On ne vit que de promesses,*' he said. '*Des promesses nebuleuses comme Nebel.*' He left for California in spite of the unions.

Spring came to America overnight. One morning it was green – a shock – and a week later the heat was already stifling. On the first day, people sat in the outdoor cafe by the zoo in Central Park and were pleased. Guislaine collected mica and quartz among the stones. The week before there had been a horizontal blizzard; now all was warmth and flowers – a continent of violent contrasts.

But I was getting nowhere. A painter called Vladimir Barjansky offered me a job. His portraits of women were flattering and commercial like chocolate box covers – they were ugly, and he was also ugly. He received me in an ornate gilt 'salon' that was probably a dream of what he wished his ancestral home had been. He wrote horror stories for Hollywood, but asked me to ghost them for him, as he could not write English properly, he said . . . well, maybe neither could I, I told him, as he poured vodka from a bottle without a label, and did not drink it himself (it must have been home-made). But what was his own language? All his languages sounded false. I did not take the job. John McCaffery, the editor of my novel at Doubleday, offered me something more serious. He had left the publishers and now had his own programme on television called *Eleventh Hour News*. I could be a speaker, he said, 'because of my voice', but it meant signing a contract and I shied from being caught, so did not take that job either.

One evening another television director from NBC called and suggested going out to dinner to discuss possible work. I had bare feet when he arrived, and was ironing. Guislaine was on the floor, sitting on the mattress which was one half of the bed, reading the Bible, to which she had taken a sudden liking. She started reading aloud to our visitor about David and Goliath. He seemed fairly discouraged, and went away, leaving his card. Previously, this feeling that there were endless job-possibilities in New York, the city of no-limit, had been exciting. But now I did not want a job that meant signing a contract; I wanted to remain available for Chim. Americans don't like people who don't want futures – they did not understand my refusal. I myself was confused. It was tempting, I needed to work – but signing a contract would be a promise to stay here . . . I started to paint.

Then Romain Gary arrived in New York, followed by the professor, and all was changed. '*Comme ce pays est rasoir*,' said Romain, continually amazed that the girls wore girdles – the most unsexy arrangement he had ever encountered.

I met him with Vsevolod. He appeared one day with a Russian friend called Sasha Kardo-Sasayev, but he knew my sister and the professor and it felt that he came from 'home'. His wife, Lesley Blanch, was due to arrive soon, after closing their house in the Balkans, where he had been consul. She was working on her book, *The Wilder Shores of Love*, dedicated to 'Romain Gary, my husband'. He must have been the wildest and most difficult, if also the most amusing husband any woman could have had. Sasha was his 'samovar', a Russian expression for a loyal and ever-present friend. He had a fine Slav face with high cheek-bones.

'*J'ai besoin de Sasha parcequ'il est con*,' said Romain, and Sasha did not seem to mind. He probably did not grasp the subtleties, and Romain was in many ways obscure. He was established as an author but not yet great; it was not for another five years that Zanuck filmed *The Roots of Heaven*. He was obsessed with women but declared that he believed in love. 'It is a duty to be happy,' he said. 'If you love someone, send everyone else to hell; stay with your person.' He was an idealist, he was a mixture, for he was also unscrupulous; he was honest enough to dislike puritans for their confusion of other duties with love – certainly much of his preoccupation was about love and sex. At times it seemed that he was playing a role, looking at himself from the outside – or perhaps looking for the idea of love more than the

150

object of love. He himself was two people; one really watched the other. He would ask with sudden anxiety: 'Do you think I am handsome?' Indeed he was, with blue eyes and nearly black hair, but the diffidence in the question was not in keeping. In the war he had been a navigator in the Free French Lorraine Squadron (attached to the RAF), and had been given the *Croix de la Libération*, a rather special decoration. He spoke English with a Russian undertone, but his true language (not his character) was French.

Driving down Park Avenue one night, we saw through the taxi window the *maréchal*, talking to two rather fearsome-looking men. 'I know him,' said Romain, 'he has business dinners in the Champagne Room at El Morocco, the most expensive place in New York. Who is he?'

I did not explain. Who was he anyway? Not the person I had known once. He had gone.

When Lesley arrived Romain's sense of proportion changed. She was very funny, and teased him for the way he fussed about his diet (which had not been apparent before). As a couple their irritations with each other were constant but entertaining. They were having a lawsuit concerning their furniture, Romain having 'lost the papers on purpose'. She gave dinners with Balkan dishes: meat with green peppers and yoghurt sauce. The Romain who made passes at women was not the same as the Romain lying on the bed in their darkened room, 'not understood', asking to be left alone. He had indigestion, during which time Lesley was in the next room (their flat in New York was small) at the head of her dinner table talking to Arabs, who never got indigestion. She was very keen on Arabs. One of her guests was the son of the Pasha of Fort Lyautey, his great-uncle was 105 years old and had been Ambassador of Morocco in Madrid in 1875 – he remembered Victoria's jubilee. Romain would appear looking tragic like an El Greco saint. He worried about his weight and his appearance, yet when he went out, or when he forgot about them, no one would have guessed from his jokes. His conversation was brilliant, and like Lesley, he was exceedingly funny. She called him the Japanese Overlord.

They lived in the Hungarian quarter, where their fishmonger played the violin. Lesley found a stray dog and adopted him. He was chocolate-brown and she named him Moony. One day she dressed him in long lace robes and asked some elegant ladies to a christening tea. They did not know if she was serious or mocking, but she really did dote on the dog.

In some ways Romain was mad. He would suggest to a near-stranger that they go off and live together far away – in Teheran for instance. (Later he was sent there as consul.) His eyes would look beyond her into the novel he was perhaps imagining and acting out, not with his pen but with his person . . . he could see himself fleeing the staid world with his imagined love. The great future Goncourt had to *live* his creation, not just write it.

The seeds of his suicide thirty years later were possibly already sown then. It is tragic to remember that he lost his laughter and that they were such an original couple. How unnecessary the subsequent events now seem. By 1980 he thought that all the world's ideals were lost, which cannot have helped.

The professor arrived to attend the American elections. He stayed at the Alrae in a room at the back that we could see from our window. Much waving ensued. He also brought his cloak of glamour with him, and took me out to dinner to the house of Ludwig Bemelmans in Grammercy Park. There were twelve people at the long table, all of whom had arrived at their destination, and had succeeded in life. I sat beside Alistair Cooke and gazed at Greta Garbo who was opposite me. The idol I used to sneak out of boarding school to see in the local cinema was not the distant statue I would have expected: surprise: she was talkative, giggling, she glittered, she chattered, she made jokes and threw her head back laughing. Alistair Cooke was kind and relaxed like an old friend. He was also one European who did not long to go back to Europe; he had become an American citizen.

I accompanied the professor to the election meetings. For Eisenhower it was organized like a military campaign, with almost Fascist efficiency. For Stevenson there was a starry-eyed feeling of amateurishness; Negroes and intellectuals formed his public. Stevenson's talk was full of jokes, which, the professor told me, Americans never liked in their political leaders.

Before he returned to Europe, there was a whole unforgettable long month when I took both my children to stay with him in a house in Rhode Island. Suddenly – like the fairy story of the table set for dinner in the wilderness – there we were. Both children were together in a house where Edith Wharton had lived in Saunderstown, with wild grapes and honeysuckle festooned along the lanes; and beyond the lawn, the inlet of the sea, there were mussels on the rocks, and swimming. But more than this: a normal family life. Shouts from the kitchen, cooking, playing the fool, hanging out the washing, driving to Wickford to buy lobsters, choosing them alive from their netted sea-water enclosure. Stuffed, baked mackerel and conversation. Rocking chairs on the veranda, and sometimes a wilder sort of swimming in the big breakers of the open sea round the headland at the Dunes Club.

After the professor left, and the summer was over, and the children back at their separate schools, it was sad and empty indeed; there was a sort of heartbreak about it. Missing a person or a place can be like feeling cold.

The professor wrote to say he had a feeling he might lose his column; perhaps I could find him one in America? It was probably only a rhetorical question, but I scuttled around excitedly, dreaming that I might help, and wanting to be busy. Richard Field in *Holiday* magazine seemed interested, but for some reason the professor was associated with Randolph Churchill, who was more than unpopular, he was a brake. They had been photographed together talking with Tito; were they partners? Nothing came of my efforts for him – and in effect he did lose his job afterwards, but not as soon as he had expected, not until Suez, when he labelled Anthony Eden as a fool. So what was the point of a political column if not to tell the truth, he asked (much later)? His fear then must already have been a premonition – yet his column was the only one not to follow a line or take orders. He was accused of 'blatancy', but this was its value.

A year had passed and we were still stagnating. The word 'lawsuit' had been used, in reference to our leaving for Europe. It was a black idea, that any two people who had once been together could be capable of such incapacity to understand each other. Chim started to fade. He must have been getting on without me.

I painted. When a painter becomes involved in his work, he takes off and the world outside the canvas becomes only the second reality.

Kimber Smith painted large abstract pictures with violent but never garish colours. He lived in the Puerto Rican district in a bare white room where there was no furniture, only piles of books against the wall, and speakers for his loud music. He made proper black coffee and his room seemed to contain its own large world that was untouchable.

Joan Higgins was a different sort of painter. She lived in a penthouse on the thirtieth floor, which was like a little hut with a terrace round four sides. The terrace was bigger than the flat, windy, with gales sometimes blowing the rose trellis away. There were views from this roof of other terraces, and people coming home from their offices, changing, in summer, into shorts, and sitting on deck chairs drinking martinis, like drawings in the *New Yorker*. 'Life is only a point of view,' Joan would say. Her own story was unusual: eighteen years before this time, a man from Hamilton Massachusetts had spent his summer in Nassau, where he met a young Englishman who was painting animals. 'Come on home with me and paint my dogs,' he said, and took the painter back to Hamilton, where he bred dogs, showed dogs, and introduced poodles into America. The painter stayed with his family for many months, walking in the snow in the woods with the oldest daughter who was then thirteen. She was Joan Griess, now Joan Higgins; the painter was Lee Elliott, and had just returned to America to paint ballet people. Joan had a huge, unclipped poodle with long, Marie Laurencin sloe-eyes. Guislaine called him a dog as big as a taxi.

From memories and desire, I painted a cafe in Auvergne, based on one old sketch. A large animal that was not quite a dog was sitting on the wall outside the cafe. When John McCaffery came to see me, he bought this painting. Lesley liked one of Asolo and said, 'Your paintings make people want to be where they are.'

But in spite of painting, our life had come unsewn; something had to happen, to change. We were pining, but what for? Maybe Europe was just an idea.

During the cold winter I saw Garbo again in Madison Avenue, wearing a mountaineering outfit: stout walking shoes, a rough walking stick, woolly hat – all very sensible in the bitter wind that came like knives through the narrow slits of streets between the tall buildings. But she did not look like the radiant creature I had dined with. She looked slightly haggard, yet she could not have been more than fifty . . . she made no more films and her life was a mystery. She was with what I took to be a funny old man, but Lesley told me he was her new Rothschild boyfriend.

In our letter box I found an invitation for us to spend a week in Mexico; this was from an acquaintance, not even a friend, totally unexpected – and perfectly timed.

We left on the last day of the year. For no reason, or perhaps because of the state of flux and low ebb, I was frightened in the aeroplane; it dropped suddenly in air pockets and the trip was bumpy. I kept praying: God tell me what to do. (He doesn't.) Do I stay in America and settle down? Should I forget the only real job I ever had? Is it foolish to go on refusing good jobs because of an idea, the *idea* of Chim? There are barns for sale in New England. We could live in the country. People buy my paintings. What do we do? There is no point in wanting something else all the time, in having a sad inside . . . so how do we know what is right? I prayed with concentration, for each child, for my family that I never saw any more . . . and for whatever was right to happen. 'Right'. To begin with, who knows what *is* this priggish 'right'? Could we perhaps be *informed*? When the saints prayed, were their prayers answered? Was there never a sign? I had always thought that if a person tried wholly, there must be a result. When crossing the German lines I had felt strong and certain. It was easy to do anything, however difficult, as long as there was *belief* . . . Now I felt so tired . . .

There seemed to be a tight, flat place stretched across the sky; it felt precious and necessary to hold on. If I held tight enough the machine would not go down – a solution would appear. I wished there would be an indication, a bright light of some sort. God was a grey abstraction. I wanted to shake him by the coat lapels like the Jews on our ship in Argentina and say, 'Look here God, what about it? How can a fellow *know* if there is never a sign?'

A taxi took us to Cuernavaca, forty-five minutes by road, and just as midnight approached and the new year arrived, we passed a huge cathedral with its doors wide open. A blaze of pink light was coming out, and a crowd of dark Indian faces with matted black pigtails turned to watch us pass. An Aztec crowd looking out of a Catholic church and on the wall outside, a crucifix with an evil eye on it. How long since Cortez had grafted Catholicism on to Indian belief . . . All the bells started clanging, the new year began: maybe this was our sign of change.

Our bedroom had a stone floor and Victorian furniture. There were many guests, none of whom knew each other, so the next day we were free to explore. Hot water came out of the cold tap, there were a few cockroaches. Outside in the garden, there was a swimming pool strewn with flower petals. In the main square there were thick ilex trees and hundreds of starlings chortling and making clamour. The Indians' bare feet were ingrained with dirt and they carried their babies on their bellies, slung in front. There were palm trees, jacarandas and flowers with clashing colours.

In the afternoon the host took us all to Mexico City. We wandered through the market where gold rings were sold cheaply. The Mexicans drove their cars in a wild and reckless way; once Guislaine and I were almost run over, then the driver got out and asked us to dinner. Two old men played a xylophone on the street corner. The host escorted our miscellaneous group to the house of a friend, where a tree was growing indoors, and where music was played by three guitarists during lunch. Then we went to a bullfight.

There were eight bulls, not six like in Spain. The arena was immense, containing perhaps fifty thousand people. There were four *toreros*, one Venezuelan, one Spanish and two Mexicans. The bulls were nasty and the first Mexican fighter, Aguilar, was hurt; he turned his back on the bull three times with a sweep of his *muleta* – and the third time, when he was edging nearer, Guislaine and I and one of the stranger-guests beside us grabbed each other like three terrified monkeys, sitting in a hunch. The bull rushed at Aguilar: two *cornadas* in the back and another attack when he fell to the ground. He was carried away. I was afraid he might die (Manolete had died on the way to the operating table) . . . and as he went, the light started to fade, the dusk crept down – then suddenly flare lights were turned on, and the sequins on the new *torero* sparkled in the half-dark. It was the turn of the Spaniard, Martorell, but we were trembling because of Aguilar.

Twice there was a weird Indian cry from high up in the top seats. Aztec faces with pigtails watched, half-animal, inhuman, immobile. I thought of Montezuma and hearts being cut out of live people. This bullfight was the host's idea of hospitality, but Guislaine was too young. Yet where could I have left her?

Martorell had grace and precision. He was master of his bull

156

and had no fear, and because of this, our fear also left us. He performed as if it were a dance, lunging forward, poised in a straight line. He was mathematical, neat; his kill was clean – there was no mess. Before the kill his passes were so close that he patted the bull's nose and pulled his tail. This joke detracted from the solemnity and made Guislaine laugh. But once the bull was dead it was sad and nauseous.

The strangeness of our visit was over a few days later. The guests all thanked their host for showing them Mexico, and left by their own means. Ours, as usual, were modest: we accepted a lift to New Orleans where we planned to get a Greyhound bus back to New York. The man who offered us the ride was an American with thick white hair. We drove through fierce country – dried river-beds, vultures, villages of mud huts with thatched roofs, faces that did not smile. The journey had the quality of a dream.

In New Orleans blacks leaned against walls. They stood under dilapidated wrought-iron balconies with washing hanging out overhead. The slums consisted of grand houses gone to ruin, with worn away shutters, and bananas and sub-tropical plants sprouting haphazardly. Tourists from the Middle West filled the old French restaurants but did not order wine (there were only Coca Cola bottles on the tables) yet to judge from the wine list there were remarkable cellars. The old generation of locals still spoke French. They were hard to photograph because they were sensitive. I took photographs of Guislaine under the signpost of Basin Street, and beside the bus with Desire written on the front, and stroking the alley cats . . . But the black mammies who were so beautiful in their bandanas, framed in windows with balconies of wrought-iron like scrolly lace, turned their heads when they saw our box Brownie. Yet with the camera put away, everyone grinned and we made friends in totally black districts; this was unexpected from what we had been told by our driver, when we said goodbye. Many cafes had 'coloured only' written outside. It was balmy, the air soft, the *vieux quartier* open all night – we would gladly have stayed on . . .

We boarded the Greyhound to return three thousand miles across the astonishing size of America – we had been as far away from New York as if we had been to Europe.

On our return (after stopping at Washington, where the bus

trip ended, and continuing by train, feeling as if we had crossed Russia), we found amazing news: Guislaine's father agreed that we could go back to Europe. He was leaving to prospect for emeralds in Venezuela and understood there was no point in our staying, since he would not be able to see Guislaine. (His mother was leaving America, which may have influenced his decision.) How simple understanding can be when it comes, and how absurd the past then appears. (Emeralds? In a way I liked his side of refusing ever to do anything plausible.) Are we not all court jesters? In spite of our feuds, I felt affection, and was sorry for him. He had such big ideas, but no backing behind them. It was bad luck. I hoped for him that this time it would work. (To this day I think of him whenever I see a Western; he loved them with such childish enthusiasm.) Also, when not frightening, he was very funny; he could have been a comedian. Yet too often he was fearsome. I had always lived in dread of his next plan.

I finished making arrangements with the school and for the departure. But such is the perversity of human nature, that when the time came, much as I had wanted to go, it was exceedingly sad, especially taking leave of friends. Suky and Maughan Gould came to say goodbye; we stood surrounded by suitcases remembering the times we had spent together. Maughan was a natural at any sport . . . I visualized him playing tennis, shussing down the ski-slopes at Stowe and appearing to fly when he jumped over the bumps. There is special warmth in American friendships.

John McCaffery was now story editor for MGM. My decision to leave was a crossroads; I saw that one way led to a path of missed opportunties, an American life I had refused partly because of Magnum. (Or was it affection for Capa and Chim? Or was I just European anyway?) How much of life is a fluke, how much choice does a person really have? Or does one only think one is choosing when really there is an outside factor at work?

'Maybe I'll be back,' I said to Suky and Maughan, because I was sorry to leave them, though burning to go – yet torn. 'Anyway no hellish goodbyes. See you soon.'

'This time I don't think so,' said Maughan, with his Astaire smile.

19

When we reached Paris there was a letter for me from Chim in the Magnum office. He was away, and would be for a long time. There was a job in Madrid which he advised me to take. Rome was still his future plan, but he was not ready yet. Capa was also away. It was only a slight anti-climax, since I still seemed to be working with them, even if in low gear. Margot Shore, who ran the Paris office, told me I would be a freelance floater called upon occasionally, but able to do other things of my own. And the future – though removed from front of stage – was still to be with Chim in Rome. Eventually.

The job in Madrid was for *Holiday* magazine. They were doing a series on outstanding women from ten countries. They had heard about a certain Mercedes Formica, who appeared to be very liberal and independent for 'backward Spain'. She was possibly a lawyer, though they were not sure. I was supposed to find her address, what she was doing, make contact and see if she would accept having a story written about her. After I had done all this they would send a photographer down. This time it would be a woman called Inge Morath, new to Magnum and to me (she was not yet married to Arthur Miller).

Guislaine and I set off with a bulging programme: not only to find an invisible woman, but also a flat to live in and a new life all over again. In New York I had listened to flamenco music with Kimber Smith. It was still a novelty and had not yet penetrated the rest of the world as it subsequently did. A fortunate coincidence with the Magnum job was that I had had a special feeling about Spain ever since crossing Aragon by train during the war, and later on the trip with the professor. I was actually longing to go there. So we arrived in Madrid in high spirits and entire optimism, both of us, for Guislaine also was a fervent traveller and filled with curiosity.

From the moment we arrived, any preoccupation about jobs or the little things of life ceased; they did not matter. Spain was grandiose, enormous, outside and above anything small. First there was the vastness of the land and sky, sepia hills with long purple shadows, and a lone monastery, lucid and sharply drawn. Then nothing – just space. On entering Madrid there was no transition, no suburbs; the open land stopped, the city began.

The light in the evenings was as if the town were lit from underneath or inside and had no substance. Even ordinary buildings looked extraordinary, for Madrid was not beautiful. It was even quite ugly, but the light before sunset was a revelation of scarlet luminosity, clarity, with the precision, yet the turbulence of a wild dream. In 1953 there were hardly any cars; only leafy avenues of trees, fountains playing, the noise of water splashing, of feet walking along the Castellana in the morning and evening *paseo*, the murmur of voices in cafes, or people sitting on little iron chairs under the big trees.

I did not care if I never left Spain again. I was willing to get lost and disappear into it forever. It was almost ridiculous to be overcome in this way with a sense of recognition, of affinity, like being in love.

Time was abundant and endless. Just one clanking taxi would occasionally pass, or a car belonging to a government official. Very few people owned cars, except someone called Dennis whom we were to meet later. The Duke of Lerma rode a Vespa. There were trams in the commercial streets, but the other streets were quiet. Ramshackle, rattling taxis were always available. There was the joke about *mañana* and nothing getting done, nothing achieved – but there was another side to it of paradoxically oriental detachment; speed was not the point. Spain did not seem entirely to be in Europe; it was an apart-place, 'somewhere else'. It had a Moorish streak, yet was not African.

After a few days we found our first, temporary flat. The sounds at night were like being in the country; the man next door had a barnyard with turkeys, cocks crowing and a donkey. After a week, we found what was to be our permanent flat through a charming old Frenchman who ran a cafe. He was called Mansard, and seeing us sitting often on his terrace, he started to chat. Through him, we visited several houses. It appeared that the owners did not let their apartment unless they liked the tenant, however much they needed the money and however much they were offered, Mansard told us. ('Pure and noble', Anouilh had said.) The old Frenchman produced *tapas: cigales* and *percebes, ensaladillas* that we ate on his terrace while he told us how he had come to Spain as a young man, and how he was descended from one of the great gardeners who had designed for Versailles. One day the talk turned to cats, and he said, 'Come into the kitchen and I'll show you mine.'

There was a black stove where a duck in a copper pan was simmering in ham stock, 'for a friend', he said. The kitchen was an enormous room lined with cupboards and drawers. There was an orange tomcat, whose whiskers Mansard pulled; the cat did not seem to mind. He pulled his tail; no reaction. Then a man came to the doorway with a large dog; the cat grew fierce, hissing with a bushy tail the size of a fox's brush. The dog fled.

'*C'est lui, le patron*,' Mansard explained, 'he knows this is his place.'

He then opened a drawer in one of the dressers and there were kittens inside, with a mother cat looking pleased and purring. As he talked he went on socking his old tomcat under the chin and the cat went on accepting. 'He knows everything,' Mansard said. 'He knows Latin.'

This cafe became one of our focal points for meetings, messages, or for Guislaine to sit and read when I was busy, under the safe protection of the old man. She was an avid reader and had got through all of Dostoyevsky by the time she was nine.

Our flat was in the Calle Fernando Santo on the top floor of the building. It had a terrace round three sides, so large and wide that one could almost go for a walk along it. From here we could see the Sierra outside the town, a reminder of the wild land beyond, and Goya's bandits. Each late afternoon the light was a continual revelation, sometimes lurid and violent, blue and vermilion, with the sky behind the red clouds as clear as if it had been washed. When darkness came it was very dark. After the uplifting sundown, it was almost frightening. There was a vein of ferocity running underneath, an acceptance of cruelty which made one think of the Inquisition, of Goya's 'noonday ghost', and of his exile. But fear was part of the power.

Apart from Mansard we knew no one at first; we had the usual introductions that I did not follow through. I tracked down Señora Formica, who was a writer. She had a column in the ABC monarchist newspaper and was willing to cooperate. I cabled Margot and Inge Morath came to Madrid where she photographed Señora Formica in her study lined with books.

I found a maid for £3 a month, the current rate. She was rough and earthy but a good girl, called Angelis. She sang a song called 'Santander' most of the day (Santander was her home) and had no notion of cooking; she would eat only bread spread with tomatoes, oil and garlic. She was covered with spots, for which I suggested meat and watercress, but she said cress was only for cows. She knew how to write, so on Saturdays her friends would come and sit at the kitchen table while she wrote their letters for them. Gradually she learned to cook and became a valuable presence.

The Lycée Français was providentially only five minutes' walk from our door, so Guislaine could continue the French teaching she had been used to.

Inge hired a car before she left and we drove out into the Sierra. The land had no green anywhere. It was apricot-brown with a sort of yellow brilliance, an almost eerie glow of twilight folding into the long shapes of the hills and into infinity. Occasionally there would be a straight poplar or a house. A woman like a black triangle in her shawl, surprised us because one somehow forgot to expect life. Old women and priests were like black heaps.

Because it was Inge's last night, we decided on our way back to make one contact, and so followed up one of the introductions I had been given. As a result we had dinner with the counsellor of the embassy, at his home. It was the only one I ever contacted, for at this dinner I met Dennis McEvoy, who happened to be there, equally by chance, he said, since it was 'not his scene'. But the meeting caused a riotous start to our life in Madrid, and there was no looking back afterwards. He was the great Madrid figure of the fifties: a lavish host, knowing everyone, living and playing wild, never appearing to need sleep – though in the late afternoon he did open his front door in a kimono.

He had been brought up in Japan, was a Black Belt in judo, and spoke fifteen languages. His father was an Irish-American writer, his mother had apparently been a Catalan dancer. He seemed entirely American, though also entirely his own eccentric self. He was president of the *Reader's Digest*, which seemed a joke – it did not fit his character. But he explained that he had enjoyed getting it re-accepted in Spain because it had been banned. He had therefore had a personal interview with Franco, pretending not to speak Spanish, and searching in his phrasebook had said, 'It does not say here how to address a dictator.' Franco had laughed and the magazine was then 'in'. After this Dennis hired many Spanish poets and intellectuals who were pleased to be well paid. He had liked the problem and the organization, rather than the content of the magazine, and once it was established he grew bored. It was apparently a large business in American money, producing millions of dollars, and second only to the Bible Society.

His body was hard and muscular, his face ugly but attractive and always about to break into a laugh. Everything was in fact a huge joke; there was no point in taking life seriously, especially not the *Reader's Digest*. He was erudite, frequently quoting the classics. He behaved like a patriarch, solving problems, giving parties for Ava Gardner and Dominguin. Once a person knew Dennis they needed no other addresses. He lived in a large flat with white walls and dark seventeenth-century Spanish furniture that he had collected. He had a manservant who was also a chauffeur. Only at times, after too much to drink, would he clown – probably because he had been a prodigy, a little too brilliant, always knowing more than most of the people he was with. He was pleased when they knew his reference or the context of his talk, but slightly bored that everything came so easily. On these occasions people would gape as he suddenly burst into song, singing opera in a tremendous, powerful and arresting voice.

Not long after our meeting, when I did not yet know him well, I told him I was going to Paris for three days to fetch some belongings and to ghost-write Mrs Snow's 'Letter from Paris' for *Harper's Bazaar*. He took charge at once, and said he would meet my plane on my return.

Two old letters to the professor in London, one describing this arrival at the airport and the other Dennis's character, can recount best if left verbatim:

The heat is sweltering. It is 5.30 and I am writing naked, in bed, planning to try to have a siesta after this letter, but first: hear the arrival. Dennis met me at the airport (he calls himself thine Dionysus) with his chauffeur, who greeted me with cries of *Coma esta?* as if they had known me for years (new friends are immediately old friends here). There were two people on the plane with me whom Dennis also knew, one a Russian with a 1900 moustache and strong accent, like Mischa Auer, the other Westinghouse, dreary but pleasant. While we waited for our passports to be returned (Spanish system) Dennis behaved as if the whole thing were a cocktail party, circulating and talking to everyone, other people from other planes too. A man arrived from Lisbon, and many Japanese, to whom he spoke in their own language and discovered they were MPs. They twittered together like starlings. Finally the Russian, American and I were driven off in the Jaguar, through the tawny land and bare mountains outside the airport – through the blank heat – but not home, straight to the Palace bar. The American was staying there anyway but the Russian grew anxious and said he had to find a hotel. Dennis said oh never mind now and wouldn't have it – his luggage was left in the car. The Palace was as usual a cross-section of the world: Jerome Zerbe (*Town and Country*), Pepe Luis Vasquez, the *torero* who no longer fights, but carries his raincoat stiffly as if it is a *muleta*, an American businessman, a Spanish marquis . . . then we were whisked off to lunch, the car waiting outside and the Russian growing desperate about his luggage, so we stopped and got him a room at a small hotel, went on to the Jockey where the food is delicious.

The others faded, and I was left alone with Dennis. Now the sign of Madrid that you would hate: sleeping-pills in the afternoon! Otherwise, how to last? I can't manage. They are coming to fetch me for dinner at 9, drinks first, dinner won't be till 11. Will leave this open.

Wednesday 8.30 a.m. (Why do I wake so early? They go to bed here at 5 a.m.)

The maid, Angelis, thinks I am not a proper señorita because I don't sleep in the mornings.

Last night drinks with Bob Hope, very funny – then dinner with John Ringling North and his talent scout, and that man with a scarred face (Skorzeny?) who rescued Mussolini.

Do you see my mother? These sorties would horrify her, tell her I work too. Am getting a press card, from Magnum. Telegram from Morath – our story on liberal women went through. The people here sleep all afternoon, I can't seem to.

Never mind, life will begin properly after the summer. We are going to Tossa – remember, where we went once? I will write and tell you if it has changed.

The first weeks in Madrid, thanks to Dennis's best intentions, were like one long party. When we did finally get away for the summer to Tossa, Guislaine and I both slept for two days.

There was an atmosphere in Madrid then, of something about to happen – the start of future big business. The Palace bar was always full of tall, beautifully dressed Spaniards, and a mixture of Americans on holiday but also some five percent operator types, last seen in Egypt or Tokyo, perching on high stools waiting . . . There had been a new American agreement with the government which brought suspense . . .

In contrast to this was the immensity and quietness of the land and the mountains surrounding the town, as reminders of something great beyond.

One early morning when I was going home from a party, it seemed that the whole population was surging out toward the south; it was the people going to work in the fields of La Mancha, on foot, on donkeys, in families, and they were singing. *Cante jondo* should be heard out of doors, since it is the song of the fields. These people must have been poor, but they seemed happy, perhaps with a type of Moorish fatalism: this is the way it is. *Es igual*.

In learning the language I found that the verb for to wait and to hope was the same: *esperar*. This seemed most indicative of their character. There was no word for the blues. Certainly the poor looked very poor indeed. There was water for fountains in Madrid but not always for drainage in the outlying villages.

The professor answered my letter to say there were people in England who refused to go to Spain because of Franco. But there were many Spaniards who did not like him either and spat out his name in disdain. Spanish disdain had a special quality: a facial expression of scorn mixed with dignity.

From the window of the aeroplane going to Barcelona (on our way to Tossa), the mountains below looked like folds of a stony, bony rhinoceros. On one side of me there was a Catalan business-man who talked and asked many questions. I learned that he owned fifteen factories, and ran them on the lines of Elton Mayo, whose book he had read in Spanish. His name was Jose Luis. He was met at the airport by his mother and a small brother in a long limousine. They drove us to our hotel, and we acquired a new friend.

Tossa was an ancient village with a Roman wall along the hill beside the beach, leading to a tower. In 1953 and 1954 the word 'tourist' meant an odd foreigner ambling about. The village, which consisted mainly of fishermen, led its own life.

We had a room above the grocer's shop. (Perhaps because of her lost empire, grocers in Spain were called *Ultramarinos*.) In early morning a van would unload chickpeas and lentils; the grocer himself, who was called Canadell, would sit outside the front door in his pyjamas. He was the owner, a man of property and leisure. I understood then why the Portuguese on our refugee ship during the war had worn their pyjamas all day: it was a status symbol.

We met a few people: an English woman, her children, the local doctor, and a burly man with gold teeth who was a very strong swimmer and also champion wrestler for France. He walked about on the beach as if he owned it, but in a nice way. He was protective; he encouraged people to swim long distances, and gave lessons to children. He wore a knife in his belt and was strong and brown like a Polynesian. When I went rock swim-ming alone, I was afraid of Moray eels and jellyfish, but with him it felt safe. He knew of a beach with rare shells, only attainable by sea; that summer I grew into the habit of swimming about five kilometres a day, and it felt as normal as walking. But on return-ing, I was shivering cold, in spite of the hot sun.

There were groves of parasol pines, olives, the maquis. We settled into a quiet summer until one day Dennis arrived. It called for a letter to the professor:

I have just had lunch with the mayor, the lorry-driver (whom we rent our room from), the wrestler from Paris (he teaches stuntmen for the cinema). We had *zarzouela*, fish soup, champagne and many brandies. This was unprecedented, it was a feast day, usually it is very quiet here. The mayor started lunch by saying he was inhibited like a Nordic, but after the brandy he sang Aragonese and Catalan songs. The lorry-driver danced, tapping the mayor's face. Franco was brought into the jokes and abused, then *veronicas* with the tablecloth, *olé* Manolete etc. and a crowd of fishermen collected to listen to the singing. The police also came, but went away when they saw it was the mayor.

It would have ended there, no more than a lunch, but just as it was breaking up, Dennis arrived in a rather grand American car (not his own) with an American writer 'of best-sellers' we were told. They joined in at once, Dennis sang *Pagliacci* standing on his head, he has a superb voice and it lost no strength for being upside down; the mayor was delighted and bought more brandy all round. Finally the American writer drove off – he has a house further up the coast and was just giving Dennis a lift from Madrid (seven hundred kilometres) and so then the whole village put Dennis to bed for a siesta. A room was found for him in a little house up a side street where a whole floor was empty. But later – we could not remember where he was, to go and fetch him. When we did find him, he had woken up and was saying: 'Where am I? How did I get here?' (A position he often finds himself in) then he added, 'I drove here to talk to you,' and it appeared it was his birthday! So we gave him a party. I ended up all over again with him and the mayor, the local doctor, the English woman and five yelling children, Guislaine, the wrestler (like a brown bear) whom I swim with. Dennis calls the doctor *le médécin malgré lui* – he certainly is always drinking in bars, but they say he is a good doctor when needed. The mayor was very merry and his wife was apparently waiting with a saucepan to bang his head when he got home.

This is what makes Tossa nice, we live with the locals. Sometimes I just sit on a chair in the street and talk with Canadell. There is an old fisherman with skin like tree bark who drinks wine straight down without swallowing, the Spanish way; he is interested in American jazz, he never heard it before this summer. There is a bar where it is played and he sits there and listens, just listens – quiet and surprised.

We eat in the grocer's shop 'garden' beside the chicken-run; wine is free!

Today sharks were sighted, but with the bear-man one feels safe; they were quite far out. We swim along the shore, with him between me and the open sea.

If you want to come here you could stay in the same place; there are endless dark rooms upstairs with large heavy furniture. It is pitch-black with the shutters closed; you sleep like you're dead. Just arrive (if you want to) and ask for Canadell or the lorry depot; he usually knows where I am. He is easy to find; he works at night and sits outside his house all day.

(It is odd that relatively few years later I wrote to the professor of that revolting Costa Brava where huge buses were bumper to bumper, Canadell's shop turned into a boutique, and the chicken-run a reception room.)

The American writer turned out to be Robert Ruark. He wrote not (yet) best-sellers, but sports columns, that were syndicated and appeared in twenty newspapers at once all over America.

We went to see him with Dennis, in his villa near Palamos; the atmosphere was very different from our village. Friends of the Ruarks had houses with floodlit lawns, beach-houses, booze and boredom. But Ruark was as hospitable as Dennis, having people to stay, offering meals, drinks, leaving all his guests for a few hours then returning, rubbing his hands together, to announce he had just had someone killed off. He was referring to the novel that he was working on, about the Mau Mau, *Something of Value*. He had many Tahitian primitive paintings and played Hawaiian music. He drank mainly rum with Coca Cola, and much ice and lemon. He had two boxer dogs who went swimming with him, and a wife called Ginny who looked as if it had all got beyond her long ago.

When we returned to Tossa, there were cries and shouts of

greeting in the streets, not only from Canadell but people we did not even know.

20

After the summer we returned to Madrid and prepared to live there forever. Guislaine walked to the Lycée and came home for lunch; Angelis learned to cook, after a fashion; our antiquated lift rarely worked, because its hydraulic system depended on rain, which was not frequent. At night, if I was late home and the downstairs doors were closed, a call summoned the *sereno*, who owned the keys of all the buildings in the quarter of his beat. He would come with them jangling on his belt and let me in, his manners gracious and dignified. It felt medieval, the way he trudged the streets like a night guard. There was something untouched and proud about Spain.

A new newspaper was being started by an ex-GI; a large man like an orangutan with orange hair. He had apparently been run out of Morocco for blackmailing people into advertising in his paper there. This time he wanted to be clean. There was no English-language paper in Spain for the Americans to read. *Time* magazine appeared only irregularly because it was often censored, and he wanted anyway to produce daily and local news. His paper was a rag, but he gave me a column in which I was free to write whatever I liked. Robert Ruark was not too proud to write in it and our columns were on the same page, which made me feel successful. In the meantime, the pay was not only small, but often failed to materialize. His finance was based on advertising, and now that he was honest there was not much of it. Also the censor would cut chunks out of articles just before they went to press, so we could not see them again in time to make sense out of the gaps. It was a mess, but greatly entertaining, and for a while it had a following, readers who corresponded, and even enough advertising to carry it limping along.

Madrid was small like a village, but without the disadvantages. Demi Gates was one of the Americans who lived there as a resident, not a tourist, and loved Spain with passion. He was against businessmen putting commercial placards on the roads. At Christmas, he had visited the village of Montejo de la Sierra with a priest, dressed as one of the three kings, and distributed toys and oranges to the children, who did not guess that behind his false beards and robe was a foreigner. He lived in the street called Desengañados, street of the Disillusioned. He was merry and funny once he knew a person, but normally shy and had invented the expression, 'cough, choke, gasp' to indicate embarrassment, which then became Madrid slang.

Vincente Bobadilla (whose family made sherry and lived in Jerez) worked for the *Reader's Digest*. He had a long El Greco face, black hair and dark eyes, and beautiful hands like the wax saints in the churches. The pallor of his skin had no pink in it; it was the whiteness peculiar to the south. He recited Lorca by heart and had something deep and tragic about him, although he attended with pleasure the wild flamenco parties given by Dennis, and would rush off with any willing foreign woman, entirely sincere while it lasted. He had a Sunday wife who did not usually accompany him – it was the Spanish system then. When they did go out together, he seemed devoted.

Dennis continued to give his parties, and to arrive at the airport saying, 'Where am I? How did I get here?' He once hired an entire flamenco family who remained in his flat for three days. Steinbeck was at this party. He had a quiet face like a sculpture, looked sensitive, and hardly spoke. Ruark visited often; he lived in Barcelona which he said was a better town to work in. He had a flat with a grand piano and a garden – Palamos was his summer house.

Then I met Alvaro.

His English was so fluent and he appeared so phlegmatic, that he could have been an Englishman. He spoke with no trace of accent, and knew all the Evelyn Waugh jokes and their context. How had this happened? He had had an English nanny, he said. There seemed no other explanation – he must have been a natural. His erudition was almost strange in such a young man, and one who had always lived in a country regarded as backward and censored. There was something about him like his land: aloof and complicated. This appearance of calm would vanish suddenly in his anger at Franco. 'He has castrated Spain!' he would shout, with a vehemence that showed a wild underside. So it was with his incredible jealousy which emerged later. There was no trace of Englishness then.

He was very tall. His entrance one day at the front door with Vicente made an impact. Someone vital had come. His coming would cause a change, something had *happened*.

He was partly Basque, but mainly Castilian. His parents lived in a flat in Madrid but also sometimes in Castile, where they owned three thousand acres of wheat fields, surrounding a farm and an old chapel. The house was near Palencia and was long and low like a ranch house, in pale stone. Alvaro preferred it to Madrid and went there frequently alone. There was a small village near, where houses with thick walls kept out the climate and goats wandered in the street with eyes like lanterns. Gaunt men looked out of the doorway of the *bodega*, where they played cards, staring from the shadows to see us when we passed. The people had stern, bony, Castilian faces, shaped by searing winter winds, capable of taking things that were tough and enduring the fierce, flattening, inland summer heat. But they were friendly, and when they smiled their faces were illuminated. Between the fields of wheat there were hillsides with groves of cork oak, broom very yellow against the clear blue sky, hoopoes perched on corab trees or on the clothesline – and always beyond, the land that stretched out in waves like the sea, not enclosing but leading on, barren like an ochre moon.

'With such a big sky overhead, and such land around, you have to believe in God,' said Alvaro, laughing. His mother went daily to Mass. He went rarely. He was Spanish, yet he was not. He was also something else besides. He had the view of a detached, much older man – until something upset it.

We started to spend most of our time together, and then, all of our time. I rode behind him on his motorbike, clinging round his waist, often terrified. We visited places neither of us had been to. He showed me his country and discovered it himself. He had never been to Cuenca, and had always wanted to see it. We set off on a long ride on his machine. Cuenca was an introverted, forgotten place, hanging over a cliff, so that some of the balconies had props under them. We were wind–beaten and cold; we drank wine in a *bodega* and ate some *lomo*. The old men, as always, made philosophical remarks about the sky or destiny. This is one of the things I remember about Spain as it was then; they were never attached to the worldly 'main chance'.

Alvaro had felt stuck in an intellectually stagnant place (no opera, plays censored, his library almost entirely English) and he was surprised and even amused by my passionate love for his country. We each made the other see a new side, the way falling in love opens up the world. Perhaps that is what was also happening.

When we got back to Madrid after this trip, there was a card from Jose Luis saying he would be in town for one day and asking me out to dinner; there was also a bunch of flowers. This was the first time I saw Alvaro's incredible jealousy. The flowers were a large spray of dark red gladioli, almost black. 'How odd the way Spaniards like funereal things, like the tortured statues in the cathedrals,' I said, making light of it, seeing a cloud. 'But Jose Luis is such a kind man, even if they are the one flower I happen to dislike . . .' But Alvaro's face was transformed, set in an expression almost of cruelty; the usually warm brown eyes were coldly dark and with a flash in them like the blade of a knife.

'You're mine and that's that. We'll have no Catalans here!' he cried, and flung the flowers out over the terrace into the street. The civilized 'older man' with detached attitudes had vanished. Here was a primitive who lay under the surface. A cave man almost. An exciting but fearsome surprise. Normally, we each criticized our own or each other's countries and made jokes about them, neither of us being chauvinistic. But he did have some personal hatreds, and Catalans were one. This perhaps made it worse – I did not know what to think. Jose Luis was a good and funny man and I would like to have suggested we all three had dinner together . . .

Later, Alvaro sat on the sofa with Guislaine and her small cousin who had come to stay with us, and read comics with them like a cosy Grandpa. What a mixture, indeed. (But the Catalan had been disposed of.)

Sometimes, in the Palace bar, a very small man called Gondarias was to be seen. He had a sallow, yellow, slightly pock-marked skin and his hair was blue-black. He looked more Indian than Spanish. His face was wicked and decadent, and he was apparently very rich, unmarried, a lavish host and the owner of one of the biggest bull ranches in Spain, near Toledo. He invited us there for lunch, with Vicente and Dennis, and sent his car to fetch us.

To the south of Madrid the land of the Mancha is flat and blank. It is Don Quixote's country – as far as one can see there is nothing. We drove through this until, in the middle of scrub and wizened bushes, there were two white gateposts (but no fence), just posts like symbols, with a lone horse and rider on guard, standing out against the sky. The house was in a green oasis, with a patio and garden; attached to this house was the chapel that Isabel gave to Columbus. There were forty people to lunch. The food was earthy: black bean soup, coarse bread, meat fried in some greasy case (which I removed) and red pimentos. There were rich almond cakes for dessert, a speciality of Toledo and much red wine from Valdepeñas and Bobadilla brandy from Vicente's family.

After lunch we went to the arena where Gondarias trained and tested his animals. It was surrounded by compartments where the bulls and cows were kept. We walked along the top and looked down at them. Since bulls are bred from brave mothers, the heifers and cows are tested for bravery before being chosen. They charge with their eyes open and are fairly nasty, sometimes more frightening than bulls.

Some of the guests went into the arena as an after-lunch sport. First Vicente, with a lazy Andalusian style as if he could not really be bothered; he made it look easy and was superbly disdainful. Then a Frenchman who lived in Spain jumped in, followed by Dennis, who was knocked down at once, but mainly because the Frenchman was in the way. Dennis was brave, but a clown with no style. Anglo-Saxons did not seem to move their bodies pro-perly, so even when making a correct pass, the line seemed wrong.

Gondarias was excellent, making intriguing noises, talking to his heifers in a low voice, calling them persuasively and alluringly: '*Vacca, vacca . . . aqui vaccita . . .*' It was a trick to get them. His face wore a beastly expression and I felt he must talk to the girls in his bed the same way. Alvaro told me he was well-known for jokes like letting a bull loose among his guests.

Dennis then rode the host's white stallion with a straight seat and complete control. Behind and around us lay the impassive land, the scrubby black trees, and far beyond to the north, the Sierra. All this time I was beside Alvaro. I was his possession, properly Spanish now in this country where women were never alone. It had happened with no conscious decision: he was there. This was a land of fate.

As we drove away, back to Madrid with Gondarias in his car, he pointed to a wall we passed and said casually, 'That's where I had thirty-four people shot in the civil war.'

Something sinister ran underneath the beauty, and at the moment he said this, a strange pain started in my hip and through the side of my body; this pain was to change our future. I did not mention it that day, pain supposedly being something that goes away best if ignored.

We went back to Fernando Santo, where we were now a houseful, since Guislaine's little cousin had come to stay. He had long, green eyes and was called Miguel. He was with us because his parents were divorcing. He was smaller than Guislaine and she called him Monsieur Moustique; they went to school together. It felt like a family. Alvaro spent all day in our flat, and was driven mad by the singing of Angelis. 'What noisy people,' he said, as if he were not Spanish himself; this was his quiet, phlegmatic 'English' side.

After dinner sometimes we went out to a little bar in the Castellana where a bearded man played the piano. We danced frequently to a tune called 'Solamente Tu'. Something must have shone around us, because when the bearded man saw us arrive he would smile and it would always be that tune.

We continued to play the 'language game' – the discovery of character through the vocabulary. There was another case of the same verb with two meanings: to want and to love. *Quierer*. 'It is odd, as if love is the same as possession,' I said.

'Of course. Who can love without wanting to own?' he almost

snorted. 'That would be some anaemic foreign emotion.'

One day, riding behind him on his motorbike, I discovered he was only twenty-five. This was casually thrown over his shoulder in the wind. It was a shock; he seemed so protective, so mature in his knowledge, bigger in every sense than me – but I was thirty. Age had not occurred to me before.

Jose Luis had told me that in Spain a woman was not allowed a passport or a bank account without her husband's permission. Jose Luis was a Catalan who admired France. He wrote me letters that were hilarious (by mistake) in broken English. He was amused by what he called my 'romance', and without meaning to sabotage, he warned me against losing Nordic independence. But it was a joke since he did not think the marriage would go through. So he would tease: be careful, a jealous man will not let you travel . . . I did not care. Alvaro had become the universe; I would have died for him. 'It may be more difficult to live for him,' Jose Luis laughed.

Apart from his jealousy, Alvaro was a mature companion. He was so amusingly indignant about the inefficiency of Spain. 'The Tagus only becomes navigable at the Portuguese frontier,' he would say. 'Yet there has been a navigation plan since the time of Philip II – why are we so hopeless?' It bothered him, yet he did not admire the Portuguese; they were another of his hates.

Alvaro's parents were not typical of the Spanish couples I had met until then, where the wife stayed at home. They went everywhere together. We spent a week with them in the house in Castile. It was unexpectedly English inside with chintz sofas. The retired nanny, Miss Lizzie, had stayed on and still lived with them. She said she had been in Spain too long to go anywhere else now. Alvaro's mother, called Maria, was much younger than her husband. She welcomed me and was warm, which was not the conventional reaction I had feared. In fact there was nothing conventional about them. The father adored ballet and had danced once with Nijinsky. He was deaf and wore a hearing aid, and he was gentle with a whispering soft voice. They were intellectuals, aristocrats and eccentrics. The great-uncle, the Duke of Veragua, sold the whole herd of Veragua bulls one afternoon on impulse because one of them gored a *torero* he liked. When another great-uncle had been ambassador in Moscow, his sister had visited him. This great-aunt was the first woman to travel alone in the Spain of those days where it was unheard of. She was an original: she smoked cigars and went to Tibet. There is a reproduction of a portrait of her on the ships that go from Barcelona to Palma. During the civil war, another uncle was taken to a village outside Madrid, where his tongue was cut off and his eyes put out – yet he was a kind old duke who always had sweets in his pocket for children. (This was the other, nefarious side of Spain.) Maria was officially lady-in-waiting to the queen, but since the queen was in exile, it involved merely going to stay with her one month each year, when sometimes they would travel; that year they were going to England.

I had thought they might mind that I was divorced, but they were above such narrowness in judging character. 'I want only for Alvaro to find his right person,' Maria said. 'I am glad it is you. I wondered whom he would find – he is so odd, in some ways – the usual girls bore him.' She was magnanimous. But there was one proviso: she was devout. We had to be married in church, otherwise it was not a real marriage in Spain and did not count. But obviously, Alvaro had planned for it to be in the old chapel there, beside the house . . . It must be ascertained, she told me, that the Catholic Church did not recognize my former marriage. We decided I would go to London for the necessary documents, and would also see my mother. Maria became a friend and I grew to love her. She also loved Guislaine and said she was 'longing for grandchildren, just as she had been longing for Alvaro to marry'. We were living in a rainbow light that was almost too good to be really happening. Sometimes I felt superstitious. I was anxious about the pain that had not disappeared, and the possible rigour of the Church . . . But I was no longer alone. I realized this only when the state of solitude ceased; there was a man, his family, and they were helping. First, it had just been Alvaro. Now this sudden family was quite unexpected . . .

Alvaro understood the reasons for my English trip but not the fact that I stopped in Paris on the way back to see Margot Shore and tell my old friends. I received an angry letter from him. He was jealous of the sheets I slept in, the clothes I wore: 'It is thunder and Wagner and spring and nothing like this has happened before.' I rang him up but cried on the telephone because he was cross. Then he was jealous of the handkerchief I wiped my tears on. 'You are crazy, you are sick,' I said.

'Yes. Come back at once.'

When I sat in the bar of the Lancaster with Capa and Gene Kelly, who had just been to a private showing of *An American in Paris*, it felt quite unreal. I missed the plane and was preparing to take the night train. Capa, who was feeling low (this happened rarely), said I had missed the plane for Freudian reasons. He took the Jose Luis view. I could not explain. There are no words for love that don't make a mockery of it. The wind on my face on his motorbike, the way Spain was grit. 'Solamente Tu'. Gene gave me some nembutal for the sleeper train; they saw me off and waved.

The next morning (after changing trains at the frontier because the tracks were a different size – everything about Spain was different) there was a sharp light on a white farmhouse seen from the train window, and anxiety vanished. Alvaro met the train, we hugged each other at the station, happiness was as large as the view, and we were starting our life together, even if he was jealous of the cat. He also laughed at himself and christened himself 'the angry man'.

In England it had been established that the 'churching' after the registry office marriage with Vsevolod was not considered to be a proper Church of England service. This rather fine distinction produced Maria's requirement: the Catholic Church accepted that I had not been married in their sense. When I told Maria, who was in London when I was there, she was joyous. She now wanted me to be converted. She was staying at Claridges with the queen, her job as lady-in-waiting being really only a symbol in exile – she was there as a friend. The old Spanish Queen Victoria (not so old, she was in her sixties) was partly English. When I met her with Maria I was wearing a straight sheath skirt and half fell over doing my curtsey. We all giggled, and there was a family feeling that can only be described as cosy. The queen's English brother (Carisbrooke) arrived for tea, Maria said I was her future daughter-in-law, and this queen, who had had blood on her wedding-dress when she married Alfonso XIII (a bomb had been thrown at their carriage), gave her blessing.

My mother was pleased, particularly by Alvaro's intellectual quality, and the fact that I would have a home. I worried about the pain, but whom could I consult? I thought I would tell the professor, but when I telephoned he was away, so I wrote him a letter, before leaving for Paris and Madrid.

After my return many things happened more or less simultaneously. When Maria also got back to Madrid I was given a family ring – an aquamarine surrounded with diamonds. We were *novios*; it was official. A present arrived from the queen. We would be married in the family chapel.

I told Alvaro about the pain, and we went to a doctor. He had just received a new machine and said he would put healing rays on to the side where the pain was. I thought it must be diathermy, but he enclosed me in a room like a cabin and supervised through a window. It seemed that these rays must have been very strong. I had twelve treatments and developed ulcers on the skin of my hip. I also started to feel weak – what was happening? There had been no cure; the pain was worse.

In answer to my letter, the professor telephoned. When I told him about the machine he announced that he would come to Madrid. Who was he? Alvaro asked. A friend, almost family, like a cousin. Why was he called a professor? Did he teach? It was a name someone had given him because he knew everything, like an encyclopaedia; there was nobody quite like him.

There is a quite special respect for cousins in Spain, so the arrival of a cousin was normal; except that he was not one – and when he did arrive there was an explosion, though not immediately.

When they first met, the professor was greatly impressed by the degree of Alvaro's knowledge on all subjects: politics, literature, trends of current thought. 'What a well-informed young man,' he said, surprised, 'and considering the difficulty of obtaining news in Spain.'

We had lunch in a club in the country outside Madrid, at the Puerta de Hierro; I was proud and happy: my future husband, my future country and home – the meeting of these two minds was a great success. I basked, though I was starting to take large doses of Codiss in order to get about. The professor asked to meet the doctor. He said the machine used sounded like deep X-ray, a radiation used only for cancer, which is why, on hearing the news in England, he had been alarmed and decided to come here. Now it seemed that the doctor was either a crook or a dangerous fool. No diagnosis had been made, and the treatment had simply been mad. Even for cancer, he said, the dose was usually three minutes – but I had received ten minutes at a time which was three times the amount. He was scathing about the dangers of Spanish medicine, and though Alvaro agreed, I could see he was becoming irritated. (The best ophthalmic surgeon in Europe was in Barcelona.)

By the time we all went to a nightclub together, Alvaro was angry at the idea that this man was not a cousin and he was staying in my flat. Added to this insult, he had a car. Alvaro followed us home on his motorbike, carrying the bunch of roses that had been on our table. When we reached the front door and got out of the car, he flung the roses which hit the professor on the stomach and then lay scattered all over the floor. 'You don't know what love is! You're a neuter!' he shouted, and disappeared, tearing off into the darkness with a noise of exhaust.

The next day the professor visited the doctor and punched him on the nose. When Alvaro heard this he was mollified. He approved, laughed, and decided the professor was all right after all. 'We could sue the doctor,' he said. But there was no point; it would not be a cure. Alvaro found another doctor who had the right idea but applied the method wrongly. He jabbed at my spine with a long curved needle like a curlew's beak; the needle broke and burned my war scar. I was humiliated, and ashamed of crying. A nightmare settled round us because we still did not know what this wracking malediction was that seemed to have come to us out of medieval darkness.

The professor left for three weeks in North Africa, handing Alvaro the keys of his car, saying he would pick it up again on his way back. They were friends now. Alvaro had discovered that altruism was not just foreign madness, that there were shades of grey, not only black and white, in friendships, and that maybe Anglo–Saxon relationships had their point. Cars were starting to appear in Madrid. Alvaro's parents had acquired one, but this car was a miracle of excitement – a Mercedes with a diesel engine – and for three weeks it was his. We could visit distant places.

We went first to Estremadura, to the village of Guadalupe where the monks grew medicinal herbs. They ran a hostelry where we stayed, and this had a Christian cloister with Arab arcades, which had been built by *mudejares*, conquered Moors. There was a miraculous black virgin who had been found by a cowherd in the fourteenth century, when he was digging the land. Maria believed in miracles. We sat together quietly in the cloister, and hoped.

In Logrosan a seventeenth-century doctor had written medicine in verse. We made discoveries, spoilt by the demon who came with us. We went to the Basque country where village churches smelled of the sea, and in one church we heard a concert by the cellist Gaspar Cassado. In San Sebastian Alvaro showed me a building his grandmother had left to the town as a gift. In small bars in the old quarter he spoke Basque with the people.

We returned to Madrid. The monk's medicine had not removed the pain, it hung over us now like a ghoul looking over our shoulders, because not knowing what it was, caused dread. We were frightened; it must be solved before we could arrange our marriage. I could hardly walk, my body was like tight elastic and knives – the Devil was at work somewhere. I drank Fundador, took Codiss tablets, and stayed at home in a crouching position. Everyday things continued: the children had lunch on the terrace in the sunlight, there were butterflies, nuns came to the door asking for money – it was just that I, personally, must have gone mad. It was rough on Alvaro, such a young man, to have the fun of owning a car spoiled by his *novia* lying on the back seat. And the *novia* knew she was healthy. It was just that there was a jinx somewhere. He bought me a ticket for London, where I went for a second opinion.

I had a feeling of doom. I had always believed that a shining thing would come one day, and the vicissitudes would all be over; this belief was the core of the earth, and my philosophy as I knew it. Obstacles to overcome, after which the world would be beautiful. Now the shining thing was here: this country, this man, with Maria waiting (as she so frequently said) for her grandchildren. So what did it mean? Health is a subject to avoid writing about – but if it changes the course of events, it is a stroke of fate, and in this case, an explanation of what followed.

21

The specialists in London made discoveries on two parallels. The first one was ridiculous: all that had been wrong originally was a slipped disc, the swimming in summer having possibly been too strenuous. But the second, weird, witchborne disease, had been artificially given by wrong use of the machine. Even when used for its proper purpose, the dose should have been half. Over-exposure had thus created an illness. But this was not all. It appeared that such large doses of radiation on to the hip would penetrate to the ovaries, and I would almost certainly now be sterile.

So what then of Maria's grandchildren – of the descendants through their only son? In other words, the marriage was off. It was all over. The premonition of doom had been true.

I returned to Madrid entirely numb, and was treated for burnt skin and anaemia. (Radiation destroys the good cells with the bad, they said, but there had been no bad cells, just bad luck.) Miguel left us. My sister wrote and asked us to go and live with them; I packed our things. I did not know what to tell Alvaro. Perhaps I thought he would persuade me it did not matter, and that we would do without children, but could not do without each other. And *I would accept*; and this would be wrong, not just for him, but for Maria. I thought he should not be in a position to make such decisions. To this day I regret not discussing it. I think he felt betrayed and his heart was broken, but I did not realize any of it fully until later, too late – because at the time it was simply a form of Hell, and I was ill, futilely and without need – because of a mistake; but I was still burnt, weak and in despair. It was six months before I could walk normally.

We both lost everything. Neither of us made a happy marriage later and nobody lived happily ever after. And it truly was the Devil's doing, because – had we known – it was not necessary. The Harley Street doctor was as wrong as the Spaniard had been; his diagnosis of sterility was not true. I had another child ten years later. So it could have been Alvaro's, and we could have married after all, and had many children – and sooner.

We reached the high peak of both our lives. Many interesting things may have happened since – but that was the top of the mountain. It was so simple. We were happy. If we could just have been left alone . . . I loved Spain before ever meeting the man, so I lost a country as well. Except that it never really left me, and neither did he. Even twenty years later . . . a hoopoe seen in Provence (they are rare outside Spain) . . . a car with a Madrid plate . . . a *paso doble* . . . *Gallito*, played in a bar in a dismal northern street . . . and if it is bullfight Sunday, it is Spain forever. (As if a reminder is needed when it is always inside.)

We went to Strasbourg, where my sister and her husband took us in out of the cold and gave us a home. Our family, working all this time as true Europeans, now had a house with a garden. The garden was a Persian carpet of my sister's creation, the house ran on a rhythm like a ritual; there was a cook, a maid, and a fat cleaning woman with a lovely child's face called Madame Kintz. The Community was still being created at the Council of Europe. Jean Monnet would make a speech and people would come to dinner to talk of their new ideas. It was happiness of the heart. Guislaine went to school and grew up now in a safe, protected home where an earthquake was unlikely. She would be disrupted no more.

Alvaro sent telegrams. I could see him in my thoughts, tall as a tree and wise, calling me Little Gael as if he were an old sage, instead of a handsome young man with an air and a *facha* all his own. I applied myself to learn the Spanish acceptance of destiny, tragedy and fate. *Valor Señorita*. Store it up and remember. All over again, like *Coragio Signorina* in Asolo, but this time it had been mature and would have been a marriage of true minds. And always, my inner sight would be seeing those farmhouses sharp white against the lucid sky, the women in doorways shielding their eyes in the fierce purple sundown, or scattering water from tin basins to lay the dust; the bare lines of land, the earth's backbone. Or a *plaza* in a small village like a stage where something might happen, and round the edge, the groups of men sitting all together, the old men with their faces used to hardship, making philosophical remarks. Ancient, barbaric Spain, so vast and so above pettiness – except when it comes to their women: these they will not share or be light-hearted about.

And Maria. We did not lose her as a person; we wrote to each other, and she became a special friend. But she was not my mother-in-law. Nor would Miss Lizzie be the future nanny. And the man: Guislaine loved the man too.

Philosophy must take over – or who could survive? Even if nothing is the same again, one must go on. . . Probably, for all people, happiness is something that only comes in short moments.

We were a family. On Sundays we went to small Alsatian villages where there were storks' nests on the church steeples and kind, fat people with sing-song voices. We ate venison and my sister and Dunstan took Guislaine for long walks in the wild woods, where there were deer and boar. I painted. Through an old doctor, who was giving me treatment, I met a *courtier*, who was a sort of travelling salesman with pictures. He had a suitcase containing paintings by Bernard Buffet (who sold then for five pounds) and Carzou, Goerg, Dauchot; he took these from town to town to his special clients. The doctor bought from this man (who has since made a fortune and retired) and showed him my work, some of which he took away in his suitcase and later sold.

When I was better I went to Paris and found a room to use as a base. Sometimes my sister and Dunstan would go away to London or for a holiday, and I would stay and supervise the house. More often I would go away about my business, and always the house was there, and they were there, in their home that now was also Guislaine's.

In Paris I found Chim again. It felt as if I had been gone a hundred years. Spain was such a different dimension, a far frontier, yet Capa and Chim had taken their first photographs there. Chim still had his Roman plan, but it was too late for me, since it would be too far away from Guislaine and the family.

Then Capa was killed in Indochina.

When the news came through, no one could believe it; everyone was dazed. He had been through so many wars, he was legendary. But this time he had stepped on a mine. . . He left a desert that could never be filled: his creased, laughing eyes; the eternal cigarette stub; the way he went anywhere, but never owned a dinner jacket (in the days before the jean age when people dressed). But he was himself, he was Capa, he needed no accoutrements. He never lent money; if a friend needed some, he gave it. Never to see him again, never to hear his voice saying, 'You are my sort of creature. . .' left a cold world. Perhaps he knew that his way of living beside guns would eventually blow him up – maybe he would not have minded dying that way. It was those he left who minded.

I attended the *Grande Chaumière*, briefly, but then followed Kisling's advice to work alone. A painting was accepted by Drouant David for their *Salon de Jeune Peinture*. A man there called Fuentes sent me to see Segovia in order to train with him. After much hesitation in calling on a stranger, I knocked on his door.

'What a lark,' he said, 'I have never had a pupil before. What are we supposed to do?'

We both laughed and were friends at once. He was stocky and strong, like a bear, with thick black hair and thick glasses like his father.

We were both broke so we shared a model called Madame Maquereau. The drawing of nudes is necessary for learning structure, but it was tedious. Segovia liked massive women with huge thighs and heavy breasts. He did not like pretty models. Pin-ups were all right for bed, he said, but they made dull paintings. I plodded on for a time before going back to working alone, but we saw each other constantly. He came to criticize and help my first paintings, which were mainly of Asolo, until Spain got into the background and filled the Veneto plain with immensity. (I am told that today this plain is filled with factories.) He gave me his best drawing of Madame Maquereau, but I changed it for a tree; Segovia is bored by nature, yet draws remarkable trees that are both strong and delicate.

It was a confused period, with return trips to Strasbourg. I painted, and wrote a novel – which to pursue? Cocteau did both, but I wasn't Cocteau. It came adrift – then moored again. My little room was a workshop.

One day Kisling was walking down the rue Royale. He was wearing a camel-hair coat and a felt hat, and looked roguish. 'Have you sold my painting yet?' he asked, shaking his finger at me.

'No,' I said, 'the wolf has not come right inside the house yet.'

He beamed with pleasure. His face had its old familiar shine, though he grimaced when he told me of his ulcers and how he had to drink milk. 'Are you painting?' he asked.

'Yes,' I was glad to be able to say.

A few years after this meeting, Kisling died in his beloved Sanary.

Two years after Capa, Chim was killed at Suez, while driving in a jeep with Jean Roy from *Match* magazine. They disobeyed an order to halt – it has never been quite clear whether this was a mistake – but they went on ahead into the minefields. Chim, with his sad, quiet face, his pleasure in books and beautiful objects, wine and food, and his love of children, would probably have aged well. Today Capa and Chim would have been in their seventies. Possibly Capa would not have wanted to be an old man. The tragedy of Chim is that he was saving up inside for the quiet time ahead, in his corner of Rome where he kept his books. . . He hated violence and was killed by a mine.

A sort of Chim ghost appeared briefly – not the person but the role: the London photographer, Baron, took photographs of me for the *Tatler* for my first painting exhibition at Arthur Jeffress's gallery. After meeting in this way he gave me the task of arranging stories for him. When all was ready he would cross the Channel. It was like the old days except that nothing is ever the same – but we even wrote a story all over again about Anouilh, who was by this time living with his new wife and small son in Montfort l'Amaury; he showed us his paintings – before this no one had known he painted. In his ancient house, he believed there were ghosts. Anouilh always had magic, and always lived in seclusion – and so this old story was new. It was published in

Queen in 1956 and also *Film Und Frau* in Germany. The Germans published the photographs of Anouilh's paintings; the English version did not.

With Baron we then photographed Mendes-France looking gloomy in his gilt salon, sitting in a gold-leaf armchair. And then Baron had an operation on an old war wound, and a few days afterwards, he, too, died. He had not accomplished his great aim which was a story about Abbé Pierre.

For the summer holidays, as Guislaine grew to be twelve and thirteen, we sometimes went back to Spain, but never Madrid. Spain was familiar like home, and we both felt drawn there, yet it was rather ghostly. We only visited new parts that we had never seen. Once, in the north, on the road near Santander, some men passed our car and then blocked us, as in a hold-up. It was Antonio Bienvenida playing a joke, on his way to a charity bullfight with his two brothers. They gave us tickets.

Antonio ate nothing all day before the fight. An empty stomach was essential to keep the nerves at their keenest. He drank black coffee and then rinsed his mouth with water, but even water was not swallowed. Like all *toreros* before the fight, he spat it out on to the sawdust floor of the bar with splendid disdain, as if the spittle contained all the trash of the world. In the bar before the fight the atmosphere was electric . . . the *peones* waiting, his brothers waiting. . .

He placed his own *banderillas* gracefully and swiftly, but it was awesome to watch a person one knows. The older brother had gained weight and probably wished he weren't there (he had actually retired, and been brought back for charity). The younger brother was classic, but neither brother had the panache of Antonio, who was by then a great Spanish figure. At a previous charity fight the two other fighters had backed out at the last moment, saying they would not risk their lives for no money. Antonio took on all six bulls alone, an exhausting feat, and then gave the money away.

After the fight that day there was a celebration dinner. A crescendo of relief, cries, and talk surrounded Antonio in the restaurant where he ate his first food of the day. In Madrid I had known him well as part of a group, but had never sat with him alone. Now I asked the Anglo-Saxon question: how did he feel about killing? He loved the bulls, he said, they were his creatures. So how could it be? Death was unimportant, he said. He did not care about it for himself either. This was the opposite of English values. He said he had tried to make it a fair sport, by forbidding the shaving of horns. Fair? The bull charges in and does not know. He takes the man head on. A fox, when hunted, is pursued, and knows it. He hears the hounds howling and baying behind him, and is clammy with adrenalin. The bull is perplexed, but not frightened. So *there* to the English: fox-hunting was worse. Man is never fair. Bienvenida fought the dangerous way, with the grace of a dancer. He gave money away; he was a liberal and believed in causes. (Fourteen years later he was gored by a cow and killed – ironic, and in his view, probably fair.)

The next afternoon – who should be standing in the square outside but Vicente . . . We were far removed from Madrid. I had imagined us to be in another land almost and *Madrileños* always said they never came here. But he was in Santander to give a lecture at the University . . . by a fluke.

'¿*Quetal*?' we asked each other, each seeing Alvaro in the other's eyes. There was an old telegram in my bag that I always kept with one of his letters. Who was living in Fernando Santo now? Where . . . was he? I was devoured with longing and cowardice, and did not ask. And around us the cool evening started with the people twittering like starlings as they came out of their houses, chattachatta – *no me lo digas* – six abreast for their evening *paseo*. The things that are over never return, Lorca said, and Vicente had always quoted Lorca: *las cosas que se van, no vuelvan nunca*, and we said goodbye and drove off into the land whose lines have no interruption and so the shadows go on forever.

22

The novel I had written was accepted by Wingate, a small publisher in Beauchamp Place where the kettle was boiling all day for tea. Having paid highly to buy *Exodus*, they went bankrupt before publishing it, because of a six week printers' strike they could not sustain. Since they had also given me the job of designing their dust jackets, this was a double dud, saved however by Arnold Goodman whom I had just met. He gave the novel to Deutsch where it was accepted.

This large, generous man, Goodman, seemed to solve everyone's problems. At that date he was particularly involved in the world of theatre and cinema – though not entirely, since he was a lawyer – but there was never a lawyer with a more human side. He used to sweep into Paris with the panache of a Roman emperor and a following of devoted friends, including the film partners Launder and Gilliat, and Marjorie Portman. Many of them were 'regulars' who formed a sort of family and we would all drive up the hill to Montmartre in a hired limousine or dine in a Hungarian restaurant. He particularly liked the Westminster Hotel in Paris because there was never anyone there. One day he said, 'I think I shall complain to the management. There was someone in the lift this morning.' When I was in London, his house became like home. I dined there at any time, usually with the same group of people, or sometimes a surprise like the writer

Colin MacInnes or Aneurin Bevan.

With the money from my first novel I paid for Guislaine's appendicitis operation, which gave a feeling of positivity, since Dunstan had paid all her dentist's bills. Her father still appeared occasionally – a dashing character in a Bugatti at one point, slightly unreal. He gave her a watch, but still mysteriously never had any cash.

The novel had good reviews, was compared favourably with Sagan, then sank into the limbo where many novels disappear. I started to write songs, and at one of Arnold Goodman's parties I sang them. He arranged an audition and I met Bryan Michie, who gave me a contract for TWW. This was just before the 1960s started. It was not yet routine for people to write their own songs, nor had guitars become standard travelling equipment, so it must have seemed funny and 'different'. But it all suddenly got under way very fast – I felt like someone in a Western movie hanging on to the outside step of a fast-moving train, not sure I could clamber in – for I had not really meant to sing these songs myself, except as a 'demo' to get them across for a proper singer. But Bryan Michie liked my voice, and I was hired with no time to train it or have singing lessons, or learn about breathing . . . So what happened? When Bryan Michie was there I was a contralto nightingale. But at other times, when nervous with stage-fright, I discovered that an untrained voice does not always come out.

Suddenly I was making a film at Elstree, in a mixture of wild excitement and panic and – like those years before with Conover – I forgot to smile. One of the songs was a new version of the 'Owl and the Pussycat', a parody where it was the cat, not the owl, who sang with the guitar in the streets at night. For this the Paris Opera had made me a cat-suit which was splendid, with a tail and whiskers. I hid inside it feeling safe, only it was hard to get the voice out of all the black velvet. For the other songs I was given Pucci trousers and gold earrings; I was a sort of gypsy. When the singing came out well, I was giddy, flying, hooked – and smiling too. But I could not predict or control when this would be. However, for this half-hour film, in which I sang six songs, I was paid three hundred guineas. In 1958 this was probably like £1,000. I had a dressing-room and a maid . . . and then afterwards, still on this high wave, I found myself alone in Elstree looking for a taxi, carrying my guitar like a tramp or a Russian refugee. Everyone had disappeared, and no one drove me home. Anyway, where was home? It had all been part of the Dreaming.

If a manager had appeared things might have been different. There were many songs, both words and music – it is only a gimmick to write them, and great fun. Some were funny, others sad – some were ballads, others jazz; I sang them at parties. It had potential, even without a manager, for I was booked for the Hylton Show. I had laryngitis, and stayed in bed drinking port with honey, which was someone's idea of a cure. Even without direction, there was a rosy future, if I had just stayed where I was. But I muffed it. This time it was no arm of fate, but my mistake.

A man had invited Guislaine and me to stay. He lived in the Jura. He was a sad man, alone and lonely in a medieval dwelling which had been wrecked by the FFI in the war and never repaired. It was a castle in the fairy tale sense, not ostentatious like the châteaux in the Loire, but older, tougher, built originally for independence from France and as a military keep, for defence. Around this place stretched remarkable countryside: in the foreground the small Fiesole hills of Italy with the straight poplars, and beyond, the far distance of Spain. Yet it was neither Italy nor Spain; it was itself, the Franche-Comté, until 1639 an independent kingdom, not yet France. But there was a truly Spanish feeling. It had been occupied by the Spaniards of Charles V for two hundred years and they left behind their grapes and method of making sherry; this wine is still made there and called Château Chalon. When we went there, traces of Spanish could still be heard in the dialect, like *merienda* for their morning *casse-croute*.

Was it the Spanish side that appealed, or was it the sad man I felt a strange desire to look after and imagined I could help – or was it even perhaps 'home', that old hoax again . . . roots . . .

Anyway the rosy future sailed past like the view outside the train window. I had managed to climb on to the train in the Western after all, but it went through the station where we should have got out and did not stop.

The man roamed through his cavernous rooms, through the ruins not only of neglect and fallen stones, but of his own life – a failed marriage, lawsuits, the hatred of his ever-absent sons . . . There was a view stretching seventy miles through the windows, and he used to stare at this view like an admiral on a bridge, like a visionary, wondering what to do. He was tremendously moving, perplexing, and in need.

The first time I had met him this had not been the case. It was at a party in Paris where he talked ceaselessly. I had not liked him then and did not see him for a year. When the invitation to stay came, I had almost forgotten him – then I remembered that also at the Paris party he had played excellent flamenco on his guitar, so well that I even thought he might have been hired for the evening. Perhaps it was fate after all, or at least a normal mistake, to think that Guislaine and I would stop off on our way back from Italy, and spend a week with him – at his home that was right on our road.

Dormice scuttled, leaving strings of turds on the kitchen table; there was a mildew smell; the plates were wiped with old damask napkins with crowns on them (these had evidently outlived the dishcloths of which there were no useful or practical remains). While the sad man was in England during the war, with de Gaulle, the FFI had drunk most of the cellar, strangled a German prisoner with the chain of the doorbell, and left dereliction and chaos. Twenty-five years of abandon had followed; the repairs would be a large job. He roamed like Don Quixote, following chimeras, inspiring pity. He was St George fighting the dragon. We stayed a week, then two, before leaving for Cornwall to join my sister and her husband. Guislaine spent her thirteenth birthday there, and by the time we got to Cornwall we brought news that I was embarked on a new sort of fight. The television contracts of England were not signed; there were other plans now.

At the end of the summer I went to Paris to dismantle my little room and pack my things. The last telephone call received there was from Antonio Bienvenida, ringing from Toulouse, saying, 'This is the voice of Spain calling! Come down here to the bullfight.' We giggled happily, which should have been a sign – with the other person the little jokes were not always right, and jokes are a sign of bigger things. But by then the net had started to enclose.

I shared St George's love for his old building, to a point where we were dominated by it. It became a Being; we lent it feelings, we were saving a life, we were going to mend it – we became obsessed and spent years on this great task. Guislaine grew up and went to America where she got a job and her own flat. The castle was St George's inherited home, but to my disappointment he did not live in it. Instead he worked for the government and lived in Paris. We used to leave on Friday nights and drive for eight hours, arriving at dawn. The next day would be spent scrubbing, painting and hammering. All our holidays, any spare time, was lain as an offering at the feet of this elephant, whose foundations had been there since Roman times.

In January the walls were wet; we slept in sweaters and ski caps and gloves and still were cold. There were huge log fires in all the rooms, but the cold was of an ancient penetrating kind, contained in the walls for centuries. Red fungus and woodworm had to be treated. After the conquest by the French in 1637 the place had been sacked and burned, and only the stone walls left standing. The wooden roof over the big square keep had then been rebuilt. It was like a huge wheel with wooden pegs in the beams. High up over these beams, the wind wailed and moaned, filling the roof like a wooden sail. The people who had lived here had fought for independence; they had held belief, and I often thought of their lost freedom after the armies of Louis XIII had won. No longer used as a fortress, it was turned into supposedly a pleasure dwelling with panelling built into the dining-room – but none of this ever quite succeeded. It was not elegant; it was a rough place and wild. In the rooms downstairs, there was an ancient silence, a feeling of truth. Five hundred years seemed to hang still inside its stone walls.

It was dominating, a colossus – and in the end it remained untamed. It was our ship to set forth in – but the search led to Charybdis. The endeavour lasted ten years.

During this time my mother came to stay. She had followed the events with passionate interest. By now she was eighty and had had a stroke. She was told by her doctor that to travel to the Jura might kill her, and it was typical of her to say, 'Never mind, I have to die anyway. I am going to the Jura first.' Luckily she came before the sad time had started, and she died before having to learn it was a huge failure. When I registered her death at the Chelsea Town Hall, I looked back over all she had told me of her life and it seemed to me very short, though she was eighty-four (or eighty-six – it was never sure) when she died, and I was only forty then.

How to explain the failure? St George's lawyers betrayed him. He was not a free man but enmeshed in vicious lawsuits and hatred – but this was only the worldly aspect. It appeared also that the dragon he was fighting was himself. From one day to the next: he was mad. In ancient times demons took possession of people. An ordinary companion cannot exorcize a demon, even if ten years is spent in trying to do so. There are people who can be helped; pity then has a result. But if the one possessed remains unchanged, it is like pouring water into sand. The helper withers and fades, to no avail – and perhaps dies. Jung says each person carries his own shadow in his subconscious, and must learn to cope and not project it on to others. It became necessary to leave.

But there was happiness before the black hole grew, and there was a positive side: we had a baby, a little girl we called Georgia. She was premature, and though tiny, she was strangely robust. She was born in the spring at the time when the flower markets in Paris were selling hyacinths and white lilac, iris and pink hydrangeas. St George wore a pink shirt – his tragedy was in his inexplicably loving other side.

We lost the castle. Its beauty remains always in my memory; the chapel bell that tolled the angelus, announcing the day's departure for hundreds of years past, as it would those to come, inside a timeless world: light fading, light returning; old day, new day – a sort of permanence – the noise rolling through the rooms like a wave, up the stone stairway, filling the roof, the wooden sail of the grounded ship – then out through the valleys and into the land beyond.

As Trollope would say, we will leave St George here and continue our journey. Why did I write it at all? Because it was out of this factor, conceived in the strangeness of our union and genes, or maybe the castle and eeriness of the whole venture – that there came this little girl with her strong character, so enthusiastic, rushing headlong into life – a child to bring up with no bombs this time, no kidnappings, no war – just my baby in peacetime and in peace.

When she was five we went to live in London.

23

Our small house in Walton Street had a garden at the back which had the rare quality of not being overlooked. There was an apple tree with white blossom, roses, wistaria, old jasmine with a thick trunk, a grape vine and hydrangeas; I planted a passion flower that grew up to the roof. Three gardens further along there was a very tall sycamore tree, probably a hundred years old, that shaded several houses and was like a wood in itself. Blackbirds and wood pigeons lived in it, and thrushes sang from it at five on summer mornings, when the street was as silent as a village. Egon Ronay, whose house was on the corner, had a terrace built in order to sit in the bower made by this tree.

Georgia and I were happy; it was a lark, like being let out of bonds. Our own house. . . We enjoyed each toasted bun, each glass of wine with special savour. We were home and no one could bother us. We took immense pleasure in the little things: the regular robin and the chaffinches that came to be fed outside the kitchen window – the earthy smell of even a city garden. From this time on, though events caused us to move house many times, we were always 'home'. Each time there were our same books, the Kisling painting and Granny's rug. Georgia referred to my mother as if she had known her, though she had missed her, unfortunately, by two years.

She went to school farther down the same street in Walton

Place, skipping past the grocer, waving at landmarks; we loved the milkman and the singing Irishman who came to clean the windows.

I had an exhibition of paintings. During the 'ten strange years' I had also written three more novels which were published. One sold to Denmark and France, but in spite of this, there was no long-lasting result. We grew poor. Independence is expensive. The contracts I had been offered ten years earlier were no longer there; the world does not wait. Bryan Michie had died, and it was no longer original to write songs and sing them; everyone did so. But we were not daunted. I sold some Meissen cups and some furniture at Christie's. It was merely a period and would pass.

One day, after a routine visit to the dentist, where a tumour was discovered, it was announced that I had cancer.

Almost everyone is afraid of cancer, for the way it is surreptitious, the unknown enemy. There are people who, with any unexplained pain, imagine they have this still uncontrolled disease. Yet when it is actually announced, it seems incredible and untrue, in a way, unacceptable – why should I have this *now*? For I now had my greatest mission: bringing up Georgia was my total occupation and desire . . .So, as the truth dawned, the fear was primeval. Cancer is associated with death. But I must not die, we were only just starting . . . is that what they had implied, that I would die?

A hot, noisy room in the London Clinic on the Marylebone Road side. As the noise made it impossible to open the window for air, the door was left ajar on to the passage. It was so sudden. There were no visitors. I preferred anyway to hide, not to announce it – perhaps that way not to accept its reality. There was a sinister parade of Arab women in black robes with masks of gold beaks across their faces. This became a familiar sight in Harley Street later, but they were the first I had seen. They looked like the carnival figures in Ensor paintings, beaks to peck with, to nip at dressings. They turned their heads and looked at me through the doorway. I stared back with respect, as a liberal, yet disliking them, because I found them ugly. They were like birds of prey when I was trying not to die – vultures circling . . . How lonely you are tonight . . . are we your only visitors? How thirsty, yet you cannot speak . . . the nurse does not understand your animal noises through the bandages that mean: water. Please water. My throat is sandpaper sore. I used to sing. You are alone, you don't sing, you won't sing any more.

The operation had been announced for nine in the morning, but was not finally done until nine at night after waiting and wondering all through the long, lonely day. Georgia was at school, and staying with a friend. The next day my sister and her husband would come, and on the third day I would get away out of this hospital . . .

Our little garden seemed like paradise. I sat on the bench and prayed not to die until Georgia was grown up. Surgeons never enquire about the home life. A person is simply discharged – back to the housework or whatever they do. Yet out of this dreadful time, a great strength grew in me – in spite of fear, and the feeling that our position was precarious, though I had thought it safe. But I also saw that if we fought, we would win. But fear had to be continually chased. Some years afterwards, I met Mr Prosser of the Westminster Hospital; he asked me to recount this, but his story comes later.

In the meantime Walton Street, on the front side of our house, started to smell of car exhaust; traffic either poured down it, or remained nearly stationary at commuter time. I had a pre-monition about the old tree, and on the advice of Robin Fedden, applied for its conservation order. But it was cut down one deserted London Sunday when we were away, and Egon Ronay was also away. We returned from Wales, where my sister and Dunstan now lived part of the time, and we saw the corner of First Street and Walton Street piled high with green branches. The beautiful smooth grey trunk was in sections, leaving only a stump. The conservation men arrived two days later – too late – and the old fellow who had taken a hundred years to reach his prime, had been cut down by a speculator in order to cram more houses into its space, and Sunday had obviously been chosen on purpose. Its absence changed the nature of the small gardens, which lost their secrecy, and the ones at the corner became overlooked by iron windows, and a new bareness.

We sold our house and moved to the country near Oxford. The delight in this house was even greater. I drove Georgia to school each morning and fetched her again at four. Tea in the kitchen, and then she would rush out on to the lawn and dance on the grass, let loose and free. There was an immense view over the edge of a long bed of roses. There was also a pool, and an orchard where two old guinea hens roosted at night – they were there like caretakers when we arrived, as if it were really their house. They stayed until one by one the fox got them. In winter we had tea and did homework by the fire, and looked out at the frost. There was an apple tree outside the window with a large ball of mistletoe on it. When the thrush got inside these branches it looked like a Victorian Christmas card.

We stayed there nearly three years and would have remained. I had borrowed money to buy our Walton Street house, and when we sold it I repaid the money and there was a profit. St George made one long-distance gesture and bought the Oxford house – but with no maintenance – so when our 'Walton money' ran out, there was no more, as we had used up our small capital. It was simple, I told the bank manager.

'Ridiculous,' he said. 'People don't live this way.'

'Well, we do.'

'No salary, no allowance, no income?'

'Sorry.'

A job was necessary but not easy to find. I had not even had time to subscribe to BUPA, having been caught so soon after our arrival in England. The hospital bills had been tremendous, and the school . . . it began to rain bills and I dreaded the post. The bank manager was kind, if also incredulous. We started to borrow on our house for the rates, the fuel, and finally every sausage too was at fifteen per cent. We ate our gingerbread house . . . gradually, like unwilling mice, hoping for a miracle to patch it with.

The average person never believes there is no money; they think it cannot be true. But Arnold Goodman, who remained always a devoted friend and followed each event, understood.

In a way, he had foreseen this situation. Years before, when I was making what he thought of as the wrong decision, he flew to Paris especially to talk. We had dinner at Fouquet's. His kindness shone around him – his safety, my friend – but the dinner was an Impressionist painting, and I did not absorb the contents of his warning. Later, he never said 'I told you so'. As we had dinners together through the years, I would wipe my tears on his very soft, voile handkerchiefs, and send him some more for

Christmas. We made a joke of it and I became Squirrel Nutkin.★
But he never ceased to follow our Gulliver's Travels.

Now at this moment of tightrope-walking with the bank
manager, he had an idea. There was a job possibility: at one time I
had written a film treatment for Launder and Gilliat ('I hope they
paid you?' he would say, and chuckle). Perhaps now I could write
dialogue for films . . . he would look into it.

The job that would save us would have to be freelance. I could
not get a job in a local town, applying to an employment bureau
in Abingdon, for instance, because my English passport had been
removed and I now had an Australian one, a new rule for those
who were born there, which in turn meant a work permit would
be necessary. (I thought of Vsevolod: the civil servants were
sticklers for red tape, a permit would require a long time, and our
meter was ticking.)

In the meantime, the bank manager said, 'You must sell your
house and live somewhere smaller.' The debts were too big. And
then I got cancer again.

Guislaine had married and returned to Europe, and was now
living in London with her husband, a tall Englishman with red
hair. We put our house up for sale and moved to a flat in Milborne
Grove. Georgia returned to her 'old school' in London where she
had friends. The bus fetched her each morning and we were at
home again, with the same books and the Kisling, but somewhere else, and anxious.

I had two operations within ten days of each other. When I was
in hospital Georgia stayed with Guislaine and her husband Miles,
and I held on to various ideas: 'Man is immortal till his work is
done,' was a line from Goethe that Lesley Blanch often quoted. I
felt animal panic, alternating with holding on.

'My daughter is nine,' I said to the surgeon. 'She calls me
Fluffy Swan and Mazoue. I can't die. She needs me. Are you sure
I will live?'

'We will know afterwards.'

The surgeon was Robin Beare. He gave no false hope or
hypocritical reassurance. His tactics were those of dead honesty;

★Squirrel Nutkin: Beatrix Potter: the improvident squirrel who does not
harvest his nuts, and instead dances in front of the owl.

some people might prefer to be lied to. Yet when he did make a positive statement it was a certainty. It gave him great strength. One counted on him, but now it was cold news.

'I will cut out a piece of your jawbone,' he said, 'remove all the glands and sever a nerve. I am afraid your face may be crooked.'

The ten days of not knowing and waiting between hospitals, after the first operation had called for a second, were the longest days I have known. I was at home, at least, but wondering and wondering about the result – not letting Georgia know anything was wrong . . . 'What a bore to have to go back to hospital,' I said, as if there was nothing to it – looking at our familiar objects in the room that now took on a separate, unrelated appearance, as if they had nothing to do with me, as if I had levitated and gone, and was looking down from the ceiling into someone else's life. I might not be here any more. Yet I loved it and I shared with Georgia the enthusiastic pleasure in any aspect of it . . . And Georgia, my mission . . . At this thought, confidence would return . . . for I could not bear, and would refuse not to be there for her growing–up. But all the time I had to *hold on*. To wake at three in the morning and remember. (They are cutting a bone out of my jaw, cutting away my glands . . . but supposing *it has spread*? They will not know till afterwards, Beare said.) Think of something else. (How can you, if you might be dead?) I tried to think of someone funny, if this had happened to Dennis he would surely have said: 'Where am I? How did I get *here*?' But it wasn't funny. (Where is Dennis anyway, is he all right? Maybe he is ill. Are all the friends in Spain all right?) It was like going crazy. Then, control again: hold on. It will pass . . . all will be well. This was only a sort of dream. But it was not a dream; it was true. Fear. Pain. Never mind pain; to live was all that mattered.

Beare had trained with McIndo after the war, repairing burned pilots. He had been a bomber pilot himself. Think of the pilots, what they went through. Remember the war . . . All the same she can't grow up alone . . . not my baby all alone . . .

The Recovery Ward at East Grinstead seemed like a cathedral: I could hear smooth music. It was a paradox, for my head was a huge, hot balloon in tight bandages, with tubes coming out of my neck – but I was indeed a balloon, soaring, free, floating over the ward like a pink zeppelin. It was over. Operation over. There

200

were people walking about the room, which was a mixed ward. There was a policeman whose jaw had been smashed. He talked to me like a companion and hardship linked us, brothers-of-the-road again, like in the war. He had had an accident but another man had only had his ears pinned back, his being simply a cosmetic case. To look nicer, or to survive, humanity was fighting or plodding or enduring. We were ward-mates; we felt like friends.

The next day I was moved to a private room and rather missed these people. The result would not be known for three days, when we would receive the pathologist's report and know whether the malignancy had spread. The wait was long – seventy-two hours – but there was no more dread of the knife. After an ordeal has been overcome, a person grows naughty and impatient, and after the strain of holding on, there is a let-down, like a long, huge sigh of relief that could lift the roof. I kept trying to claw away the maddening bandages. The nurse insisted on eight pillows since it was necessary to remain sitting. Sit and endure.

Beare came to tell me the report was all clear. Outside the window, the leaves on the autumn trees seemed to be in some celestial light, a tapestry of gold luminosity – and Beare standing quiet beside the bed, the focus sharp on him like a beam out of the heavens in an old master when there appears a prophet's message. I could stay here. It was my picture too, not the lost world. Georgia and I were safe together.

'I am lucky,' I said, and Beare looked astonished.

'That's one way of putting it,' he said, and we both laughed.

We could laugh and make jokes again. The raft had stopped rocking. The balance was back.

'So you smashed up my face for nothing?' I said.

'We had to be sure.'

'You are a genius.'

'No. My hands do what I tell them, that is all,' he said modestly, and went loping off down the pasage with his quiet walk, like a distinguished lion.

In the following days I learned that he had a workshop where he made small beam engines function, and he also made silver jewellery. 'We are just artisans,' he said. He was a geologist and could recognize rare stones. He grew orchids, he felled trees on his land, and at the moment he was clearing a stream and was up to his waist in mud each weekend. He was a sort of Leonardo da Vinci. He was also a great surgeon. He could remove a tumour from an eye, then implant the cornea from this eye on to a man who would otherwise have become blind. He could save sight, save lives . . . Without cancer, I would not have met him. Illness usually changes the course of events badly – as it did in Spain. But sometimes it can bring faith.

Because of our finances, I did not stay in hospital long. After five days I was taken home in a car driven by Peter, a chauffeur I had found to take Georgia to school while she was staying with Guislaine, out of school-bus range. He was a New Zealander misfit who drove minicabs. He had given me a filigree crucifix as a talisman, which had been passed from sick people to each other as a ritual. I gave it back – there was a collective presence of others in this gesture, a feeling that trouble unites.

Leaving hospital felt like leaving a prison – the world outside looked new and unfamiliar. We drove through the yellow autumn into the grey suburbs of London, its leaves soot-bronze and tired. The driver said Guislaine would not bring Georgia home until the evening, after school and her supper. Surprisingly he asked if I would like to hear some jazz. It was an amazing suggestion, and as I considered it, I grew excited by the idea that I was saved, alive, would live, and it seemed like a fitting cele-bration, instead of waiting at home alone. We went straight from hospital to Ronnie Scott's in Soho – and found there a live legend, whose hammock-swinging Hot Club de France rhythm I had heard in France during the war. Now he was here and in person twenty-five years later: Stéphane Grappelly, bent over his violin like an elderly insect, practising in the afternoon.

He seemed to represent the miracle of life restored, except that I was bent over now too, and dizzy. The violin grew double, like an orchestra, bumble bees playing the double bass, wasps sawing at the cello, crane-flies plucking with their long legs at the violas . . . We had celebrated living, but the New Zealander was mad. Now we went home fast. We reached the house just as Guislaine arrived with Georgia, and we all seemed to be sitting on each other's laps, and crowing and laughing and hugging. Then: to lie still in the night and know it is all right. To hear Georgia breath-ing, and see the shadow of the cherry tree across her bed. To think: it is almost, not quite, but *nearly* worth the agony. And ever after I associated Grappelly's strange, swinging violin with a burst into recovery.

24

The Micawberesque optimism had been premature. Two weeks later I went to see Beare for a check-up. I went down the passage to his consulting room, singing happily. I had brought him some stones from my collection, to ask him their names. He knew them all: jasper, coalite, agate, jade, limestone threaded with quartz. But then he had an announcement to make: I was going to have radiation.

Hiroshima returned.

'Radiation! But I can't! They burned my head with it as a child! My hair all fell out! In Spain they burned my hip. It lost my fiancé for me. It took away my country. I can't have radiation, I hate it, I am terrified of it, it has only brought me harm.'

He could not understand why I was quite so anxious. How could he know? I was hysterical with suspicion, with anti–climax and disappointment; the primeval panic was back.

'They told me I have reached saturation point,' I said, 'and should not even have X-rays at the dentist. Surely it is not necessary? What are you hiding? Am I not cured then after all?'

'It is only a safety measure,' he said. 'Your enemy is cancer, and it did come back. It has gone now, and this is just routine, to make sure.'

'Routine! That scorcher that gave me ulcers?'

'Only because it must have been done badly.'

'But if I am cured, *why?*'

'To make quite sure.'

The celestial light turned to dejection.

Georgia started to wonder if visits to hospitals were part of other people's lives, other mothers of girls at school, and whether our house would be sold. She overheard talk of money disappearing. She did not worry; she had a merry disposition. But she did wonder, which is different, and as she grew up, she noticed. We should get a small cottage in Sussex, someone suggested, and not stay in London paying the rent. But the Oxford house had not sold, even at auction; so what with?

I told her we had a star to follow, and as I told her, I believed it. It was then that our star was born, or perhaps then that I noticed it was there. It would be a futile education for a child, to pretend that everything is always all right, but it seemed wise to accept that trouble is something that happens, and can be coped with – and so remove anxiety. In the years that followed we did truly have a star which shone especially when the road was perplexingly tortuous. We would hold to the star, and as Georgia grew older she frequently referred to it, calmly and confidently.

Beare sent me to Mr Prosser in the Westminster Hospital. He seemed at first to be dry and sardonic. He was a tall man, and the scars on his neck told that he had been through some horror himself. Later I made great friends with this deadpan Scot, who had a sudden twinkle in a very blue eye. But the beginning was fearful.

'Perhaps,' I said, grasping at straws, 'it will just be three or four times?'

'More like forty to fifty,' he said. 'Every day for six weeks.'

(Sick. It can't be. It isn't real. Suppose I refuse? Please, not after all the holding on, keeping tight control of myself, positive thoughts till the finish – then winning. So not any more. If I have won, can't I be left alone?)

I just said: 'I am afraid of the machine.'

He was surprised and quite interested to learn of the abuse of radiation I had had, even on my hands as a child. He became kind.

'Cancer is a tiger,' he said. 'When you shoot, it turns round and bites you.'

'You mean it might come back *again?*'

'Not if we make sure it can't.'

That made some sort of sense. So did his calm, unmoved tone of voice. We were hunting together then. We made somewhat corny but reassuring jokes about shooting in Sussex, where he went at weekends. He instructed the Japanese assistant who worked the monster-machine to be careful of my hairline, so that my hair would not fall out . . .

But closed up in the room, locked into a science-fiction space-ship cabin, the machine set at my throat, the jaw marked with blue crosses like Jewish doors under Hitler – the line from the ear down the whole jaw . . . I was frozen with all the old fears. What is courage? Trying to have no imagination. But imagination is stronger than mental discipline. Could the enemy really be back in my body? The room anyway is full of rays, so that no one can stay with you. The Japanese operator looks through the port-hole. But when his face disappears you are alone and clamped in and cannot get out. The rays must be harmful, if a person has to receive them alone.

When I went home and lay down, the bedroom was full of black dogs, whirling, flying. I felt mad. How could I look ahead to this for six weeks? I shivered and trembled, with a cold feeling and clamped throat. The curtains flew out in the draught. I was quite alone all day when Georgia was at school, and thank goodness she was – because by teatime when she came home we read aloud and played the gramophone and I had hold of myself. There comes a point beyond endurance, one thinks, but this is not so. It passes, and there is nothing one can do but accept – and even in this dragging down of the spirit (for the machine is tiring and depressing), there is a sort of peace. Accept. What can you do? *Es igual*.

The dreariness of the waiting-room in the Wesminster base-ment became an interesting reflection. We all sat waiting our turns in this grey room with the dog-eared magazine (there was usually only one) . . . What could be done about it? A fresco of a large view? The fact that these rays went on underground made the place particularly airless and enclosed. I wondered about the staff and the doctors who spent their lives in this dirty old womb . . . with never a window to open. And the other patients wait-ing, were they all frightened? Where were their homes, how far did they come each day? Should we not speak to each other? We were all going to die sometime, so why should we fear? (Remember Bienvenida . . . Yes but Georgia – give me at least ten years. *Please*. Anyway I like it here. You *need* people like me. Who am I talking to; is it God?).

I studied the faces near me, but did not speak. It was absurd. How could I console or comfort them? Surprisingly, they did not look anxious. They just looked like people waiting for a train, except for one wan woman.

Horseferry Road and the way home. Every day. The Tate Gallery was next door. Sometimes I looked at paintings and stared once into one of Bonnard's gardens – but I was usually too tired. I reflected on organized help for the patients – useful help, not just a chatty amateur – and then gave up the idea; a doctor I spoke to found it superfluous, and looked at me as if I were slightly nutty. Each person has to carry his own burden, he seemed to say. Let them get on with it. Yet surely they all thought about death as they waited for their saving rays? Apart from suicides, who wants to die before their season comes? And even then it is 'not minding' rather than wanting. If people race cars or hang-glide, they risk death but do not believe it will happen and do not think of it anyway because the excitement of their action is life for them; they are living to the full and do not consider dying. But cancer is to be told you have a killer in the house of your body. There is no action. All you can do is wait while it stalks, to see where it will strike. 'There are ways of fighting,' Prosser said, 'and some people win.'

Another doctor appeared now in our lives, by a fluke. He had given the anaesthetic four years earlier and was not involved this time. He had only happened to hear the news and telephoned out of kindness. The timing was at the low ebb; he must have guessed because he called on us often then and greatly helped through the dark time. Horseferry Road was a drag. I was an old horse and my neck had started to burn. I had given up wondering how to help the other patients because I was a zombie. Food had no taste yet I retained the sense of smell and was hungry. A roast cooking made me ravenous, but I could not swallow because food tasted like sawdust, wodge to force down and choke. The new doctor, our friend, brought me lichees because they were cool. What did he actually do? Nothing, or everything. He was there. Sometimes he stayed away – he seemed to know when. He never imposed. He telephoned. He asked if I needed anything. The feeling this gave was unprecedented.

He had no conversation, which was restful. Normally it might have been dull, but now it was water in a desert. He was silent furniture in a cool room, quiet in a house after loud noise – after a voice that 'droned on somewhere' (as Meredith said of Willoughby Patterne) 'and ceased not' – after clamour . . . the hallucination of our only visitor from abroad, when Guislaine had asked for help and it was refused . . . and there were voices shouting and her tears . . . He suffered too – but could only see his own kaleidoscope colours – he never noticed the tears of others, and it had become Munch's *Scream*.

I felt this doctor might be like the description of the Jane Austen man by Stuart Hampshire: 'Men of few words and contained feelings, who always mean more than they say. They do not chatter or gush, their prose is lean . . .'

Whether he was really that way did not matter; the timing of his appearance was miraculous. He was usually untidy in crumpled clothes and had lost his glasses. He had an exceedingly sweet expression and his hair was thick and shaggy like an airedale – when it stuck on end Georgia called him Gollywog, then later she called him Shaggy Doc.

'I like his speed,' said the professor one day when he came to see us; it was well observed. He always walked fast and with underlying energy. He would run and bound up the stairs when I stood waiting at the top, with eagerness, like a young boy. So finally Georgia called him Dash because he dashed everywhere he went.

And so life settled. Milborne Grove, a flat on the first floor overlooking gardens – and as the spring came, the green shoots appeared. The yellow bus came to fetch Georgia each day to go to school. It was full of little girls, wearing their Hampshire School hats, twittering like birds and waving out of the window as the bus drove off. We were back in place. At night we heard owls, there were three colours of lilac in the street, and one garden had iris of five different colours. *I will live* was happiness. The machine did not matter; I put up with it.

We had brought our small piano with us from Oxford, and while Georgia was at school I started to write songs, then the story for a musical. It grew absorbing. To the songs I had sung on television I added others. After working out the melodies on the piano, and fitting the words, I took them to a man called Louis Mordish, who had played at Guislaine's wedding. This man was a natural and could play anything. He arranged the orchestration. He was musical director for Dickie Henderson but had spare time. We arranged harmonies together, and he shaped the music. It felt like making a film: 'Try this in ragtime Louis,' and there it was. 'Now try it slow.' He was brilliant. I was brilliant. We were shooting a movie in the Sahara. Or the Gold Coast. Or Hong Kong. I wrote the words and music, but without him it would have been nothing; we were a team.

Each day I would drive out to Wembley, where he lived high up near the park. I hardly needed to drive – I felt drawn, and the car was drawn by remote control – I could hardly wait to hear him play, to create together and sing. Singing was fascinating; something had been given back to me. 'I Live on Windfalls and Dreams'. New songs in a major key, not sad ballads. 'What's Money? It's Only a Commodity' (this title from a remark of Lord Goodman's). We would work for hours, for days. Louis's appearance was slightly like Chim's.

'Good morning, what awful news today,' I would say, (it was at the time of the miners' clash with Heath and the three-day week) and with ancient Jewish wisdom he would answer, 'The news has always been bad.' It was a Chim joke.

When I went home, Georgia was there to tea. We were safe. Each morning, after hospital, it was regular, like going to an office job . . . through Shepherd's Bush, past the Balzac Bistro, the North Pole Road, wondering about the origin of these names given to the grey, greasy suburbs of the world's largest capital city – and each turn of the road led to the green hill where we made music: Mayo and Mordish, like Gilbert and Sullivan.

For a (fortunately therapeutic) time I floated in a Walter Mitty haze, remembering the excitement when Gene Kelly made *An American in Paris* and the feeling that singing and dancing always gives, and forgetting that it was twenty years ago, or that I had only met Frank Loesser once and he would not remember who I was. Never mind. We belonged together. Creation is always in the present tense. I longed only to sing and dance, and forgot radiation.

We made a recording of these songs that was slightly hysterical, having hired a studio for one hour only. We were told rather late that pop groups allowed one hour for each three-minute song, in order to go over it and get it perfect. We went through all our fourteen songs in the hour – and in any case did not have the money for more time. There was no repeat, no time to correct a mistake – and considering this, the tape was splendid. The piano of Mordish could make anything all right – though our method would certainly have been described by Demi Gates as 'Cough, Choke, Gasp' . . .

It was satisfactorily finished, and nothing came of it. I gave it to an agent who put it in a drawer. I did not care about the 'book' or scenario, which was not very good (about two couples whose fate was changed by the strange presence of an enigmatic man) but I was sad about the songs, because people would hum them after hearing them only once, and I knew some of them were good. Lord Goodman always whistled 'Poor Charlie', and my sister and Lesley Blanch cried at 'Lost People', Dash liked 'I Live on Windfalls and Dreams'. It seemed a waste, but waste is a large part of life.

The radiation was over.

'You'll feel great in a year,' said the Japanese Sandman. 'It takes about that long.'

When I said goodbye to Prosser, there was a faded beauty visiting him, with what appeared to be a younger and healthier husband, but both looked stricken: the verdict must have been bad.

When we were alone I asked Prosser if I could not say something to encourage.

'I got through it somehow, shall I tell her? She can be a winner.'

He was strangely cold. 'No,' he said. 'She has the Devil behind her. She left it too late.'

It was amazing: this kind man, my friend Prosser sounded unkind. He indicated no sympathy because, it seemed, she had not tried. She had allowed the tiger inside her house and not cooperated . . . (perhaps refused radiation?) She was evidently not new to him. It seemed a harsh vindication. Was she damned just by the mathematics of her failure to act? Was it just bad luck? Or did she have the incurable type . . .? No, for then he would not have been unkind. How difficult it seems, to give help – real help – not just charity.

'*But*,' said Prosser with a certain violence, 'you are to tell anyone and everyone, whenever occasion arises, that you have been cured. You must come here for check-ups regularly so that it is down in the files. This gives courage. There are people who must know – the fighters must know. Tell it, spread it.' This, presumably, might be of real help . . .

So: write it, and I have done so here.

25

One day after eighteen years, and out of the sky, Alvaro
telephoned. How could this be possible? I looked at the receiver
as an unreal object; but it was true. It was really his voice . . . A
friend he had run into in the street in Madrid had given him our
telephone number. Suddenly it was like yesterday, only a generation later. He had married but it had been a failure, over and
done with. He had two grown children. He had been to America,
had worked in a Coca Cola factory in Belgium, and was now
running the Castilian land as his full-time work. His parents were
dead. It was 1974. My daughter was ten.

He suggested that we meet, and my thoughts were off like an
arrow, agreeing to anything. Georgia was due to spend a holiday
with a schoolfriend in France, visiting her father and her aunt and
speaking French. I said I would go to Spain.

'I am fat with grey hair,' he said. 'Will you recognize me?'

'My face is crooked and my neck is burned – will you recognize
me is more to the point? Horrorshow.'

We arranged that I would drive to Biarritz, and he would be
waiting, in a certain cafe . . .

When I told Dash about this, he was fascinated. He knew the
story and thought this was to be the happy ending. He had
business of his own to attend to in Spain – a flat to sell near
Marbella – and with typical kindness, said he would go at the

same time, in case I needed anything, in case something went wrong.

When I reached Biarritz and stopped outside the cafe, there he was. His hair was indeed grey but thick, and he was brown; he had gained weight but was not fat. Always before he had dressed carefully and worn beautiful suits; now he was in a blue cotton shirt and jeans, but not anyone's jeans – they were neat and clean and special. He was a man in a Spanish Western, yet not, for he looked like no one else. He was superb. He did not mind my crooked smile, and said it hardly showed, adding, 'My God, as if it would matter anyway . . . don't you remember *Cornered*?' We sat down at a table for lunch, staring at each other curiously and in a way, shy – and I did remember *Cornered*. It was an old film we had seen together, the first in which Dick Powell played a straight part. There was a great love in his life, and when asked (by someone curious and slightly jealous) what she had been like, he had said quietly, 'She never had the proper food, she was thin, she had crooked teeth . . .' It was foolish and feminine, I suppose, to have felt anxious because when he had known me I had not been crooked – but it was not the point – only that when two people meet after many years, with things of overwhelming importance to say, they often start off by discussing the time of the train or whether there are clean sheets. Is it nerves? . . . or just the absurdity of life . . .

We drove off in two cars, stopping in San Sebastian where again, in a bar in the old quarter, he spoke Basque to the bartender, who knew him. Why had I left him, and Spain, he half asked me, but only half – and maybe again by some mistake (or perhaps rightly, who could ever know?) I did not explain or go into it all again, when the present and possibly the future seemed shining, and that old past so dire. I was vague. (Why think again: how different it could have been? How much had Maria been hurt? She was dead now and it was too late to make up for it.) Instead I asked how his parents had died, and what had happened to our various friends. There was an old couple in the bar who apparently came regularly and had done so for years. They were the worse for wear and both had slightly purple skins. Alvaro found them endearing, and said he loved the way they loved each other. How understanding he was, and now the jealousy had gone, he was mature. Though he had always seemed older than his age, his character seemed to have settled. How was the professor, he asked, and when hearing he had lost his job, said he had always liked *fracasados*, failures . . . and we played the language game again; it sounded like fricassee, something – 'worn out' in a stew. There was a word for the blues after all: *la morriña* – but it was a Galician word and so did not quite count; Castilians must endure, he said, and Castilian is another word for linguistically pure Spanish . . .

When we reached his house the *encargado*, the old farmer, recognized me. Could it be *Howards End* – coming home? There was no telephone in the long ranch house. He listened to music when he was here, and was purposely away from the world. The bedrooms had linen sheets and thick bedspreads, chosen by Maria; one could feel her still here. It was very hot by day but cold by night. We slept with warm blankets. There was a log fire, music, and talk. We cooked our own food. Some invisible person from the farm came occasionally and cleared and cleaned – but never disturbed. Outside, the broom was yellow everywhere, in full flower, and when we saw a golden oriole Alvaro was excited. He was interested in birds, but when it came to visiting the land, he preferred to sit in his jeep – so I walked.

The old man was going along a track beside the fields in a cart, with a rust-coloured horse and a dog following. The dog stopped sometimes, sniffing the air, pretending importance. Alvaro said he was foolish and *sympathique*, but the old man said he was most useful, *bueno* by day and *malo* at night. And he got out of the cart to help the horse up a hill, singing to himself in snatches of a sad primitive song.

Alvaro had business in Madrid, so we had to leave. When we arrived, our old city was unrecognizable – I could not even find my way about. Traffic, noise, smell. 'Yes it is hideous, is it not?' Alvaro said. 'Spain has grown up. Everyone now has cars, everyone lives together without being married, everyone on the beaches wears bikinis . . . remember when the *guardia civile* tried to arrest you?'

Then I told him I had been dreaming of the ocean, in the basement of the Westminster Hospital, and would like to swim. But when I talked of the south (the only beach in Spain not yet ruined was on the Atlantic, south of Cadiz), he suggested I go

214

alone while he finished his business. It was so normal and yet so strange – as if we had been an old couple all along – and here was his 'English' side again. I remembered him once meeting my bus, eighteen years before, after I had been to Valencia to write my column. All the peasants with their live chickens and chatter tumbled out, followed by me – and Alvaro was standing there immaculate in his clean suit, the English Sunday papers folded under his arm, and with faint annoyance said, 'Noisy people, aren't they?' as if I too were Spanish, but he was not. Now it was a continuance of the same joke. He did not like the south; it was far too hot. But it seemed peculiar to go away, after coming all this way to see him. 'But we have all our lives,' he said. 'Are we not going to make them together?'

We telephoned Dash, who was already in Marbella, and he said he would look after me. He was longing to leave his repulsive town and said he would meet me at the beach near Zahara, where there were lilies. So Alvaro and I had acquired many different habits – normal in any couple – but all the same, somehow, the wheels seemed to have slightly left the tracks.

'But you *must* be with Alvaro. It has to end that way,' said Dash a few days later, walking along the windblown sand near Trafalgar, where there were shells and white crests on the waves. We went into a cafe in a village, full of old men, and drank thick, black expressos and tried to get through on the telephone. Dash asked Alvaro to change his mind and come down here – but the line was bad and he could hardly hear – so instead Dash said I would be back the next day. Dash then discovered Chinchon, the strongest, driest anis, and later also the splendid Spanish word *resaca* (undertow), meaning hangover.

We drove to Madrid, where Dash was planning to take the plane back to London, but by the time he arrived, with Chinchon all the way, he went to the Ritz for the night, appearing there in a wild state, and was refused entry to the bar without a tie. He said he thought his mission had failed.

Alvaro took me to dinner with his cousins. He said, 'She loves Spain,' with a mixture of amusement, surprise, and pride. Then it was time for me to fetch Georgia from her holiday and start back. He drove the car for me to Barcelona, a long six hundred kilometres, and we rested for a few days in the house of a friend of his who lived on the Costa Brava. This friend was Basque. His name was Jesus, pronounced Shoos in Basque and he lived in one of the few remaining unspoilt villages, inland from the sea, and was angry at the smell of pigs. But it was ghostly; there was an echo of 'before' when Robert Ruark had been at Palamos, because Ruark was now dead.

In the mornings we drove a few miles to the coast and Alvaro accepted this northern sea. He sat on the beach while I swam, reading *Time* magazine and looking angry with the world. We had dinner under the trees with Shoos and his lady and many friends, and we talked most of the night, every night. Staggering up a stone staircase out of the village square to go home, Alvaro groaned once, 'I feel so *old*, Little Gael,' and I had to tease him and laugh – he was only forty-six. But he was so physically lazy, riding while I walked, reading while I swam. His mind was the agile part of him – his swimming consisted of flopping into the sea and out again. (I had sometimes wondered about our age difference, but it would not have mattered.) I felt well, and brown, and whole again. But sick of no sleep . . . We agreed he would come to London in the autumn. I drove away the next day to fetch Georgia, and went to bed in a hotel in Perpignan, unashamedly, at nine p.m., and slept like a hibernating bear.

He came to England. He came by car, but since he said he always got lost in the London suburbs (never unstuck from the South Circular Road), I took the train and met him at Dover and we stopped on the way to London to have lunch in the village of Chilham. He had sherry first, and the publican started telling him about the different brands. Never did he guess that this English-looking fellow in the tweed jacket was a friend of the Domecq he was speaking of, and had known all about sherry since he was born, because he was really a Spaniard. The joke never wore thin, because it worked every time.

We did not make our lives together, though both of us wanted to. A mist must have risen, that cannot be explained. I have a green bathing towel that he bought me in a shop on the way to the beach – so I know it is true and really happened because it is there in the linen cupboard, Alvaro's towel.

He stayed with us in Milborne Grove. Georgia loved him and polished his shoes. He had huge Spanish siestas in London, in the autumn, when people went to bed quite early, but he woke up at six, hoping for a proper evening.

He took Guislaine and Miles out to dinner at the Mirabelle. When he had last seen Guislaine she had been ten, the age Georgia was now. It was continuity, and he was family, in his too-small dressing-gown (his dressing-gowns had always been too small). I still wear the medal of Fatima that his mother gave me, and have kept her letters, which are in my desk. We went house-hunting in Sussex, and it was with Alvaro that we found the cottage we moved to with the remains of our gingerbread money.

But dreams do not come true; it is rather that real things become dreams.

26

'Go and say hello to Vsevolod,' Stephen said to me in the Dunes Club, Rhode Island, in August 1978. 'He would love to see you.'

'Of course. Where is he?'

It was twenty-six years since I had seen him, or been back to America. There were various people sitting on the wide wooden deck, under parasols, with the strong white American sunlight around them and the blue ocean behind. Jean was there, seeming unchanged. There were a few elderly men in flowered shirts of wild, Hawaiian design, and an old fellow with wisps of white hair blowing in the breeze. Could that be . . .?

'Vsevolod.'

He turned to look at me with a faint smile, and a steady, deep look out of very brown eyes, and it was indeed his same but lined face, once I was close. Jean had told me he had been ill, after his mother had died ten years earlier. The power of this small, dominating woman had suddenly been withdrawn. She had idolized him, rather like Romain Gary's description of his own mother in his autobiography, and had brought him up in the golden image of what she believed him to be, and required and expected him to become. Even without this burden, it is probably not easy to be the only son of a widow whose husband has left her. Her absence had caused him vast depression, and co-incided with his old age. He had then had a mild stroke, about which the doctors were not explicit. They had prescribed drugs that Jean thought were too strong, and perhaps this was what had damaged his brain – for something had happened to him. He was better, yet had not recovered, and his face was affected on one side.

His family surrounded him: wife, daughter-in-law, grand-sons. One of them started to help him put on his shirt, for he had been sitting in the sun with a bare chest. His arm would not go through the sleeve. With them pushing and struggling with him, he suddenly looked at me and laughed. The laugh was tremendous, the gleam in his eye held all his old humour. How diminished was he really then? Or was the joke on us? Had he perhaps recovered, but was forgetful . . . or was he just bored with convention? Had he opted out because he could not be bothered?

'Vsevolod, put this on, you've had enough sun. Stand up a minute . . .' Why not leave him alone? He didn't need his shirt. He was used to a lot of sun. He went on smiling his cuckoo's nest smile – maybe having his joke outside us.

The next day he was in the garden in Saunderstown, with the roses and the picket fence, opposite the house where Edith Wharton had lived. There was a book on his lap. He smiled again his faint, enigmatic smile. Jean was in the kitchen in her bathing suit, the August heat was heavy like a damp blanket. She was brown – the constant swimmer with ash-blonde hair pulled straight back showing her good bones. She glanced frequently through the window at him with a mixture of anxiety and hope, and sometimes – impatience. This talkative husband, who had fascinated her with his European glamour and sophistication, was now silent. This love she had lived with for thirty years, often unfaithful and absent, was now stuck at home; she had to dress him, pot him out at times, to wash him when he forgot. He would roam no more. It was ironical that she would have wished it some other way: home, but differently.

He talked a little in his green garden, with the ropes of honey-suckle and wild grapes round the edge, and what he said was to the point. His malady was certainly puzzling and paradoxical – at times he seemed entirely himself, only a bit mysterious. At other times he was absolutely not there. The book on his lap was poetry that he had written. I borrowed it to read that night in bed. It was in the classic French tradition. It seemed odd that here was this man who had been saved, given a nationality, allowed to work, found his perfect wife . . . and yet France still gnawed at his heart. (Romain Gary had said, 'I have not a drop of French blood, yet France runs in my veins.') Ironically, in spite of his happy life in an American homeland, Vsevolod's poetry contained nostalgia and even pain.

> *A la gloire, à la mort, j'ai préféré la vie*
> *Renaître avec Paris valait bien une messe*
> *Trop tard, hélas, car j'ai vendu mon droit d'ainesse*
> *Pour l'exil sans retour, par delà des Antilles.*

There was another poem called 'The Scar'.

> *Cicatrice:*
> *Europe! Ma maîtresse abandonnée*
> *Du puits sans fond où glisse l'anneau d'or*
> *Monte la clameur de nos randonnées*
> *Mais déjà près de moi, calme, captive*
> *L'Amerique mon epouse s'endort*
> *Afin que mon identité survive*

As so many times before, I wondered why the French had behaved so strangely with their White Russians. For what logical purpose? The French always see themselves as logical, lucid, Cartesian. Why not have accepted the devotion of these refugees and put it to good use? It was such true devotion, and loyalty. Vsevolod chose a French *nom de plume*, Jean Deneveure, rather than his own Russian name; a pity – but it was probably his love of the language that made him want a name that belonged to it. Again he showed this unused longing to belong. It seemed mad to have forced him out of France, and yet, he had found Jean.

That night he appeared again in the Dunes Club. This time his hair was not flying in wisps but had been combed and was smooth like a silver cap on his head. He was dressed elegantly in white flannel trousers and a blazer – and as always, he wore his small, private, Mona Lisa smile. He danced with Jean. The floor was open along one side on to the dark ocean and the night sky.

The orchestra played classic old jazz tunes against the faint rasp of surf. The room was full of Americans in their parrot-coloured clothes, except for this one man who was different: a distinguished elderly Russian, placing his feet neatly in a classic tango, with a woman who had visibly danced with him for years; they moved like one person, swooping, reversing, wonderful to watch. Unfaithful or not, he had loved her truly, and he called her Rose.

The last time I had watched him dance in a ballroom was when we had crossed the equator, on the boat full of saved refugees. He was thirty-one. Where had it all gone? Thirty-eight years dissolved into the Dreaming.

When he was young, he was politically a liberal and stood up for the underdog. Though he was funny and loved by his friends as a 'good chap', I used to think he talked too much and I hated his lewd jokes. At seventeen I did not understand. Also I was a late developed seventeen, and thought his various sexual obsessions both boring and uncomfortable. But now this familiar old fellow was endearing and rather likeable – he made me feel maternal, somewhat too late. The new silence he had developed made a strong impression, and the occasionally precise phrase he spoke would indicate he seemed to follow conversation. He had been an open book; now he was a mystery. His family could not fathom the blank – what was it hiding? Was he a little gaga, or very wise? He certainly listened when they referred to Dad as having to be led to the lavatory, or when his dessert (chocolate cake) was ordered for him as for a child. He heard, but his face muscles did not move. Then suddenly there would be the laugh. Peals of laughter at someone's joke, taking it in. Whether crazy laugh or true, it was infectious and made one immediately laugh too. What the hell, something or other was very funny indeed.

Georgia had her American summer that we had been planning since she was ten. It came true when she was fourteen. She saw America, her brother and sister again (for Guislaine and Miles were now living in America too), and their families and their homes; at fourteen Georgia was an aunt.

Newport . . . the Jamestown bridge, grey houses with white shutters . . . the reflected light of the sea coming into Stephen's house in Saunderstown, built on to the land where we had stayed long ago with the professor. The garden slopes down to a bay where there are mussels and clams on the rocks. Stephen and his wife Wendy have three boys. We picked wine-berries with them, scrambling through the woods, avoiding poison ivy, respectfully stalking the bull in the field on the way back. We lived all together for two weeks taken out of the Dreaming, like a small life set down apart. Wendy is a botanist, so she knew the names of all the flowers, grasses and rushes. She is the great-grand-daughter of the French actress Réjane, whose daughter married an American surgeon in the Great War. Stephen became a businessman in New York, but Saunderstown is where the heart is – where they grow vegetables and flowers, swim, wind-surf, cross-country ski in winter – and where the children ramble off and lead their own lives, American fashion, which they have done since they were small.

We also stayed with Guislaine and Miles and their two small daughters, in their house in a tall, silent forest in Katonah. Miles won a scholarship to Radley and was an Oxford blue; there is a large oar over the fireplace in their hall. Their forest is wild, the trees immense – yet in one hour he is in Wall Street handling high finance, with a view of big sky and sea from his office window.

Georgia saw Chinatown, Little Italy, the soaring buildings; she looked up, standing at their feet, craning her neck back in amazement to see them move in wheeling circles against the sky. From Radio City Observation Roof, the pinnacles were floating in grey August smog; they looked like mountain peaks in a lake. On the street corner below, young musicians played 'Stardust' . . . Demi Gates was in New York; a misty light came into his eyes when Spain was mentioned . . . We saw Capa's little brother Cornell, who was always known as Corny. He took us to the photographic museum on Fifth Avenue where there is a bronze bust of Capa, the legend who never really died . . . the painter Joan Higgins, with her long blue eyes . . . Suky and Maughan Gould whose house we managed to stay in for two nights (you stinker, why did you take so long?) . . . Bob Harbach ('I Want to Be Happy') . . . 'Where are we, how did we get here?' as Dennis would have said . . . But already we are no longer here, and the plane rises up over the long American coastline, flying back over the places where we stayed: Nantucket, the whaling port with cobbled streets, grey houses

with white shutters . . . over the cousins we never reached in
Maine . . . on toward the wild islands of Newfoundland. A three
week excursion ticket, the time is up . . . it is already last
summer.

'Unreal,' said Georgia, as we drove along the roads of France in
our little old blue car, back to routine. 'Did it really happen?'

In Paris we visited two publishers (whose letters Jean had
shown me) to see if we could have Vsevolod's poetry published
in France – the book I had read had been published in Canada. (In
a strange, nonsensical way, he still seemed to be my first, and
now rather ghostly mission.)

Jean also gave me Meerson's address: I had lost him completely
ever since the war. 'He managed to escape to the south of France,
where he married,' Jean told me. 'His wife hid him in the woods
and took him food. He decided to dress like a workman, but
ordered such well-cut overalls that he looked more like a fashion
drawing. One day the Germans did arrive. He came out to speak
to them, thinking, well, if the game is up, it has to be . . . But all
they wanted to know was the way. He gave directions, and said
to his wife afterwards, "You see, one should always face the
Germans." "Yes dear," she answered, "but don't ever show
them your profile."

Thirty-five years later we sat in a cafe below his office in the Place
de la Madeleine, and he told me the rest. He had used our *passeur*
for the escape, had gone to a landowner friend in order to hide,
and had married the daughter of this friend. Today he is art
director of Mode International. But he is still bitter, even these
many years later, about what he calls the French betrayal of him
in the war, recalling that it was the French police who took him to
the Germans. But he has managed in his fashion. 'Each time I got
a kick in the arse I advanced a few yards,' he said.

I told him I was writing some of the things that had happened
to us all, but the difficulty was there was so much to leave out, yet
still too much to put in . . .

'Yes,' he said, 'life is on several parallels. We could all write
three or four versions of our autobiographies, all different, all
true.'

The philosophy of this remark was a relief from his bitterness.

It filled me with resignation and fatalism, and therefore peace. It was all so long ago still to be so bitter, yet it had passed so quickly. Suddenly – we were thirty-five years older. Looking back on Meerson's escape and the German occupation was like seeing an old documentary film. I no longer felt the violent hatred I had for Pétain in my youth, and saw him in retrospect rather with pity. He was an Arras peasant, brave in the First World War, but in the last war he was senile. They propped him up and used him as a puppet, then stripped him of his decorations; and he died, bemused. Disgraceful he was indeed, in the last war – but he still deserved a soldier's burial for his courage in the Great War, and did not get it.

We sat and drank our coffee in silence before returning to the present, and then by some coincidence, Meerson said, 'Spain is the place.'

He looked at his watch and stood up. 'I must go back to work. That is where I would live, if I could choose, but it's too late now.' And he went back to his office, taking his long strides, in a beige corduroy suit and high-necked blue sweater, appearing just as outstanding as when his looks had caused him to hide.

Too late now. One life is not long enough. Spain is like a love affair that never really ends. But France is reason; not the passionate and erratic politicians, but the good sense of life and the way of living it. It is a sort of central balance in the middle of Europe, where the head rules the heart – in spite of the paradox of being unsafe or unstable in time of war. It was not really the French people who mistreated the White Russians, but their bureaucrats – the same 'race apart' in any country.

How to understand the sadism of civil servants – those small, safe men? In Normandy another sort of small man tends the gardens of the war cemeteries, where his brothers lie under the ground in the name of freedom; that old fight which is still not won. One hopes they did not die in vain, but the world seems so dissatisfied now, even though human conditions are so improved.

Like a small piece of patchwork in an immense tapestry, man builds or knits his inch into the pattern. His passage here is just a flash visit even if he lives to be ninety. The mountains are geologically aeons old; the cathedrals built by man for God – though also for other men – took hundreds of years to complete.

But that was in the days when man was not in a hurry for an immediate result.

What happened to the White Russians? They have nearly all gone now. The club in the rue Boissière, run for naval officers of the Czar, has been closed each time I have passed in the street this year. Inside, on its dusty gothic walls, there hang photographs of Nicholas II and Alexander III. Last time I was there the dinner was served by a creaking princess, to superbly handsome old men with very blue eyes. Anglo-Saxon blue eyes look grey at night; but there is a quality in Russian blue that remains brilliant in the evening, whether by electricity or candlelight. Yousoupoff had this bright blue look, and so apparently did Nicholas II. So does Ala, widow of Ter Abramov. But the last Czarist admiral must have died, for the door of number 40 rue Boissière, the *Foyer des Officiers de Marine Russe*, is always closed now.

On the last night of 1981 in France, there was a programme on television about Poles. Still freedom – that old goal; always fought for, hoped for, despaired of and believed in again, perpetually escaping just ahead of the butterfly net like a lure. Yet sometimes for a period it is there – the vision of the future. One day surely the earth must open and all brothers be amalgamated into a non-political understanding.

As it was New Year's Eve, we waited, expecting reviews of the past year, Sadat, the Pope – and suddenly instead, there were Astaire and Kelly singing: 'All the world's a stage and we're here to entertain you on it' – and there was a fifty-year procession of dance and song in a collage from 1929 until 1981. We looked at the dream of every man who ever interpreted show business as the circus pageant of his own life, like a documentary of the futility yet greatness and pathos of man. Everyman was the edition of poetry books my mother travelled with: Everyman I will go with thee and by thy guide. And here ends this book, the skeleton story of about forty years that I have sped through. It is not so much to tell what happened to each individual destiny, as to tell the importance of their overcoming. Survival. To hold on and not give up. 'First you gotta last,' said Hemingway, in spite of the fact that he did not manage, nor did Romain Gary. One would hope the end of something is the beginning of the new dream or the next plan.

As Georgia and I left forever our house in Sussex, we looked out of the kitchen window on the last morning, at the pond we had designed and dug – almost a small lake, with a grassy island like green fur in the middle, that had gradually grown reeds and tufty bushes where the birds could nest – and on this last morning, when the west wind was blowing the rushes into a grey sheen, for the first time there were not just coots and moorhens – but a swan had come. It was a young swan with grey, downy feathers still on its white plumage, swimming quietly in the morning, alone.

It was tremendously nostalgic that it should have appeared on our last day, as we waited for the car to take us away from our house, and yet it was like a sign of continuity. We had a star to follow, and if we were going away, we were also going on. The sky on this morning was clear, and the water round the swan was blue. The swan was a legacy for someone else who would live here, a legacy we left for Sussex.

Conclusion

Cartier-Bresson has remarried and has a daughter of nine. His wife is a Magnum photographer called Martine Franck, but for him, photography is over, buried and (emphatically) done with. He is drawing. He attends the *Grande Chaumière*, is due to have an exhibition, and is working and studying with all his accustomed energy. When the new photographers of Magnum gather round the master, he tells them how very different it is now from when it was started, when 'no assignment' meant 'no dinner', and though he is glad that they can feel safe, one feels he finds its size less human.

When the young visit a Cartier-Bresson exhibition, they may not know that though his photographs look familiar, because many people now take the same kind of pictures, it was he who started this vision. Capa took war photos, Chim portraits and children – but the geometry of bicycle leaning against tree, the light on puddles, the haze, the romantic mystery of everyday things – this was his view first. In the way that Hemingway started the short, abrupt dialogue, or Proust the stream of consciousness, Cartier started the Bresson vision, and if it has now become part of the normal scene, expressed equally by other photographers, it is like the way people quote Shakespeare without knowing it; he has been absorbed into the language of photography.

At the Magnum retrospective exhibition in 1981, in the

Luxembourg Gallery in Paris, where I ran into him with his wife, he had the same candid, innocent look, in his old tweed cap – the same level gaze as always.

Segovia has never changed; he paints to the exclusion of all else. He hates Sunday lunch or holidays, is bored by nature (though such a splendid draftsman of trees) and does not know how to drive a car – but he paints. No fresh air, but he is never tired and always looks as healthy as if he has just skied down a mountain, yet the air he breathes on the short walk from his home to his studio is the grey pollution of the Boulevard de Clichy. He goes to the cafe for lunch, or between times for coffee. He talks and laughs with other painters there and is immensely jolly and fond of his friends. Then he returns and paints on.

Luckily no one says to him, 'There is someone at the door,' or 'Where are the clean sheets?' or 'You really should see more of *me*' – except, unexpectedly, his father. Occasionally Segovia the Elder will telephone from Geneva or London and ask, 'Could you come here for the day? I need you.' If his son goes, he finds when he gets there that it is just to post some letters or some equally trifling task. 'I might as well be in the moon,' he told me, 'as far as seeing London or making an outing of it; my father says, "There is no point in going to the dining-room, we'll just have the dinner sent up" – so the hotel bedroom is all I see.'

But the old man is still giving concerts at the age of eighty-eight. Both Segovias, who are both called Andres, have the same strong working-pattern and health; they are what the French call *forces de la nature*. At the age of seventy-eight, the elder Segovia produced a son, now ten – also called Andres.

During a police round-up in the war, Segovia (the painter) was picked up on the Champs-Elysées, and the fact that by chance he did not have his identity papers with him caused him to be deported to Germany, where he was put to work in a factory for the duration. As a result, he speaks perfect German and has twice married German wives; the incident changed the whole course of his life.

One night I dreamed of Prosser, which reminded me when I woke that I was due to report. I telephoned the hospital in the morning for an appointment, and they told me he had died during the night. During the time of my dream he had been on his way. Kind Mr Prosser – my old warrior with scars on his neck, always helping the fighters and with no time for those who did not cooperate. There is a last line to be said on this subject: I did have cancer again in the winter of 1980, and though the weeks before the operation were as terrifying as can be imagined, once it was done, this time it was, truly, routine: the machine had become my friend. I write this for Prosser's sake, to keep my promise to him: to give courage. People must not imagine that the sleuth is winning the battle – though it still too often does, but less frequently. There remains the last part of the enemy to be destroyed, and there is an army of knights fighting it – Dr Newton in the Westminster Hospital, Professor Westbury, the onchologist (my surgeon last time) at the Marsden, and they need help. It is not easy. In fact it is easier to be overcome with terror at the sign of any lump – but safety is given by the sure knowledge and kindness in Westbury's hands as he feels the map of one's jaw and neck. 'I am cautious,' he says, keeping watch, taking care, quelling fear. Constancy from the patient also, is what Prosser asked.

The understanding of my GP, Dr Richard Petty, should also be mentioned. He said quietly, after thoughtful reflection while I sat in his room, 'You must not think . . . that you are slowly dying.' I was startled; his insight was worthy of Elton Mayo's technique ('Listen to what they *don't* say') because it was what I had in fact been thinking, the third time round, but had not realized it. Thanks to this remark, I left his rooms uplifted.

Marcel Rochas told me he would have starved without a manager. His talent was great but his business sense nil, like many artists. Rochas not only designed clothes and his famous lace bottle – but made a magic inside the flat where he lived in the rue Barbet de Jouy. It was unlike any other dwelling; it was like entering another land. He created – his manager coped. So when he fell dead on his front doorstep one night coming home from a party, he left his widow an empire.

Money, or its lack, weaves its own web. There is a train in Australia called the Ghan. It crosses into the Northern Territory and goes through the queer, empty land where the most ancient of the earth's creatures live. Kangaroo and emu leap and gallop beside it, imagining they are getting away but often going parallel and unknowingly following alongside before losing ground. The Ghan is the name Georgia and I gave for the reason we had to leave our three houses in the English countryside: the rates, the fuel, the bills – we could not keep up. We galloped alongside but the Ghan won. Many people criticized us: 'Oh they love moving house, they can't keep still,' but they never knew about the Ghan. The people who criticize do not usually know the facts. We moved, we were always at home in our Bedouin tent with our same books and possessions, we *made* it happy – but we would have preferred to stay. The peasant who never leaves his village is luckier than he knows.

At each of our two Sussex houses we had a large pond dug by a bulldozer (instead of buying a washing machine which would have cost the same). There was an island in the middle, over four feet from the edge at any point, this being apparently the distance a fox will not swim, so the island made safe nesting for waterbirds. The soil was clay, so the water held, and in our part of Sussex the water table was in any case high. The first pond was fed by a small stream, which ran through and out into a neighbour's land. We put two couples of fish into the pond. They multiplied and swam to the neighbour, an old general who was most pleased and said it was biblical. The second pond was in a bare field with no stream, like a dew pond, fed by rain. The level was lower in summer but because of the water table never dry – only in this pond heron came and ate the fish. In each case the gradual ecological growth of reeds and rushes came of its own accord, taking about two years. The second pond was in an unsheltered windy place. It often had waves, and in storms it even had squalls – but the rushes grew high and protective.

It was necessary to landscape the mud that was dug out of the ponds (five feet deep in the middle) and this was put on one side and squashed into the shape of a natural slope. In the first case, at an old cottage called Mopeshole, we made what we called an Italian hill by planting roses and cypress trees. We also planted an orchard of apple trees and plum, a white and a red horse chestnut, a weeping Huntingdon elm, muscat grapes in the greenhouse (to celebrate the Common Market referendum in 1974) and Riesling outside on the south wall, and always a passion flower, in

London, Oxford, Sussex and now Provence.

The vegetable garden required digging in heavy clay soil. Each spadeful felt it would break one's back but we were helped in this by three unforgettable old men, Mr Stillgoe in Oxfordshire (where the soil was also clay), and in Sussex, Edward Birnie and Mr Evered. They worked in all weathers, understanding the land, knowing how to light a bonfire in the rain when the leaves were soggy. The ritual of growing, and the season when the first broad bean shoots were eaten by the wood pigeons, or the peas eaten by mice – this all became more important than any politics.

At Mopeshole, before we came, there had been a plantation of a thousand fir trees, as a Christmas crop; they had been cut down and sold but their stumps were left behind. Gradually, after gazing despondently at this wilderness of spikes, we dug them up by amounts of thirty to fifty a weekend, when friends like Dash would come to help. With old men scything, the cows grazing in the next field, the downs blue in the distance – quietly and peacefully a garden grew.

Elton Mayo was an agnostic: his faith in the outside factor was implicit. Faith is not rational and does not depend on intelligence; it is the non-believers who argue the most. My mother did not believe until late in life. She would say, 'We are too small, we are dust, how can we matter enough to continue?' One day when she was eighty, she announced: 'Man has his place in the cosmos.' But their view was large and abstract and did not conform to any ecclesiastical shape. They had affinities with Santayana.

No one was wittier, more hilariously funny or better company than Elton Mayo, no one braver or a better sport about the aches and pains of old age than my mother. She improved with time – the older she grew, the more relaxed she became, with all former agitation gone. She was enthusiastic, well-informed, and thrilled by the smallest thing like a bird singing. She had been brought up in what would now be millionaires' surroundings, but was anxious about money. She was careful in her rather lonely old age to a point of almost depriving herself. She never took taxis unless absolutely necessary, even after her first stroke when she was often giddy. We teased her about being so economical, but after she died we found in her desk drawer a list of thirteen charities which explained where her money went. They were as varied as

'Radios for the Blind'. 'Wireless for the Bedridden' – to Hungarian Relief in 1956. She also paid for the fare to Australia for several Jewish people she had met in Austria at the time of the *Anschluss*, when she had been looking for a school for me.

Elton Mayo, by contrast, was a spendthrift in his fashion, but he never had debts. He earned, he spent. Hired cars with chauffeurs in which he crossed Europe (rescuing me once from school in Lausanne where I was stranded with furniture under dust sheets, after the other girls went back to England – we drove from there to Asolo, always admonishing the driver to go slowly), privacy and comfort (he liked Palace hotels), good claret.

He was a nervous man and a chain-smoker, waiting at the window if a member of the family was even ten minutes late, but he never needed sleeping-pills and could sleep instantly like Churchill or Napoleon. In the height of battle – in mid-afternoon during an intense work discussion – he would sleep ten minutes and wake refreshed, solve the problem and proceed to the next question. He liked jazz; my mother liked classical music and went to concerts alone. Once I saw them waltz together; they were like skimming birds.

When he died, a waitress in Boston said, 'He was one of us.' He understood the boss and the workers so well, people sometimes wondered which side he was on. Harvard University, in their Memoriam presented to the family said, 'He has left an imprint that will never be erased.' He was not photogenic, no photograph shows the very dark blue of his eyes, their expression on the verge of laughter, or their depth of human understanding; nor can it show the white smile with his strong teeth that never had one filling. I hope that my description of him can somehow replace a photograph for the reader. A special attraction shone out of him, perhaps also because he had been a waltzer, tennis- and cricket-player, and a strong swimmer – in other words a physical as well as an intellectual man. This kept him lean and wiry into his last years. The *Fortune* magazine photograph accentuates the splendid dome of his wise head, reflecting in his study, but it does not show either his radiance or his laughter. Most pictures of him young (and before he went bald, he was a platinum blond) have unfortunately been lost, and in any case there was only one that I thought did him justice – in white flannels, a blazer and boater hat, and with the famous smile. (For that matter there are no photographs of my mother, who was, apparently, a great beauty when young, according to contemporary accounts. The miniature does not do her justice either. Her bust exists in some unknown museum – rather typically of her, she could not remember where.)

In May 1982 there was a meeting at Harvard under the heading of 'The Mayo Mystique'. Professor John Smith of Southampton University, who is writing Elton Mayo's biography, said, 'Mayo was a catalyst, he caused things to happen. If he had not existed we would have had to invent him.' Mayo's ideas live on. They are studied in A-level sociology, in management courses and in the French *baccalauréat*, and the translations of his books continue – yet he did not enjoy the writing up of his work; his enthusiasm and pleasure were in research and the excitement of discovery.

We were brought up to believe in ideas, not worldly success. (I say brought up, because although we only saw our parents in summer, the excitement of their company was as strong as our affection and longing to be with them.) Money was something that must exist, but in some other uninteresting area, never compromised for. They probably expected we would have a large Australian inheritance. As I said earlier, the erosion of absenteeism (albeit unwilling) and the traditional bad luck of the manager made this over to the Bunyip.

What becomes of the wisdom people only gain with age? Maurice Genevoix, in the year of his death, after writing what the critics called his best book at the age of eighty-nine, asked, 'Is one life long enough to make a man?'

Often I see Alvaro walking in the street ahead of me, but when I reach him, it is someone else.

St George remained in our life like one room in a large house. Georgia, writing to her sister, said, 'He is an amazing mixture of five people in one body.' It would take many writers to explain him: Sybille Bedford for his lonely heart, Balzac for his lawsuits and the meanness of his life, Ivy Compton-Burnett for the cruelty and the bitter dialogue in his family. He did not kill his dragon, but it grew older and quieter. I could never (nor would I want to) describe this tragedy, nor the pain and scars it left on those around him, of which he had no idea. A complex character indeed, there would be sudden gaiety and wit, and he himself would then inspire pity and also love – so the one who had suffered would feel mad in turn.

A quiet time is the hardest thing to obtain, or be understood by those who dislike or dread solitude, of whom there are many. One summer I happened to spend a month alone in a farm building in Spain. There was no electricity, and the water was in a well outside the front door. There was no radio and I did not have a watch; I guessed the time by the light and the sounds. The family from whom I rented this dwelling lived half a mile away across an almond orchard where goats wandered. In the day they did various jobs and chatted to me. When evening came they filed away in a processional departure, carrying a lantern. At first it was eerie to be entirely alone, but I grew accustomed, and a strange peace descended. Georgia O'Keefe, the American painter aged ninety-two, said, 'No one can teach you to paint, you learn by trying.' Ivon Hitchens said, 'Art school training is suspect. Technique should follow no rules.' I painted, swam and read; sometimes I walked a mile into the port and ate grilled prawns and talked with a friend.

What is luxury? Not necessarily the Ritz; perhaps just a place where the spirit is quiet. This month remains in my memory as absolute freedom – a peace that was almost a drug, though drug is the wrong word, for it was truth, not illusion, and it grew to a state which was hard to leave.

As Europe becomes overbuilt, a *postscriptum* on Menton revisited: Georgia and I stayed with Lesley Blanch this year in the spring, in her jasmine and roses in the exotic vegetation of Garavan – to find that the Waterfield garden is due to be bull-dozed, as also the Italian villa next door where Napoleon stayed, with its terraces of bananas – and Lesley Blanch's view of the sea is now blocked by a puce- and mustard-coloured slab of cement: new flats, 'studios grand standing' – in the place of a small now demolished hotel with shutters and wistaria, the blue Mediterranean showing over its roof. It was far below, the flats have soared to a height above and beyond any nightmare. It seems as if locusts are crunching away the ancient gardens Menton was famous for, leaving only lava-spittle, buildings that look like solidified vomit.

The saddest part of the coast is Menton, because of the rare plants that grew in its near-tropical climate, sheltered from the Mistral – but the most shaming part is Monte Carlo, where an asphalt jungle of cliff faces has arisen, each excluding the sunlight and the sea from the other's view, causing noonday darkness in streets like chasms.

When one asks why Monte Carlo is so mutilated, the answer always comes: 'They needed money.' But why must money bring ugliness? Could not 'they' have made a plan? Since the cliffs and hills rise high behind (and surrounding buildings are placed on pinnacles of rock with remarkable skill) – could there not have been a design, like a Roman amphitheatre – apartment blocks graded in terraces like steps – so as not to hide each other? Or crescents, like in Bath? Perhaps even an international competition of architects could have been organized; the final result would have been Monte Carlo fame, instead of shame, to the young, like Georgia's friends, who say in surprise, 'Is *this* Monte Carlo? Who wants to live here?'

Not only Lord Rothermere's villa with its gold mosaic bathrooms has gone, but many of the original *palais* with specially beautiful gardens (pointed out with regret by our taxi-driver, so this is not a 'highbrow view') and also the small, simple waterfront houses. Near the Palace there is still a row of chrome-yellow villas in an avenue of orange trees. The difference in old and new is not just the question of taste – whether there are people who like skyscrapers – it is in the way they are jerry-built, without care – only hurry – not lovingly stone by stone, to create places to love and live in.

A Russian prince whose life left him stranded in Monte Carlo had a lung disease, diagnosed by his doctor as caused by cement dust. Something happened outside his peaceful balcony, drills and bulldozers arrived overnight . . . in the city of uprooted palm trees, where cranes fill the skyline like a modern forest – and blocks spring up anywhere and awkwardly, like clothes that do not fit.

Graham Greene advises people to avoid settling in the region of Nice because of crime (though Nice has remained architecturally intact, once one reaches it; all new building is in the hinterland) – but there is another sort of crime, albeit accidental, through carelessness and greed, along the rest of the coast, in allowing the merciless destruction of trees, gardens, and a unique spiritual beauty it took generations to grow.

Aborigines in Australia, who never built houses like the Maoris and have always been nomads, have a sixth sense and knowledge of where the animals are grazing; they can always know and foresee changes of climate, and move ahead of them. These men and animals are adapted to the ecology of the oldest continent with its years–long droughts. Kangaroos can decide or order their own gestation. In drought they do not give birth, but unlike rabbits, who abort, they keep the baby indefinitely in the pouch – then when it rains and the grass is green, two or three babies may be born at once. This is why aborigines believe that rain brings babies. In drought kangaroos drink their own urine. The chemical process that turns green fodder into protein is higher in them than any other animal; there is no fat in their bodies except in the tail.

Sir Benjamin Rank, (the Australian surgeon who informed me on this subject) told me that aborigines, who are natural sportsmen and win easily at games (Goolagong) have no sense of competition – once they have won, they are bored with going on proving the point, unlike Western athletes. White man has something to learn from this human quality – and even more usefully, from the animal's adaptation to drought. Hopefully it will not be lost in the rush to take back the aborigine's reserve in the Northern Territory – where uranium has been found.

Roderick Cameron once said that a person born in Australia – even if they leave and do not live there – aways feels a sense of isolation, and an outsider in small countries.

The day we finally get to Cressbrook, even if Reugny and Harold are old ghosts, they are probably still galloping and cantering in the paddock below the garden, in the Dreaming. Harold – the champion trotter of Australia, never beaten, lived to be twenty-three, and Reugny – sleek father of generations of race-winners. The land will be vast, the light as brilliant as Spain.

In the meantime, Georgia became eighteen in 1982 – so the star that appeared in Milborne Grove did take us on a safe journey.

Epilogue

Dear Mr Prosser: P.S. I have kept my promise. But to be honest, the first time I wrote it, I did think: touch wood.

I had the malady again, and now apparently in a milder but lingering fashion, it is back a further time at the end of 1982. (I have said milder, because in effect the operation is smaller, but also I have decided that is so: *I won't accept it any more*.) Georgia has As for her A-levels, I am back at work, and we are through the tunnel of our twelve-year hole, the incredible stress of the unwritten part of this book. We are in place and we are happy. So I add here more than your message, Mr Prosser, the repetition of my own: hold on, overcome. By trying, man can hope to last out his season, until his work is done, and only afterwards and then, to accept is peace.

Shariat, Tarikat and Hakitat – the law, the path and the truth – this is the religion and philosophy of the Sufi mystics – rules for the community, leading to Maarifat as a person grows higher into a final degree of abstraction, freeing the spirit from the flesh, liberating from terrestrial doubts and fears. The final degree is called the Kh'al. This religion was established in the Caucasus by Arabs, in the eighth century, but it has not even yet come into its final stage. It is still in the height of violence misguidedly called faith – but it is laid down as the eventual state to acquire. *Whosoever does not acknowledge that it is immaterial whether he is a Moslem or a Christian has not achieved the truth and knows not the essence of being.*

adapted from Lesley Blanch, *The Sabres of Paradise*, p 57.
Her italics.

I have had to fight all my life, but there was also laughter and love and luminosity and magic. The sword and the fight are for the beginning. Later, I hope, is for the folding of hands, the flowering and the fruit.